HUMAN BEHAVIOR HOW INFLUENCES SERVICE NEED CHANGE

JOHN LOK

Copyright © John Lok
All Rights Reserved.

Contents

PREFACE

Preface

How social change influences human behavioral change ? Why human behavior may be influenced by social change? Our individual behavior whether can be influenced to bring negative or positive attitude by social change? I shall attempt to indicate cases to explain whether our individual behavior can be influenced to changed by social environment change. Readers can have more understand how and why social change may influence our behavior in possible. Behavioral economy is one useful and fun social subject. Behavioral economists ususally research how and why human behaviors may influence economy growth or recession, or how and why economy environment changing factor may influence human behavior changes.

This book is a business psychological teaching book. This book aims to indicate some sample different kinds of client individual psychological emotion challenges to give opions to let these businesses how to solve these psychological challenges and how to attract clients' concerning to their products or services. Also, I shall explain how to use psychological methods to predict clients' emotion in order to attract more clients to choose to use these businesses' services or buy these businesses' products. These product or service businesses include space exploration relative product, natural energy resource product, environment pollution product, road transportation design service, airline fuel product, Disney entertainment service, travel agent service, education service etc. I feel any businesses can keep longer time to grow up if businessmen can know how to use psychological methods to predict their clients' positive emotions. I shall give my opinions to answer how to predict these businesses' client emotion, such as how Disney can attract more visitors; how to predict clients' emotion to consume space travel entertainment and/or space relative products; how to increase student numbers, how to predict traveller individual's travelling destination choice etc. client psychological choice behaviors.

I write this book aim to let readers to raise knowledge how to predicts service industries consumers needs and research what factors can influence their needs change.

The first market concerns travel industry: How to predict future travel behaviour from past travel behaviour for travel agents benefits. I shall indicate how to predict travel behavioural consumption from psychology view and computer statistic both view points and qualitative of travel behavioural method to achieve how to operate travel business more successfully.

The second market concerns school education industry. I shall indicate what the factors can influence the final grades of academic students. I shall give examples to explain why these factors can influence the final grades to be bad of academic students easily. Those factors include: tutoring method factor, class attendance and academic performance factor, drinking and academic motivation factor, the link between sleep quantity and academic performance factor, the relationship between physical fitness and academic performance factor, the relationship between student's learning style and academic performance factor as well as the relationship between time management and academic performance total seven factors.

The third market concerns outsourcing either manufacturing or service strategy. Although, nowadays, outsourcing is popular strategy to any global organizations. But they neglect outsourcing strategy has also disadvantages. I shall explain why outsourcing strategy can bring benefits to some organizations, but it can also bring disadvantages to some organizations. I shall indicate evidences to explain what the reasons are not right when the organizations choose outsourcing strategy. I shall explain why any organizations need to analyze their situations whether are suitable to apply outsourcing strategy to operate their management, before they decide to make outsourcing strategy.

The fourth market concerns multi-level market. Pyramid scheme of the economic analysis of the criteria is used to distinguish what the difference is multi level marketing sale channel and direct personal sale channel . I shall utilize economy theory in reaching the opinion what the difference view points were between direct personal sale and multi level marketing, toward determining whether the reasoning can also generate false positive. I also discuss the welfare implications of different tests that might be used to distinguish a legitimate direct seller (pyramid scheme) and multi-level marketing from a fraud. The, I shall dicate the different types of consumer frauds by calculation and considerations which both employ to detect whether pyramid and personal direct sale fraud both are occurring. Finally, I shall explain whether Multi-Level Marketing can assist global economic growth in our societies.

The fifth market concerns travelling road driving market. I shall explain why it has close relationship between travellers number influence and the crisis of road traffic fatalities to any countries. I shall indicate Japan travellers' road driving behaviors. I shall apply rational choice theory to explain why drinking alcohol of drivers' behaviours can cause Japan's economic development indirectly. I shall give reasons to explain different country government's transportation and travel development departments ought need to concern their traveller road driving behavior how to influence their traveller visitor numbers.

The six market concerns MTR (underground train) transportation strategy. I shall explin why MTR underground train transportation needs to know passenger behaviour. What are the factors to cause passengers who choose to catch other transportation tools? Indicating methods how to solve passenger choice challenges to attact many passengers who will choose MTR to catch more than other kind of transportation tools. It is suitable to any readers who have interest to learn how to use transportation behaviour strategy to solve passenger behavioural choice.

The seven market concerns airline market. I shall let economic students who can learn how to use behavioral economic method to solve the fuel price rising risk to global airline industry. Also I hope any airline company management leader who can learn how to apply behavioral economic method to predict when fuel price rising to avoid its risk and how to avoid the fuel price rising bad influence to cause whose airline businesses failure for long term. Finally, I shall indicate what factors cause the fuel price will raise as well as I shall indicate what the other external threats can cause risk to airline industry and I shall also compare the fuel price rising factor and other external threats whether which is the most effort to influence airline industry failure. Then, I shall give recommend how global airline industry can apply behavioral economic method to avoid the fuel price rising bad influence.

The eight market concerns entertainment park market. I shall explain how Walt Disney theme entertainment park which how applies knowledge management strategy to solve strategic and human resource problems successfully as well as I also give reasons to prove why it can not be theme park leader to influence USA economic and employment growth in the future and give recommendation how it can raise its ability to be the entertainment theme park leader in the future. The first chapter concerns what Disney background was and what my research aims were. The second chapter concerns what my research and analysis results are and what Disney knowledge management strategy had been implemented. The final chapter concerns to explain why Disney needs to change its internal strategies to raise its competition if it wants to be theme park leader to influence USA economic growth in long term.

The nine market concerns space technological industry. I shall indicate what space business's benefits will be contributed to human . I shall research whether what economic factors are influenced to our daily living by the space business main country players. Awareness of the space industry is critical of public policy is to support it. As the impact of climate change makes survival for the human species increasingly problem, the imperative to develop the means to evacuate planet Earth and sustain human existence becomes critical. The first chapter explains a conceptualization exploration of space how is presented from a globalization perspective. The Second chapter indicates what the benefits are managed to international cooperation in space exploration. The third chapter indicates the impact of space exploration activities upon society. The final chapter indicates the benefits stemming from space exploration. I shall provide a comprehensive review of how space technology can be used to resolve fundamental environmental, technological, and humanitarian challenges that we are experiencing on our planet.

This book final market concerns foods and product manufacturing market. I shall indicate how to predict customer' emotion to judge whether how to produce or design your foods or products to sell to them successfully. I want to give my opinions to let businessmen to know how to
predict consumer emotion to avoid the risk to spend excess investment to invent the new products or produce the bad taste foods or soft drinks to promote to enter to sell wrongly. I shall use three science and psychology methods to explain what suitations your products or foods can sell from online more acceptable. So, this book teach students to learn how to use the suitable strategies to achieve to manage any business more success. In my this books which indicate some business concepts and theories how to apply to these kind of buiness markets to achieve more accurate

strategical methods effectively.

- Prediction travel behavioral consumption from psychology view and computer statistic view.

- Whether climate change can influence travelling behaviours.

- Whether individual habitual behaviour can influence travelling behaviour: e.g. renting travel transportation tools

- How to determine future travel behavior from past travel experience and perceptions of risk and safety for the benefits to travel consumers?

- What is push and pull factors to influence any traveler who chooses where is whose preferable travelling destination.

- Why expectation, motivation and attitude factor can influence travelling behaviour.

- How to use qualitative of travel behavioural method to predict future travel consumption.

- How to apply advanced traveler information systems (ATIS) to predict future travelling behaviour.

- How does online tourism sale channel can influence traveling consumption of behaviour.

- Actively based patterns of urban population of travel behavioural prediction method.

●
What is environmental uncertainty factor?

●
Whether outsourcing will bring
what kind of work skills.

● Bibliography
　　　Chapter 4
Internet Multi-Level Marketing

●
What are the differences between multi level
marketing and direct personal sale? p.117-147

●
Whether multi level marketing can assist
economic growth.

●
Why the internet has positive influence on direct
sale industry in multi level market to assist
economic growth.

●
Whether multi level marketing can influence
economic growth in poverty countries.

Chapter 5
MTR (UNDERGROUND TRAIN) TRANSPORTATION
SERVCE MARKET
　　● Why MTR underground train transportation needs to
know passenger behaviour. p.148-173
● Why route choice can influence passenger
● behavioural choice.
● Why trip time reliability and crowding factors
can influence MTR passenger choice.
● What is the crowding difference between
train and MTR underground train.
● How MTR can attract many passengers.

Chapter 6
AIRLINE TRANSPORT INDUSTRY
　　● How positive or negative social
change can influence any airlines' air ticket prices
to be risen or fallen. p.174-194
● What is the relationship of oil price
and terrorism to airline industry?
● Why does airline self-organization
exist in airline industry?
● Why tourism and airline industries

have close relationship to influence their profitability
between of them.
● Why oil fuel raising price factor
can cause risk to airline.
● Methods to solve rising air fare
prices demand
I. Why will biofuels energy be demanded ?
II. Whether the relationship between terrorism
III. and oil prices has close relationship.
IV. What factors will influence airline industry's
V. price elasticity of supply and demand?
Chapter 7
DISNEY ENTERTAINMENT THEME PARK
What factors caused Walt Disney strategic and
human resource problems p.195-220

Knowledge management strategy

● Whether Disney knowledge management
strategy can influence America tourism
economy growth in the long term.

The development of the travel and tourism
Industry to change customer needs and expectation to cause amusement park industry development after world war
II
The economic and social impacts of America
Theme park Tourism industry

The background on how people view the
theme park industry in America

Characteristics and hierarchy with
respects to economic importance of the theme
parks to the region in USA.
The impact of America Disney tourism
on local government expenditures
What is Disney theme entertainment
park unique characteristics and image in USA
How Disney increases employment chance
The factors what are contributed to
Disney's successes on its way towards becoming
the world's largest family entertaining company
Conclusion and Recommendation
Bibliography
Chapter 8
SPACE TRAVEL ENTETAINMENT INDUSTRY

● p.221-232

A conceptualization of space exploration

●

The benefits and Values are managed to international cooperation in space exploration

●

The impact of space exploration activities upon society.

●

The benefits stemming from space exploration

Chapter 9
Facility management how influences airport and logistic employee performance
● Facility management assists employees reduce maintenance service expenditure
● Facility management role in p.233-250 organization
Facility management how influences public service transport service performance
How (FM) space moving management brings employees efficiencies
● Predictive the choosing right data asset and (FM) analytics solutions to boost public transportation service quality
● The relationship between facility management and productive efficiency
● The relationship between facility management and consumer behavior
● Facility management influences consumer satisfactory service feeling
● Facility management how influences employee Psychology to raise productive efficiency

● How to impact of workplace management on well-being and productivity
● Facility management technological factor how influences workers performance in construction industry
● How organizational facility environment factor influences new and old employees long term performance
Chapter 10

Psychosocial and medical interventions
for mental and physical health facility
management strategy

● What is the new model of healthcare facility
management p.251-259
● What is the tradition facilities management
model to hospitals
● Approach to reducing costs
● The path to a solution
Reference
Chapter 11
Strategy plan implement
● Economic factors influence
to meet strategic management? p.251-265

Management factors influence organizational strategic plans

● Organization strategic plan challenges
School strategic plan challenges
Service organizationsveffectiveness
and efficiency challenges
Electronic health record system
to health care organization challanges
● Benefits of rationalization from
strategic plans
Reducing costs and improving
service for strategic plan
to service organizations
Brand strategy
Human resource plans to space
exploration organization
The direction between business
and tactic models and tactics
Strategic communication
plan
● Reasons need strategic plan

Why organizations need strategic plan
What is strategic management?
Why needs strategic versus
non-strategic cooperation
Strategic plan tangible and
intangible benefits

● Reference

Chapter 12

I

TRAVEL ENTERTAINMENT MARKET

What factors can influence travel behavioural consumption

Prediction travel behavioral consumption from psychology view and computer statistic view.

How to predict travel consumption? It is one question to any travel agents concern to use what methods which can predict how many numbers of travelers where who will choose to go to travel more accurately. I think that who can consider how to predict travel behavioral consumption from psychology view and computer science view both.

On the psychology view, It has evidence to support the relationship between self-identify threat and resistance to change travel behavior to any travelers, controlling for whose past travelling behavior, resistance to change if a psychological phenomenon of long standing interest in many applied branches of psychology. Past travelling behavior has been acknowledged as a predictor of future action. Such as travelling behavior that is experienced as successful is likely to be repeated and may lead to habitual patterns. Some psychologists differentiate habit between two concepts, such as goal oriented and automatic oriented both. Although repeated past travelling behavior is addition goal oriented and automatic oriented. Further non-deliberative nature of habit may make appeals to judge and to predict future individual traveler's behaviour accrately. However, repeated travelling behavior without a necessary constraint of goal orientation and automatic oriented both. So, it seems that psychological factor can influence any individual traveler why and how who choose to decide whose travelling behaviour.

On the computer statistic view, structural equation modeling is an extremely flexible linear-in-parameters multivariate statistical modeling technique. It has been used in modeling travel behavior and values since about 1980 year. It is a software method to handle a large number of variables, as well as unobserved variables specified as linear combinations (weighted averages) of the observed variable.

●

Whether climate change can influence travelling behaviours.

The flexibility of human travelling behavior is at least the result of one such mechanism, our ability to travel mentally in time and entertain potential future. Understanding of the impacts is holidays, particularly those involving travel. Using focus groups research to explores tourists' awareness of the impacts of travel own climate change, examines the extent to which climate change features in holiday travel decisions and identifies some of the barriers to the adoption of less carbon intensive tourism practices. The findings suggest many tourists don't consider climate change when planning their holidays. The failure of tourists to engage with the climate change to impact of holidays, combined with significant barriers to behavioral change, presents a considerable challenge in the tourism industry.

Tourism is a highly energy intensive industry and has only recently attracted attention as an important contributions to climate change through greenhouse gas emissions. It has been estimated that tourism contributes 5% of global carbon dioxide emissions. There have been a number of potential changes proposed for reducing the impact of air travel on climate change. These include technological changes, market based changes and behavioral changes. However, the role that climate change plays in the holiday and travel decisions of global tourists. How the global tourists of the impacts travel has on climate change to establish the extent to which climate change, considerations features in holiday travel decision making processes and to investigate the major barriers to global tourists adopting less carbon intensive travel practices. Whether tourists will aware the impacts that their holidays and travel have on climate changes.

When, it comes to understand individual traveler's behavioral change, wide range of conceptual theories have been developed, utilizing various social, psychological, subjective and objective variables in order to model travel consumption behavior. These theories of travel behavioral change operate at a number of different levels, including the individual level, the interpersonal level and community level. Whether pro-environmental behavior can be used to predict travel consumption behavior in a climate change. However, the question of what determines pro-environmental behavior in such a complex one that it can not be visualized through one single framework or diagram.

Despite the potentially high risk scenario for the tourism industry and the global environment, the tourism and climate change ought have close relationship. Whether what are the important factors and variables which can limit tourism? e.g. money, time, family problem, extreme hot or cold weather change, air ticket price, journey attraction etc. variable factors. Mention of holidays and travel were deliberately avoided in the recruitment process, so as not to create a connection factor to influence traveler's individual mind. However, the dismissal of alternative transportation modes can be conceived as either a structural barrier, in the sense that flying is perhaps the only realistic option to reach long-haul holiday destination, or a perceived behavioral control barriers in that an individual perceives flying as the only option open to whom. The transportation tool factor will be depend to extent on the distance to the destination. This can also be interpreted in a social perspective as an intention with the resources available where much international tourism is structured around flying. To increase the availability of different transportation modes, tourists could choose holiday destination closer to home.

Finally, also how to predict future travel behavioural consumption. I feel that travel agents need to predict whether any country's random daily variation of weather factor is also important to influence travel behaviour. e.g. in weather, temperature, rainfall adn snowfall with traffic accidents factors will have relationship to cause travel demand. Some scientists estimate suggest that when warmed temperatures and reduced snowfall are associated with a moderate decline in non-fatal accidents, they are also associated with a significant increase in fatal accidents. Thus increase in fatalities and temperature. Half of the estimated effect of temperature on fatalities is due to changes in the exposure to pedestrians, bicyclists and motorcyclists as temperature increase. So, if any countries have rainfall, snowfall and low temperature to cause traffic accidents, whether this accident occurrence will influence the travelers who liking climb snow hills, riding bicycle, running sports who will avoid to travel to these countries' bad weather after occurs. So, why I feel that this natural climate factor will also be one serious factor to influence travel behavioral consumption.

● Whether individual habitual behaviour can influence travelling behaviour : e.g. renting travel transportation tools

Whether habit can be intended to predict of future travel behavior to people are creatures of habits. Many of human's everyday goal-directed behaviors are performed in a habitual fashion, the transportation made and route one takes to work, one's choice of breakfast. Habits are formed when using the some behavior frequently and a similar consistency in a similar context for the some purpose whether the individual past travel consumption model will be caused a habit to whom. e.g. choosing whom travel agent to buy air ticket or traveling package; choosing the same or similar countries' destinations to go to travel ; choosing the business class or normal (general) class of quality airlines to catch planes. Does habitual rent traveling car tools use not lead to more resistance to change of travel mode? It has been argued that past behavior is the best predictor of future behavior to travel consumption. If individual traveler's past consumption behavior was always reasoned, then frequency of prior travel consumption behavior should only have an indirect link to the individual traveler's behavior. It seems that renting travel car tools to use is a habit example. So, a strong rent traveling car tools useful habit makes traveling mode choice. People with a strong renting of traveling car tools of habit should have low motivation to attend to gather any information about public transportation in their choice of travelling country for individual or family or friends members during their traveling journeys.

Even when persuasive communication changes the traveler whose attitudes and intention, in the case of individual traveler or family travelers with a strong renting travel car tools habit. It is difficult to change whose travel behaviors to choose to catch public transportation in whose any trips in any countries. However, understanding of travel behavior and the reasons for choosing one mode of transportation over another. The arguments for rent traveling car tools to use, including convenience, speed, comfort and individual freedom and well known. Increasingly, psychological factors include such as, perceptions, identity, social norms and habit are being used to understand travel mode choice. Whether how many travel consumers will choose to rent traveling car tools during their trips in any countries. It is difficult to estimate the numbers. As the average level of renting travel car tools of dependence or attitudes to certain travel package policies from travel agents. Instead different people must be treated in different ways because who are motivated in different ways and who are motivated by different travel package policies ways from travel agents.

In conclusion, the factors influence whose traveler's individual behavior either who chooses to rent traveling car tools or who chooses to catch public transportation when who individual goes to travel in alone trip or family trip. It include influence mode choice factors, such as social psychology factor and marketing on segmentation factor both to influence whose transportation choice of behavior in whose trip.

● How to determine future travel behavior from past travel experience and perceptions of risk and safety for the benefits to travel consumers?

How to determine future travel behavior from past travel experience and perceptions of risk and safety for the benefits to travel consumers? Why does individual traveler avoid certain destination(s) is(are) as relevant to tourist decision making as why who chooses to travel to others. Perceptions of risk and safety and travel experience are likely to influence travel decisions. If travel agents had efforts to predict future travel behavior to guess whether travelers will feel where is(are) risk and unsafe to cause who does not choose to go to the country to travel. Then, the travel agents will avoid to choose to spend much time to design the different traveling package to attract their potential travel consumers to choose to travel. The reason is because in the case of individual traveler's tourism experience, the traveler whose past disappointment travel experience (psychological risk) will be a serious threat to the traveler's health or life (health, physical or terrorism risk). The past safety or unhealthy risk to the country(countries) will influence the traveler decides to choose not to go to the countries(country) to travel again in the future.

●

What is push and pull factors to influence any
traveler who chooses where is whose preferable travelling destination.

How to predict individual traveler's behavioral intention of choosing a travel destination. Understanding why people travel and what factors influence their behavioral intention of choosing a travel destination is beneficial to tourism planning and marketing. In general, an individual's choice of a travel destination into two forces. The first force is the push factor that pushes an individual away from home and attempt to develop a general desire to go somewhere, without specifying where that may be. The other force is the pull factor that pull an individual toward in destination, due to a region-specific or perceived attractiveness of a destination. The respective push and pull factors illustrate that people travel because who are pushed by whose internal motives and pulled by external forced of a destination. However, the decision making process leading to the choice of a travel destination is a very complex process. For example, a Taiwanese traveler who might either choose new travel destination of Hong Kong or another old travel Asia destinations again or who also might choose any one of Western country, as a new travel destination. The travel agents can predict where who will have intention to choose to travel from whose past behavior and attitude, subjective and perceived behavioral control model.

The factors influence where is the traveler choice, include personal safety, scenic beauty, cultural interest, climate changing, transportation tools, friendliness of local people, price of trip, trip package service in hotels and restaurants, quality and variety of food and shopping facilities and services etc. needs. So, whose factors will influence where is the individual travel's choice. It seems every traveler whose choice of travel process, will include past behavior. e.g. travelling experience, travelling habit, then to choose the best seasoned travelling action to satisfy whose travel needs. This process is the individual traveler's psychological choice process, who must need time to gather information to compare concerning of different travel packages, destination scene, climate change, transportation tools available to the destination, air ticket price etc. these factors, then to judge where is the best right destination to travel in the right time.

●

Why expectation, motivation and attitude factor can influence travelling behaviour.

Social psychology is concerned with gaining insight into the psychological of socially relevant behaviors and the processes. For instance, on a global level bad influence to global warming, it influences some countries extreme cold or hot bad climate changing occurrence, then it ought influence some travelers' behavioral decision to change their mind to choose some countries to go to travel at the moment which do not occur extreme hot or cold climate (temperature). e.g. above than 40 degree in summer or below than 0 degree in winter. Due to the extreme climate changing environment in the countries, it will cause them to feel uncomfortable to play during their trips. So, the global warming causes to climate changing factor will influence the numbers of travel consumption to be reduced possibly. This is global climate changing environment factor influences to bad or uncomfortable social psychological feeling to global travelers' mind of traveling decision. What is individual traveler expectation, motivation and attitude? Tourism sector includes inbound (domestic) tourism and outbound (overseas) tourism both incomes to any countries. According to recent article, a tourist behavior model has been developed, called the expectation, motivation and attitude (EMA) model (Hsu et al., 2010).

This model focuses on the pre-visit stage of tourists by modeling the behavioral process by incorporating expectation, motivation and attitude. Travel motivation is considered as an essential component of the behavioral process, which has been increasing attention from the travel; industry. The economic approach defines "tourism" is an identifiable nationally important industry. It includes the component activities of transportation, accommodation, recreation, food and related service. So, tourism behavioral consumption is concerned the individual tourist's usual habituate of the industry which responds to whose needs, and of the impacts that both the tourist and the tourism industry have on the socio-cultural, economic and physical environment.

However, travel motivation means how to understand and predict factors that influence travel decision making. According to Backman and others (1995, p.15), motivation is conceptually viewed as " a state of need, a condition that services as a driving force to display different kind of behavior toward certain types of activities, developing preferences, arriving at some expected satisfactory outcome." So, motivation and expectancy which has close relationship to any tourist before who decided to do any tourism of behavior. Some economists confirmed motivation and expectancy which has relations, such as expectation of visiting an outbound destination has a direct effect on motivation to visit the destination; motivation has a direct effect on attitude toward visiting the destination; expectation of visiting the outbound destination has a direct affect on attitude toward visiting the destination and motivation has a mediating effect on the relationship in between expectation and attitude.

● How to use qualitative of travel behavioural method to predict future travel consumption.

I also suggest to use qualitative of travel behavioural method to predict future travel consumption. Methods such as focus groups interviews and participant observer techniques can be used with quantitative approaches on their own to fill the gaps left by quantitative techniques. These insights have contributed to the development of increasingly sophisticated models to forecast travel behavior and predict changes in behavior in response to change in the transportation system. First, survey methods restrict not only the question frame but the answer frame as well, anticipating the important issues and questions and the responses. However, these surveys methods are not well suited to exploratory areas of research where issues remain unidentified and the researched seek to answer the question "why?". Second, data collection methods using traditional travel diaries or telephone recruitment can under represent certain segments of the population, particularly the older persons with little education, minorities and the poor. Before the survey, focus group for example can be used to identify what socio-demographic variables to include in the survey, how best to structure the diary, even what incentives will be most effective in increasing the response rate. After the survey, focus, focus groups can be used to build explanations for the survey results to identify the "why" of the results as well as the implications. One Asia Pacific survey research result was made by tourism market investigation before. It indicated the travel in Asia Pacific market in the past, had often been undertaken in large groups through leisure package sold in bulk, or in large organized business groups, future travelers will be in smaller groups or alone, and for a much wider range of reasons. Significant new traveler segments, such as female business traveler. The small business traveler and the senior traveler, all of which have different aspirations and requirements from the travel experience.

Moreover, Asia tourism market will start to exist behaviors in the adoption of newer technologies, a giving the traveler new ways to manage the travel experience, creating new behaviors. This with provide new opportunities for travel providers. The use of mobile devices, smartphones, tablets etc. and social media are the obvious findings to become an integral part of the travel experience. Thus, quality method can attempt to predict Asia Pacific tourism market development in the future.

However, improving the predictive power of travel behavior models and to increase understanding travel behavior which lies in the use of panel data(repeated measures from the same individuals). Whereas, cross-sectional data only reveal inter-individual differences at one moment in time, panel data can reveal intra-individual changes over time. In effect, panel data are generally better suited to understand and predict (changes in) travel behavior. However, a substantial proportion was also observed to transition between very different activity/travel patterns over time, indicating that from one year to the next, many people renegotiated their activity/travel patterns.

● How to apply advanced traveler information systems (ATIS) to predict future travelling behaviour.

Nowadays, information can impact on traveler behavior and network performance. For example, when steadily growing levels of vehicle ownership and vehicle miles traveled information has been identified as a potential strategy towards man aging travel demand, optimizing transportation networks and better utilizing available capacity. Toward, this goal to predict further tourist behavioral consumption. Many countries, government tourism development institutes has applied advanced traveler information systems (ATIS) which travel behavior models and high-fidelity network performance models made increasingly feasible through the rapid advances in computer power. Crucial components of this problem domain are the modeling of individual tourist drivers' response to travel information and the development accurate guidance of relevance to real would trip makers. So, this advanced traveler information systems (ATIS) can assist the tourist who like to rent travelling car tools to travel in any countries own free traveler information systems service conveniently. Also, this travel information system can be intended to assist travelers to make better travel choices. e.g. this system can improve the decision making of individual traveler rather than improvements of network performance overall. So, we need to understand how tourists make their travel plans. Also, understanding decision process that lead to booking of the trip is equally important, as it allows of a potential behavior.

●

How does online tourism sale channel can influence traveling consumption of behaviour.

Nowadays, internet is popular, it seems that booking air ticket behavior of using internet is predicted to influence overall tourism air tickets payment method. Tourism industry has grown in the previous several decades. Despite its global impact, questions related to better understanding of tourists and whose habits. Using online travel air ticket booking benefits include booking electronic air tickets can be made from entering any electronic travel agents websites in the short time and electronic travel ticket payers do not need leave home, who can pay visa card to pre booking any electronic travel ticket from online channel conveniently.

How to analyze activity based travel demand ? Nowadays, human are concerning the traffic congestion and air quality deterioration, the supply oriented focus of transportation planning has expanded to include how to manage travel demand within the available transportation supply. Consequently, there has been an increasing interest in travel demand management strategies, such as congestion pricing that attempts to change aggregate travel demand. The prediction aggregate level, long term travel demand to understanding disaggregate level (i.e. individual levels) behavioral responses to short term demand policies, such as ride sharing incentives, congestion pricing and employer based demand management schemes, alternate work schedules, telecommuting limitation of travel agent traditionally work nature shall influence oriented trip based travel modelling passenger travel demand indirectly.

Finally, online travel purchase will be popular to influence the number of travel behavioural consumption nowadays. Any travel package products can be sold from websites to attract travellers to choose to prebook air ticket for any trips conveniently. In the past ten years, the internet has become the predominant carrier of all types of information and transactions. Regarding travel decisions, internet has also become an important sales channels for the travel industry, because it is associated with comparably lower distribution and sales costs, but also because ir adapts to hign supply and demand dynamics in this industry. Consequently, the travel and tourism industry tries to increase the internet sale specific share of sales volumes. So, internet sale channel has changed travel consumption behavioural pattern and characteristics and travel experience. For example, Switzerland has one of the highest population-to-computer ratio in Europe. It is also one of the most highly internet penetrated countries in terms of use of the WWW on a day-to-day basis, with more than 75 percent of the population older than 14 years using the WWW daily (ICT, 2005).

The reason of booking online tourism may include: convenience, fast transaction, finding traveling package choice easily, more airline seats available. So, online booking tourism will influence the traditional tourism agents visiting of sales and air tickets and travelling package numbers to be decreased. Finally, the online booking tourism market shares will be expanded to more than traditional tourism agents visits sale market in the future one day. So, the travel agents who still use the traditional tourism visiting sale channel which ought raise whose features to compare to differ to online tourism sale channel if these traditional touriam agents want to keep competitive ability in tourism industry for long term.

●

Actively based patterns of urban population of travel behavioural prediction method.

Actively based patterns of urban population. It is a method of motivational framework means in which societal constraints and inherent individual motivations interact to shape activity participation patterns. It can be used to predict one city or urban the numbers of travel demand in the year. It has two elements: First, capability constraints refer to constraints are imposed by biological needs, such as eating and sleeping and/or resources, such as income, availability of cars etc. to undertake the urban or city's family activities in the year. Second, coupling constraints define where, when and the duration of planning activities that are to be pursued with other individuals. So, this method needs to gather information (data) to get the relationship between activities, travel and spending work time and space time to evaluate whether there are how many families who have real needs to spend time to go to travel in the year.

●

What is trip based versus activity based approaches?

What is trip based versus activity based approaches? The fundamental difference between the trip-based and activity based approaches is that the former approach directly focuses on trips without explicit recognition of the motivation or reason for the trips and travel. The activity based approach , on the other hand, views travel as a demand derived from the need to pursue travel activities. So, it is better understand the individual or family behavior basis for individual or family travelling decision regarding participation in travelling activities in certain places or cities or countries at given times and hence the resulting travel needs. This behavioral basis includes all the factors that influence the why, how, when and where of performed activities and resulting individuals and household, the cultural/social norms of the community and the travel surrounding environment.

Another difference between the two approaches is in the way travel is represented. The trip based approach represents travel as a collection of trips. Each trip is considered as independent of other trips, without considering the inter-relationship in the choice attributes , such as time, destination and mode of different trips. As tours are chains of trips beginning and ending at a same location , say home or work. The tour based representation helps maintain the consistency across and capture the interdependency and consistency of the modeled choice attributed among the trips of the same tour.

In addition to the tour based representation of travel, the activity based approach focuses on sequences or patterns of activity participation and travel behavior, using the whole day or longer periods of time is the unit of analysis. Such as approach can address travel demand management issues through an examination of how people modify their activity participation, for example, will individuals substitute more out-of-home activities for in home activities in the evening of who arrived early form work due-to a work schedule change?

The major difference between trip based and the activity based approaches is in the way, the time dimension of activities and travel is considered. In the trip based approach, time is reduced to being simply a cost making a trip and a day's viewed as a combination, defined peak and off peak time periods. On the other hand, activity based approach views individuals' activity travel patterns are a result of their time use decisions with a continuous time domain. As individuals have 24 hours in a day or multiples of 24 hours for longer periods of time and decide how to use that travel among or allocate that time to activities and travel and with who, subject to their socio-demographic, transportation system and other and scheduling of trips. So, determining the impact of travel demand management policies on time use behavior is an important step to assessing the impact of such policies on individual travel behavior. The final major difference between this two approaches relates to the level of aggregation. In the trip based approach, most aspect of travel, e.g. number of trips etc. are analyzed at an aggregate level.

Consequently, trip based methods accommodate the effect of socio-demographic attributes of households and individuals in a very limited fashion, which limits the activity of the method to evaluate travel impacts of long term socio-demographic characteristics of the individuals who actually make the activity travel choices and the travel service characteristics of the surrounding environment. So, the activity based models are better equipped to forecast the longer term changes in travel demand in response composition and the travel environment of urban areas. Also, using activity based models, the impact of policies can be assessed by predicting individual level behavioral responses instead of employing trip based statistical averages that are aggregated over defined demographic segments.

The future travel target behavioural consumption

●

Why senior age will be main travelling target.

In the past, Germany government had established tourism survey analysis to analyze survey data in order to arrive at reliable conclusions on future trends in travel behavior. To aim to find how demographic change will influence the tourism market and how the industry can adapt to those changes. The travel analysis provided data on tourism consumer behavior, including attitudes, motives and intentions. Since, 1970 year, it is based on a random sample, representative for the population in private households aged 14 years or older. Then, a continuous high scientific standard combined with a national and international users makes the travel analysis a useful tool and reliable source for tourism industry and policy decisions. It aimed to gather statistical data. e.g. on the age structure and on demographic trends, quantitative and qualitative analysis with time series data from the travel analysis. It shows e.g. not only the future volume , quite different from today's seniors, or how who will travel of family holidays will change, e.g. single parents of low, but grandparents of growing significance for tourism.

Demographic change is said to be one of the important drivers for new trends in consumer traveling change behavior in most European countries (e.g. Lind 2001). Because the growing number of senior citizens in the European Union and other industralised countries, such as the USA and Japan, looks to become one of the major marketing challenges for the tourism industry. United Nations statistics predict that the share of people being 60 age or older will grow dramatically in the coming future, and is expected to rise from 10 percent of the world population in 2000 year to more than 20 percent in 2050 year (United Nations Population Division, 2001). From its statistic, some data showed that travel propensity increased throughout life until the age of about 50 years of age and was then kept stable until very late in life 75 age. The most important results is that the travel propensity when getting older is not going down between 65 and 75 age of course, the overall development of this variable is influenced by a lot of other factors which are rsponsible for quite a variation over time. It is now possible to suggest that the general pattern of travel propensity is one of the key indicators for holiday life cycle travel behaviour, includes three stages. The growth stage tends to increase from early aduithood until 45 age old or when reaching some 80%. The next stage is stabilisation from the ages of around 50 age,until 75 age old, starting with a lower increase. Finally, the decrease stage is a slight decrease occurs once people reach the more advanced age of 75 age to 85 age old (Lohmann & Danielsson 2001).

So, it seems Germany government tourism prediction to future travellers' behaviour indicated these findings, such as on how future senior generations will travel, who had used survey data to examine the patterns of travel behaviour of a generation getting older and applied the findings to draw conclusions on the future. Also, it predicted that on the future of family trips, family semgmentation will be the travel behaviour patterns in the future. These findings together with the statistical data on demographic change allowed for a better understanding of the coming tends in family holidays. It's aim developed in consumer behaviour related to demographic change and predicted what will happen future of tourism one had to consider other influences and drivers as well, for example, trends on the supply side. e.g. low cost airlines or in travelling consumption behaviour in general whether how the past may provide a key to predict travel patterns of senior sitizens to the future.

Given the projected growth of the senior citizens market, designing specific marketing strategies to meet the prospective needs of elderly tourists will become increasingly important. It has been an implict assumption that it will be a close relationship between the travel behaviour of today's senior citizens and the those of future ones. The growing number of senior citizens in the world. e.g. China, Hong Kong, Japan, USA etc. countries. Global senior citizen tourism market will be based solely on demographic predictions about the future of the population's age structure. However, many of these seniors won't only live longer but will be fitter and more active until later in life. Many of the will also have plenty in life. Many of them will also have plenty of time and money to spend on travel. So, will these new seniors behave like today's senior citizens? Will they adopt the same travel behaviour as the previous generation or become a new market of oldies for the leisure and tourism indudtry? However, to determine the actual number of senior citizens who will be travelling and to sought to evaluate and specify certain difficult to predict the actual numbers of senior citizen to any country. However, they can be based on the implicit assumption that there is a close relationship between the travel behaviour of past, present and future seniors. But is this a valid assumption? As the reiseanalyse travel analysis survey, which was conducted in Germany every year, offered some interesting data possibiltieis. It was designed to monitor the holiday travel behaviour, opinions and attitudes of Germans and has been carried out since 1970 year, questions in the questionnaire. Data are based on face to face interviews, with a representative sample of more than 7,500 repondents, the interviews being carried out in January each year. All results refer to the average for the defined generated, which ranges generally over ten years. The group of people then at the age of 60 to 69 age is described. This corresponds to the same generation ten years ago, when they had an age of 50 to 59 age. When this methodological approach is not necessarily very sophisticated, it does have the important advantages of being cost effective.

●

How to psychological method to predict
travel behavioural consumption.

On the psychological view point, I think individual traveler's character will have those kind of personal characteristics. First, simplicity searchers value above everything ease not transparency in their travel planning and holiday making, and are willing to avoid having to go through extensive research. Second, cultural purists use their travel as an opportunity to immerse themselves in an unfamiliar looking to break themselves entirely from their home lives and engage. Sincerely with a different way of living. Third, social capital seekers understand that to be well travelled is a personal quality, and their choices are shaped by their desire to take maximum of social reward from their travel. They will exploit the potential of digital media to enrich and inform their experiences, and structure their adventures always keeping in mind they are being watched by online audiences. Finally, reward hunters seek a return on the investment who make in their busy , high-achieving lives. Linked in part to the growing trend of wellness, including both physical and mental self improvement who seek truly extraordinary and often indulgent or luxurious' must have experiences.

Why needs to know the personal character of individual traveler's characteristics. Because if travel agents could feel which kinds of individual traveler's character, then who can predict which kind of travel package to design to them more easily. For example, how to determine future travel behaviour from past travel experience and perceptions of risk and safety? We need to concern that the influences of past international travel experience, types of risk associated with international travel and the overall degree of safety feeling during international travel on individual's travelling experiences likelihood of travelling to various geographic regions on their next international vacation trip or avoidance of those regions, due to perceived risk. Because individual traveler's experience of safety risk degree to the countries, it will influence who chooses to go to the countries/country to travel again.

Why travellers avoid certain destinations are as relevant decision making as why who choose to go to the country(countries) to travel. Perceptions of risk and safety and travel experiences are likely to influence travel decisions; efforts to predict future travel behaviour can benefit to individual tourist's decision making. As Weber & Bottom (1989) defined risky decision is as "choices among alternatives that can be described by prodability distributions over possible outcomes" (p.114). Some psychologists judge subjective perceptions of physical reality, i.e. image of a particular tourist destination, whereas value judgement refers to the way individual rank destinations according to whose attributes. i.e. attractiveness, safety, risk etc. factors to form on overall image. So, if the individual traveler had unhappy and worried and unsafe experiences to go to where the place(country) to travel during whose vacation time before. Then, this negative travel experience will influence who is afraid to go to the place (country) to travel again. Risk of place, country, destination or region means the danger is relatively high to the place, ie. increasing in airplane accidents, crime or terrorist activity targeting citizens of potential traveler's nationality or the probability of occurrence is great , ie. recent occurrences involving travel regions/destinations under consideration or effective actions to control consequences exist. i.e. selecting safe regions and destinations, taking extra precautions when traveling to risky destinations. These risk factors will influence the individual traveler who chooses to cancel travel plan to go to the country again.

Another interesting research, how to predict behavioural intention of choosing a travel destination, which has focus of toursm research for years, but the complex decision making process leading to the choice of a travel destination has not been well researched. The planned behaviour model using its core constructs, attitude, subjective norm and perceived behavioural control, with the addition of the past behavioural variable on behavioural intention of choosing a travel destination.

Understanding why people travel and what factors influence their behavioural intention of choosing a travel destination is beneficial to tourism planning and marketing. Understanding travel motivation is the push and pull model. The idea of the push and pull model is the decomposition of an individual's choice of a travel destination into two forces. The first force is the push factor that pushes an indvidual away home and attempts to develop a general desire to go somewhere else, without specifying where that may be. The second force is the pull factor, that pulls on individual toward a destination, due to a region specific travel location or perceived attractiveness of a destination. The respective push and pull factors illustrate that people travel because who are pushed by their internal motives and pulled by external forces of a destination. Nevertheless, how push and pull factors guide people's attitude and how these attributes lead to behavioural intentions of choosing a travel destination have rarely been investigated. The decision making process leading to the choice of a travel destination is a very complex process. The planned behaviour model is as a research framework to predict the behavioural intention of choosing a travel destination. The model based on the three constructs of attitude, subjective norm, and perceived behavioural control (Fishbein & Ajzen, 1975).

In conclusion, the factors can influence travelers who decide to choose to travel the country, which include personal safety was perceived to the highest motivation factors among the important factors which include, scenic beauty, cultural interests, friendliness of local people, price of trip, services in hotels and restaurants, quality and variety of food and shopping facilities and services. The factors include both push and pull. Push factors include knowledge, prestige, and enhancement of human relationship etc., whereas, the most significant pull factors include high technologic image, expenditure and accessibility etc. For example, Japanese travelers visiting Hong Kong. Push factors are such as exploration dream fulfillment and pull factors are such as benefits sought, attractions and good climate city. It will be the factor of future travel patterns and motivations of sub-cultural and ethic groups for Japanese choice to go to Hong Kong travelling.

Bibliography

Backman, K., Backman, S., Uysal, M. And Sunshine, K. (1995). Event Tourism : An Examination Of Motivations And Activities. Festival Management And Event Tourism, 3(1), 15-24.

Fishbein, M., & Ajzen, Z. (1975). Belief, Attitude, Intention And Behaviour: An Introduction To Theory And Research, Boston: Addison Wesley.

Hsu, C.H.C., Cai , L.A., Li, M(2010). Expectation,
Motivation And Attitude: A Tourist Behavioral
Model. Journal Of Travel Research, 49(3),
282-296. http://dx.doi, org/10.1177/004728750
9349266.

ICT Information And Communication Technology Switzerland, 2005. ICT Fakten (ICT facts).
Available from http://www.ictswitzerland.ch/de/ict%2fakten/factsfigures.asp(retrieved Dec.12, 2005) in German.
Lind, (2001): Befolkningen, Familjen, Livscykeln- Och Ekonomisk Tillvaxt. Institutet For Tillvaxtpo-litiska studier/ Vinnova/Nutek.
Lohmann, Martin (2001): The 31 st. Reiseanalyse-RA 2001. Tourism: vol. 49, no.1/2001;pp.65-67, Zagreb.
United Nations Population Division (2001). World Population Prospects: The 2000 year Revision, New York.
Weber E.U., & W, P.Bottom (1989). "Axiomatic
Measures Of Perceived Risk: Some Tests And extensions." journal of behavioral decision making, 2 (2): 113-31.

II

SCHOOL EDUCATION MARKET

What are the factors which can influence the final grades of academic students ? I shall indicate as below:

● Tutoring method factor

The tutoring method factor includes self-determined tutoring, academic advisor schedules tutoring, group tutoring, one-to-one tutoring, peer tutoring and professional tutoring. These different kinds of tutoring method can influence the final grades to any academic student. As the cognitive learning theory and humanistic theory both are for this study conceptual framework. The results of a one-way analysis of variance determined there were significant differences in final grades of students who received group tutoring compared to one-to-one tutoring and peer tutoring compared to professional tutoring.

In fact, many colleges and universities have had to provide tutoring to attend to the needs of all students' aims to teach them how to write assignments and how to exam to get higher grades. However, any methods of a tutoring will have benefits and weakness to any students. For example, students who attend group tutoring may have an advantage because other students may contribute additional information relevant to questions, whereas one-to-one tutoring will give the students the undivided attention of the tutor. In addition, students who attend tutoring provided by their peers rather than professonal tutors may feel more relaxed and relate to them differently then professional helpers. What methods do tutors use? Tutoring methods usually include self-determined, academic advisor, determined programs group, one-to-one, peer and professional tutoring. What is the relationship between final grades and tutoring programs. I suggested that academic programs, particularly professional tutoring are successful and may lead to increase student persistence in course completion. In fact, students who activity participated in the tutoring program had greater academic success compared to those who did not participate in the tutoring program. Further, no researchers had compared outcomes for students who received tutoring in a group setting rather than one-to-one settings.

In addition, no researchers had compared outcomes for students who receive tutoring from peer tutors rather than professional tutors. Also no research was found that outcomes were for students who were required to participate in tutoring services, but allowed to self-determine that schedules. However, research has shown that students who voluntary received tutoring service regularly most often received a passing grade in the course for which who received tutoring.

● Reading habits among students and its effect on academic performance factor

Reading habits are well planned of study which has attained a form of consistency on the part of students towards understanding academic subjects and passing at examinations. Both reading and academic achievements are interrelated and dependent on each other. Reading habits involve personal investigation, self-study, self thinking and analysis to each bok's content. So, reading habit is the student himself/herself motivation, it is not motivated by teachers, who need to spend their leisure time in reading both English and literature. However, the problem most students have that contributes to their poor performance in tests and examinations is lack of proper reading habits. For an excellent performance, there is the need to the student to form good reading and study habits. Whether what are the reading habits among students? Has reading habit effect on academic performance? Is there a relationship between student's reading habits and academic performance? What kind of materials to students read when who visit the library? Why do students engage in reading? People read for different reasons and purposes, some of which include for pleasure, leisure, relaxation and for knowledge.

In student view point, reading is an essential tool for knowledge transfer and the habit of reading is academic activity that increases skills in reading strategies. It seems reading habit can help any student to raise knowledge and writing ability to prepare to write their assignments for those different subjects and examinations. It is possible that examination grades and study habit has close relationship.

● Class attendance and academic performance factor

The major reasons are given by students for non-attendance which include external influences of assessment pressures, poor delivery of lecturers, timing of lectures and work commitments and financial constraints. Indeed, web-based learning approaches have become popular instead of some classroom attendance universities in our societies. So, it causes students who don't need to attend to classroom regularly. Although, some existing evidence points to a strong correlation between attendance and academic performance, no effect of the studies citied above demonstrate a causal affect. However, the levels of motivation, intelligence, prior learning and time-management skills is a major limiting factor to the utility of causal affect. However, these relationships are contingent upon a number of factors, such that it is nearly impossible to predict academic performance using socio-economic. To conclude, the non-attendance or attendance factor influences academic performance is difficult to measure, such as student motivation, socio-economic status and attendance is required to influence why the student choose to attend or not attend the classrooms.

The conclusion to drawn from this study is that gender, age, learning preference and entry qualifications did not cause any significant variation in the academic performance of students. Although, some students' academic performance were not significantly different from the rest of the students. It seems some talent students who don't need to attend any classrooms and their non-attendance behaviors won't influence their academic performance to be bad. Otherwise, some foolish students who need to attend classrooms to achieve passing grades.

● Drinking and academic motivation factor

Whether academic motivation can be a mediator for achievement. It was hypothesized that heavy drinking decreases academic motivation, which subsequently also decreases academic achievement. The effects of drinking on univerity grades: Does academic motivation play a role? However, academic achievement can be influenced by a number of factors and the effect of alcohol consumption on achievement has been of particular interest to researcher. Heavy drinking habit of students, e.g. weekly drinking alcohol, and/or consumption six or more alcohol on each occasion of drinking, these heavy drinking alcohol behaviour can influence these drinking wine students whose grades to be gone down in possible. High drinking wine or alcohol habit can cause day time sleepiness, unhealthy behaviours, like unhealthy sleep patterns because they may be linked to behavioural consequences. Due to students who regularly drink alchohol, then whose drinking behaviours have interrupted sleep cycles: They go to bed late, wake up late and experience increased daytime sleepiness. All factors of which were found to be associated with decreased academic performance. It seems heavy drinking alcohol habit of intelligent students will get the bad academic performance also.

● The link between sleep quantity and academic performance factor

Whether has it close relationship to link unhealthy sleep habits and academic performance. Such as current study examined the relationship between grade point average (GPA) and sleep, in terms of quality and quantity. In general, human need have four different aspects of sleep quantity. These aspect included number of nights spent with less than five hours of sleep during the past week, as well as during an average week, number of hours of sleep obtained in an average night, as well as the number of all nighter's the students. Results indicated a significant positive correlation between amount of sleep per night with GPA, and a significant negative correlation between average number of day per week that students obtained less than five hours of sleep and GPA.

Health sleep habits can defined , such as self-rated satisfaction with sleep, enough sleeping during the night non difficulty sleeping at night and non over sleeping. If students are unsatisfied with their quality of sleep, who will encounter studying problems, due to who lack nervous to attend any classrooms to listen any lecturers' speaking to remember any important contents of their different subjects every day. So, their non sleeping bad behaviour which will cause them to get the bad academic performance in possible finally.

● The relationship between physical fitness and academic performance factor

Whether can lacking enough physical fitness sport cause students to get bad academic performance? In fact, human needs health physical ftness of life to carrying on working or studying. Physical movements of the body are vital for normal brain development to children or young adult. So if the child or young adult chooses to spend whose time to often play video games to watch television or occupies himself/herself on the computer on the weekends and after school, instead of any physical fitness sports in whose relax time to spend time to do. It will have chance to cause blood pressure, depression and other diseases to him or her. It seems any student ought have enough time to do physical fitness to keep him or her mental health benefit to prepare to have health body to learn. Otherwise, lacking physical activity will cause lower levels of self-esteem and lower levels of anxiety to cause lower academic performance in the classroom to any students. For example, the mathematics and science students who need have health body to go to classroom to study. So, enough physical sports activities are important to these students. Due to a more focused mindset on academic performance has hindered the quality and quantity of these mathematics and science students to learn in classroom everyday. So, physical fitness has close relationship to academic performance.

● The relationship between student's learning style and academic performance factor

The student's personal factor, such as level of motivation, persistence, responsibility and need for structure, whether these factors can can influence whose academic performance. Which is learning style? It is the way a person processes, internalizes and studies new and challenging material. Student's performance may be related to learning preferences or styles as learners. Some experiments indicates that college students taught in their preferred learning styles scores higher on tests, fact knowledge, attitude and efficiency than those taught in instructional style. So mismatch of teaching styles and learning styles could give negative impaxt to students.

In the psychological view, due to students tend to be bored on inattentive in class, do poorly on tests, get discouraged about the course and may conclude that who are not good in the subject. As a result, students' success in classes may depend an understanding the learning style characteristics of students who enrol in the respective courses.

● The relationship between time management and academic performance factor

Managing time is any student's responsibilities. Time management is a skill that every student should not only know, but also apply. A lot of university students complain about running out of time when who need to do a certain assignment or prepare examination. They get frustrated beause who are not able to finish it before the due date. On the other hand, they spend a lot of time to meet their friends or playing, so who have no enough time to enhance their learning of productivity in order to get low grades. For example, a subject assignment needs have a important due date to finish to submit because who lack time management skill to predict the size of assignment, who need how long time to finish. So they won't have enough time to finish the assignment to submit before the due date to cause to get fail grade of the assignment.

In conclusion, any university students ought need to considerate these bad behaviours can influence their final grades. So, you ought to avoid to do these bad behaviours to reduce your bad grades risk occurrence.

III

OUTSOURCING SERVICE

Information Technology Outsourcing

In any organization information technology department, information system operations remain the predominant function outsourced, other functions are also being performed by external service providers and the relationship is between outsourcing and certain demographics: size, industry is formation intensity. The results suggest that system operations remain being performed by external service providers. Further, industry and information intensity has some influence on the extent of outsourcing of certain functions.

The first reason is cost reduction, trying to remain competitive and up-to-date is becoming a financial burden to many organizations. This is true particularly in fields, such as banking and financial services, health care and manufacturing. Hiring outsiders to handle part or even all of its information system often helps an organization to provide better services and maintain a competitive advantage. The information technology industry choice of outsourcing factor is related to size, industry type and information technology.

The second reason is technological and/or human resources in the management of the information technology infrastructure skill improvement. The information technology department outsourcing service to external service provider, includes the degree of internalization of technological resources and the degree of internalization of human resources. Some economists defined internalization of outsourcing service is as ownership is by the focal organization which takes on full control with profit and loss responsibility. Also who define outsourcing is as involving a significant use of resources, either technological and/or human resources, external to the organizational hierarchy in the management of the information technology infrastructure. So the information technology external service providers includes: applications development and maintenance, systems operations, networks/ telecommunications management and user computing support, system planning and management purchase of application software, but excludes business consulting services, after-sale vendor services and the lease of telephone lines etc. outsourcing services.

The third reason is economics of scale in areas of hardware, software. This pressure is seen as the most significant factor driving today's corporate interest. An outsourcing service provision might be in a position to exploit economics of scale in areas of hardware, software and staff since it pools different kind of technological projects from many service receivers. Outsourcing information technological service can reduce the corporate's cost with the high level of IT investment, there are increasing pressures to move away from fixed expenditure, corporate overhead towards a more direct variable cost approach to control the IT operations. The IT costs can become predictable for overruns is often placed on the service provider. Outsourcing service can allow the service to gain immediate access to competitiveness in delivering products or services as well as to avoid of obsolescence risk, due to the changes in the nature of the IT infrastructure, the risk of obsolescence is high. Outsourcing can allow the service provider has the ability to diversify these risks across a broad range of service receivers. However, long term contracts might in spread the risk, the weakness is back to the receiver.

It seems outsourcing IT service has also these disadvantages: such as, loss of flexibility or managerial control. Outsourcing reduces real or perceived control over both quality real or perceived control over both the quality of software and the timetable of project since the work is now being carried out by people not under direct supervision. It also threats to long term career prospects to information system professionals because many of them do not find suitable. Is jobs or promising career paths in both areas of the corporation. Outsourcing also increases coordination cost. It may requires increasing time to communicate and coordinate with the service provider. Traditionally, the formal meeting cost of negotiating and monitoring the outsourcing contract are potentially wide ranging, indirect and substantial increasing, such as, additional releasing or transferring employees, in license transfer by software vendors and in re-negotiating contracts costs. So, the IT industry of profit motivates service provider might not be in the least interests of the outsourcing service receivers. Some IT service providers are in the business of maximizing their profit at any cost, this could run counter to a service receiver's interest.

●

Outsourcing or insourcing in human resource supply chain factor

To choosing of outsourcing or insourcing in human resource supply chain factor of the controlling service demanders needs to concern this issues: Should human resource activities be provided in house or should all or past of those activities be outsourced? The relationship between organizational structure and the HR function is an important variable. The individual activities that comprise HR systems include not only the employee life cycle from recruiting to termination, but also planning for organizational staffing needs and improving organizational effectiveness. How organizations need to outsource HR function to not care employees knowledge and skill is a factor to influence any organizations choose to outsourcing non core employees when which have no any right employees to be promoted to do the position. For example, firms engage in HR outsourcing to reduce management access HR expertise, achieve workforce flexibility, focus managerial resources and keep up with changing workplace negotiations. Also, supporting the tend is the availability of common technology platform, which can reduce costs for organizations and risks. However, organizations are afraid of losing some control over delivery of outsourcing services and finding themselves dependent on the vendor or liable for the vendors actions where there are both benefits and challenges may be informed by the structure of the relationship between client firms and these organizations offering the outsourced activities to client firms.

What variables are impacted by HR outsourcing of staffing? Which include: administrative costs for labor expense, client firm to HR relations, HR regulatory competency requirement, knowledge of cost factors, e.g. billing and pay rates, vendor markups and margins, vendor management competency requirement, client and vendor relationship, communication is between client managers and staffing vendor, employee data-available, data quality control, data security, match with job requirement, employee quality, inter-vendor competition, mining of client talent by vendor, quality content for preferred staffing vendor, standardization of business process (intra-company), strategic focus of client firm, demands on client managers vendor competency and external economic environmental viability.

However, it has dynamic relationship between the client firms and staffing vendors. Moreover, the models of human resource supply chain, every has different set of advantages and disadvantages for the client firms. The models can be relate to the decision making process on outsourcing of human resources. As strategic services tactic decisions have an important impact or selecting the particular HR outsourcing model that a client firm adopter. The another model is the balance of power and control over managing the control workers differ to decide what every worker individual skills or abilities outsourcing demand. Moreover, local contracting is also the predominant traditional model for outsourcing staffing with non-core employees. A client firm usually uses several staffing vendors to meet temporary staffing needs for seasonal functions, employee absences and special projects. The advantages of local contracting are high touch and high quality of service by staffing vendors, minimal bureaucracy, empowerment of hiring any high qualified employees to get the job done, and a relatively better fit between specific staffing vendors and functional needs.

The disadvantages of local contracting can increase costs from non-standardization of hiring practices and procedures across the client form, a significant amount of word of mouth and subjective quality issues, high local costs and client firm us subjected to the capabilities of the staffing vendors and contract employees. However, local HR contracting is the most flexible, high quality, but expense, inefficient and ineffective HR outsourcing model for the client firm. Another model is the working period to be decided to outsource HR contracting. In this situation, in the short term and on a day-to-day basis, the client firm aims to achieve on economy of scale with its staffing vendors. The total costs of temporary workers as well as internal costs for contracting with several different vendors are higher than if it needs one staffing vendors to meet all its needs. So, the client company can set the reasonable pricing that it pays for its temporary outsourcing staffs. Each staffing vendor secures a different rate range with each vendor as opposed as one contact. In the long term, it is benefiting, each specialized staffing vendor is able to fully work with each function needs temporary utilization is better than the average. Mismatches are fewer. Functional departments are able to receive a high quality / high touch service in any time period. Another model is the centralizing is when the department standardizes the staffing process to drive costs down of temporary workers. This tends to occur when a percentage of non-core employees reach a certain ratio of core employees. The advantages include more uniform standards in hiring process, billing rates and pay rates, departmental hiring managers can refocus their effort to choose outsourcing staffing, criteria may be established for a performed suppliers list and greater security for the staffing established vendors that offer higher quality services. The disadvantages include new departmental responsibilities in HR which decreases outsourcing efficiencies for the organizations daily administrative direction is rather than long term strategic direction. Usually lacking qualifications to fulfill the responsibilities, overall, centralizing of HR outsourcing is that firms can achieve more standardization which additional bureaucratic costs and the necessary non-core jobs do not get done as a need. Another model is purchasing HR, which manages staffing vendors from HR to the purchasing unit of an organizations. The goal is to continue cost reductions by increasing efficiencies. In conclusion, the main benefits of HR outsourcing include maintaining organizational control over the hiring process, application of purchasing capabilities for greater standardization in hiring processes pay rates and bill rates. So, any outsoucred HR organizations may be reduce hiring process cost.

●

Global outsourcing source strategy
in a value supply chain

What is global outsourcing source strategy in a departmental role? In a highly competitive global environment, many manufacturers are responded by setting and outsourcing relations for components and finished products with lower cost producers on a contractual electronic commerce department, (original equipment manufacturer basis). Outsourcing strategy is part of the value supply chain of corporate activated. Nowadays, global outsourcing increases organizational and technological capacity of firms and cooperating a network of remotely located external suppliers performing. These understanding the important roles that product designers, engineers and production managers and purchasing manager etc. play in global sourcing strategy empowerment. Specially, electronic commerce is popular to supply chain. For example, Toyota car manufacturing company, owns unique capabilities by designing and manufacturing certain car components in-house , i.e. insourcing. Toyota also outsource manufacturing activities, Toyota adopts purchasing necessary, but no strategic inputs from independent component suppliers on obtaining a lower cost for these inputs. For example, products would be belts, tires and batteries to vehicle products that are not customized and do not differentiate its products from its competitors. Toyota's outsourcing strategy is car strategic inputs provide differentiation, e.g. engine, transmission etc. are sources from suppliers based on strategic partnership to gain to access to suppliers' capabilities and it is also a conceptualize global outsourcing sourcing strategy to Toyota car manufacturing company.

How value chain outsourcing affects firm level performance. Global outsourcing strategy means to identify which production units that will serve which particular markets and how components will be supplied for production and thus included a number of basic choices, companies can make in decision how to serve various markets. Either choice relates to the use of inputs, assembly or production within the country to serve a foreign market or decides to use of internal or external supplies of components or finished products. In this outsourcing source input situation, the term sourcing is needed to describe how multi-national companies mange in of components and finished products in serving foreign and domestic markets. Sourcing decision making is both contractual point of view, the sourcing of major components and products are occurred by multi-national companies. First is from parents or their foreign subsidiaries. Second is from independent suppliers on a contractual basis. The first type of sourcing is known as insourcing. Otherwise, the second type of sourcing is referred to outsourcing. How to achieve economies of scale by outsourcing or insourcing sourcing input strategy? Therefore, the two outsourcing strategies are multi-faceted and require careful examination.

●

Outsourcing benefits in economic view

The two economists (Abrahamson & Rosenkopf, 1993) indicated that In long term, outsourcing can help to reduce fixed investment in finance view point, in-house manufacturing facilities and thus lower the breakeven point, which subsequently helps boost an outsourcing company whose return on equity (ROE). Thus, if any one corporate performance is evaluated on the basis of its contribution to the company's ROE. Also, in the short term or long term on resource inputs outsourcing view, early adopters of outsourcing strategy indeed experienced efficiency gains as they were able to reduce fixed investment in in-house manufacturing facilities and lows their ROE. But, later adopters may have different to gain institutions legitimacy or because of competition pressures in the industry, despite some inherent uncertainties about the long term costs and benefits of outsourcing strategy. It seems that outsourcing strategy was devised as any organization's policy makers to access trade linkages of benefits for short term or long term. Outsourcing strategy is a systematic analysis of the economic, political and regulatory implications indicates potential benefits along with a number of potentially negative side effects to any organizations. Then, outsourcing strategy will be caused this question: How to assess the risks and benefits of outsourcing for organizational sectors and nations both? The decision to change outsourcing behavior to carry a business activity may have profound implications for outsourcer and outsource receiver both, but little impact of the sector level. The common occurrence of industry decisions to outsource most manufacturing, including sale of factories, it created a new sub-sector, contract manufacturing. Otherwise, at a national level and public sectors become less distinct to outsourcing strategy. Public policy on outsourcing has stimulated extensive debate, privatization social justice and value for money etc. challenges.

●

What motivate outsourcing what is being outsourced risk and concerns?

Whether what motivate outsourcing, evidence of what is being outsourced risk and concerns? Outsourcing activities include: outsources manufacturing components and other value adding activities. Some focused on employment is outsourced another firm's employees carrying out tasks previously performed one's own employees. Outsourcing is an activity outside the organization's chosen core competencies. It seems outsourcing is a sub-contracting relationships between firms, all foreign production, hiring of workers in non-traditional jobs, such as control workers and temporary and part time workers.

What are the motivations for outsourcing reasons? Why outsourcing is needed to any organization. For example, it can enable firms to focus on core activities. The concept of focus originates in operation on a small, manageable, number of tasks at which the operation becomes excellent to specific technologies and as a risk of vertical integration advantages. Other benefits of outsourcing appear is literature on strategic management, operations management, purchasing and supply and innovations. Moreover, outsourcing can improve flexibility to meet changing business conditions, demands for products, services and technologies by creating smaller and more flexible clear evidence includes improved creditability image, greater workforce flexibility and avoiding being backed into specific assets and technologies are harder to measure. How outsourcing can improve company performance. For airline manufacturing industry example, Hill & Jones (1995) showed that the manufacture of a large portion of the Boeing 767 is Boeing's third largest commercial aircraft, which is outsourced to Japanese manufacturers, which include Fuji, Kawasaki and Mitsubish. As a result, only 10% of the value of the 767 Boeing is produced in-house. So, outsourcing is an attempt to enhance manufacturing air place industry competitiveness.

●

How can choose smarter outsourcing?

How can choose smarter outsourcing? Organizations hope to do sight options to save money, among themselves staff layoffs and a reduction of overhead costs, such as office space. Private companies have long outsourced in order to save time and money. During periods of economic growth, many organizations began to use outsourcing more frequently and staff workloads grew in proportion to increase budgets. Tasks such as conducting needs assessments, reviewing proposals, conducting site visits, monitoring and creating evaluations systems were increasingly given to outside contractors, consulting firms and independent consultants in the belief that external specialists could do the work more efficiently and effectively than company itself.

Nowadays, there is a growing stream of organizations need to research into the outsourcing of innovation activities within the innovation, management, marketing and economics disciplines. These organizations need to understand how with the outsourcing practice becoming more commonplace in their industry. However, their behaviors bring these two questions: Whether outsource or internalize innovation activities and the performance implications of this decision can support for both transaction cost and resource based arguments is examined with both theory bases showing substantial attention? Whether outsourcing innovation activities can lead to faster product development and cost savings? On advantages hand, it is possible that outsourcing may lead to higher costs and slower new product development. Further the technological uncertainty may have conflicting impacts on the outsourcing decision that are not yet well understand. When outsourcing product development has reduced costs and has proved speed to market. On disadvantages hand, outsourcing has also reduce product development time delays and higher quality concerns. Why to cause performance implications of outsourced innovation activities in transaction in cost economics and the resource-based view point? When outsourcing product development has been to reduce costs and has improved speed to market, outsourcing product development is not unlike other make or buy decisions. So, make vs buy decision is similar to logistic and IT outsourcing. Internalization of product development will be preferred when transaction costs are excessive. Otherwise, the market i.e. outsourcing will be selected when transaction costs are low. Transaction costs can include adaption, safeguarding and measurement costs. Adaption costs represent efforts to adjust contract to change conditions and are a result of environmental uncertainty. When a firm may have to revise on agreement with a partner company, this facing substantial penalties, due to an unstable market environments, the firm is likely to perform this function internally. Safeguarding costs characterize the costs of an outsourcing provider acting opportunities after investments have been made in the inter-firm relationship and are the result of transaction specific investment. Measurement costs include all expenses with confirming that contracts have been fulfilled passably. The contracting firm may face substantial costs to estimate quality for contractual services. When the sum total of these transaction costs is substantial, internalization will be favored.

●

What is environmental uncertainty factor?

Environmental uncertainty refers to unanticipated changes in circumstances surrounding an exchange in market uncertain and technological uncertainty. Market uncertainty is the fluctuation and unpredictability of demand. With respect to innovation projects, market uncertainty may cause frequent changes to the development, complications and adding expense to external contracting. These changes may necessitate renegotiation or cancellation of innovation contracts, which will likely carry prohibitive penalties (a term) transaction costs. These transaction costs promote internalization under high levels of market uncertainty. Otherwise, technological uncertainty environments, selecting market governance allows firms the flexibility to end relationship should technical requirements shift. It seems that market and technological external change factor will influence to benefits to any organizations to choose outsourcing strategy. On the other side, outsourcing can bring this question: Whether the offshore outsourcing of information technology jobs choice is suitable to any IT organizations? Nowadays. The offshore outsourcing if IT jobs from the United States has been enabled by a powerful influence of global economic demographic and technological forces. In fact, many IT companies were drawn to offshoring outsourcing because of the need for programmers to fix the Y2K problem in the late 1990- year. It is shortages of US programmers. Other factors driving this phenomenon include the wage gap between the US and developing countries, e.g. China and India, advances in technology, labor availability, expanding foreign markets and foreign government incentives. The spread of the offshoring phenomenon from low skill manufacturing to high wage white collar service industry jobs reduces the country's IT jobs critics, it represents the mobility for many US workers who saw post-secondary education as the route to a higher standard of living. The offshoring outsourcing of manufacturing and service jobs from the US to lower cost foreign nations become a national issue in a very short time. The impact of offshore outsource on the information technology sector gives outsourcing potential loss of millions of jobs at all wage levels and the critical contribution is the IT sector to US productivity growth. However, decisions about the locations of manufacturing or service facilities reflect market forces key factors include the size of local markets, capital availability and costs, labor availability skill levels and cost, logistic issues, reliability and infrastructure and IT in particular relationships with research institutions. All these factors will influence the choice of offshore outsource IT jobs strategy top any organizations.

●

Whether outsourcing will bring
what kind of work skills.

Whether outsourcing will bring what kind of work skills. Many employers choose outsourcing to employ employees. This core of our work is identifying trends which will transform global society and the global marketplace. How it influences our nature of work form health care to technology, the work place and human identity. A decade ago, workers worried about jobs being outsourced overseas. Today companies, such as Odesk and Liveops can assemble teams " in the cloud" to dosales, customer support and many other tasks. It seems outsoucring can influence many high technological job of changes. Global connectivity, smart machines and new media are just some of the drivers reshaping how we thank about work, what constitutes work and the skills, we shall need to be productive contributors in the future. As computer technology in the cloud will be used popularly to society. A signal is typically a small or local innovation that has the potenial to grow in scale and geographic distribution. A signal can be a new product, a new practice, a new market strategy, a new policy or new technology, such as online cloud computing files storage service method. It is an innovative social science method to computer users. However, this new computer files storage method influences outsourcing service of needs increasing. It will have key drivers and skills areas that will be most relevant to the technological workforce of the future.

It is estimates that by 2025 year, the number of Americans over 60 age will increase by 70%. The challenge of an aging population will come. What it means to age, individuals will need to rearrange their approach to their career, family life and education to accommodate their life plan. Increasing, people will work long past 65 age in order to have adequate resources for retirement. Multiple careers will be commplace and lifelong learning to prepare for occupational change will see major growth. To take advantage of this well experienced organizations will have to rethink the traditional career paths in organizations, creating more diversity and flexibility. As the high technological cloud computing storage method is invented. Any organizations can save their files to the central cloud computer storage system website to save or find their files from website more easily. It will reduce their computer department expenditure and staff salary. So, outsourcing computer file storage service demands will be influenced to increase to any organizations as well as organizations will reorganize their computer department job nature to shape the kinds of social, economic and political organizations which inhabit. Outsourcing is a good solve method to assist organizations to pay cheap salary to employ many retired high age workers by contract or temporary or part time method to reduce their computer department's number of employees and the retired labors only need to pay cheap salary to learn how to use internet to help whose employers to save their files to their outsourcing computer storage service provider's central computer storage system every day efficiently. So, organizations do not need to employ many computer department staffs to avoid to pay much salaries to this computer department expenditure. They can choose outsourcing to pay cheap salaries to employ many retirement labors to assist them to do simple office storage job from internet channel efficiently and effectively. Hence, internet high technological innovation can influence office outsoucing of job duties increasing.

Whether domestic outsoucing in the America, what assesses trends and effects on job quality. Nowadays, US firms' use of contractors and independent contractors and its effect on job quality and inequality. Why firms choose contract out for certain functions and assess their predictions about likely impacts on job quality, stagnant wages, growing inquality and the deterioration of job quality are among the most important challenges facing the US economy today. Although any country's domestic outsourcing , firms' use of contractors, franchises and independent contractors any one of these factors is a potentially important influence to companies reduce compensation and shift economy risk to workers. However, the domestic outsoucing takes place on a much larger scale and effects many more workers than has been recognized ranging from low wage service workers, security guards, warehouse workers and hotel housekeepers to professionals and technical workers, such as programmers, health care technicians and accountants. These tends are part of structural change in the organization of production to influence quality of jobs and the nature of employment contract after outsourcing jobs are popular. The quality of jobs include wages, benefits, employee skills and training and mobility opportunities and job security as well as inequality across jobs. Domestic outsoucing concerns these issues: such as employment and labor law, the provision of health, pension and other workplace benefits. However, any companies choose outsourcing of employment reasons include, such as that it relates how management choices to pursue value added or cost focused strategies. Contracting out is difficult to define because a large part ot economic activity has always occurred through business-to-business transactions, as captured in macro-economic input-output models. Outsoucing job employment method can influence any one labor's individual quality of jobs. Usually, international companies choose the offshoring of work in global supply chains. Until recently, the domestic counterpart outsourcing employment method has grown supply chains to domestic or regional outsoucing employment.

What factors cause domestic outsourcing and whether firm decisions about what to retain in-house and what to outsource have changes over time. Some evidence suggests that firms have responded by focusing on their core competencies and outsourcing low value added tasks as well as higher value added specialized functions. Advanced technologies have facilitated this process by allowing firms to outsource entire functions ans more easily monitor contractors as well as employees who work, leading to new forms of networked production and rise of specialized outsouring employment firms. Domestic outsoucing influences the changes of job quality, benefits, hours, workload, job stability, schedule stability and occupational safety, health, incidence of wage theft and access to training and promotions. Predictions are less clear for job requiring professional or technical or specialized skills or those that are outsourced to large and diversified outsourced contractors. Types of outsourced contracts include: suppliers or vendors of products, such as manufacturing inputs or services, such as business services or staffs service or staffing firms, franchisees and independent contract, such as freelancers, independent contracts or non demand platform outsourced workers. It is significant restructuring of domestic manufacturing supply chains will greater reliance on suppliers and subcontractors. In addition, the potential growth of on demand outsourcing work as well as other forms of job fragmentation. It causes this question: How outsourced workers are multiple forms of income generating work to achieve economic security and how outsourcing workers can build career across jobs and over time.

Firm in every sector of the economy contract with other firms as part of their production process, as do governmental entities. The functions that are outsourced vary widely. For example: human resources ans research and development functions, building services, recycling, regulation and compliance, accounting, credit card collection, call centres, mortage and check processing, information technology and data processing, logistics and transportation, machine maintenance, cable installation, food services, food processing, parts manufacturing and assembly, laundry and housekeeping etc. outsourced jobs causes.

Whether what business impact of outsourcing will be caused? Nowadays, IT outsourcing was clearly a part of an effective management strategy that the companies felt IT outsourcing strategy can bring to achieve positive results. Information technology outsourcing providing servicers will be predicted to provide services that is expected to raise over the next five years minimum. The companies demand clients expected benefits of IT outsourcing and determined that cost reduction, increased operation, efficiency and improved IT effectiveness. What are the impacts of outsourcing to influence better long-term improvement in the business performance? It is impossible to being benefits of significant reduction and lower growth in sellings, general and administrative expense to IT outsourcing company demand clients. Also, pre-existing corporate cultures are focused on business improvement to IT outsourcing company demand clietns. In the past researches, some economists indicated that points can be used to reflect the actual numbers increase or decrease in percent. However, their prior researches shows that prior to outsourcing, the annual growth in selling, general and administration expenses of eompanies in the study was already 4.2 points lower than sector medium. Moreover, within one to two years after IT outsourcing these companies improved even most. Annual growth in selling and general administrative expenses for them was 9.9 points lower efford to assist any IT outsourcing will have selling and administrative expenses for long term. Also, almost two-third of the companies studied outperformed in increased growth in return on asset two to three years after IT outsourcing commenced. Prior to outsourcing, the annual ROA growth rate for companies in the study ws 7.5 points lower than the sector median. After outsourcing, however these companies experienced 8.6 points higher median a substantial change of 16.1 points. Also, nearly two to third of the companies studied grew earnings faster than their peers. Two to three years after IT outsourcing, companies experienced an annual rate of growth in earnings 11.8 points higher than the growth rate of the sector median. Thus, it seems IT outsourcing can assist the IT outsourcing demand clients to reduce expenditure and to raise income both as the same time. Then, it will cause these questions to IT outsourcing demand clients. Is outsourcing influencing in an economic downturn to finance sector in the short term? Is the finance sector's renewed change for outsourcing just a temporary cost-cutting measure? Will today's economic climate initiate long term financial and productivity gains? Whether what are benefits and disadvantages of outsourcing finance sector IT. I shall demonstrate why outsourcing open source software support and maintenance can be a good choice to start. Firstly when company plans to budget cuts expenditures, IT outsourcing is often the first choice. For example in 2003 year, Zurich Financial services' sprawling IT department consisted of more than 7,500 employees. After posting a record loss of 3.4 billion the year before, Zurich decided to cut down on in those staff and outsource nearly half of its IT work. Outsourcing has successfully cut costs by 45 percent and cut the number of in house IT staff by 60 percent. Here are some of the benefits that companies enjoy when they outsource information technology functions to competent, reliable vendors.

In fact, it can be too expensive to maintain, company's own information technology, especially during a recession. Fortunately, many IT functions can be easily and efficiently outsourced, positively impacting individual company's bottom line. Employee costs are much higher than just salary and benefits, keeping employees happy, productive and busy takes time, effort and money. Although, many IT staffs will be dismissed, it will increase the unemployment ratio in societies. But, moving an IT service out of house means financial organizations don't have to worry about technology refresh costs in the future. It also cuts down on human resources requirements, specialist IT service provides which can provide the newest technologies and deliver quality service more than company itself in house information provides are the most effective to develop and implement and upgrade their clients' software or the launch on a new platform, due to the expert's time is wasted on day-to-day duties for whose other IT outsourcing demand clients. However, instead of IT outsourcing service outsourced offshoring in that service sector, how economic impact to influence the outsourced offshoring country. For example, United States continues to run an international trade surplus in services. Many Americans are particularly concerned about the loss of skilled, well paid jobs in such fields as computer programming and accounting etc. positions. These jobs seemed relatively secure at a time when many manufacturing jobs were being cost to import competition. Similarly, telephone call centers, once viewed as an esonomic development opportunity in some areas, increasingly are moving low wage countries, such as India and the Philippines. Thus, offshoring raises many questions for policymakers and general public. For example, which service jobs will be affected most by import competition. What are the likely effects of service-sector offshoring on U.S.A. output, employment and our standard of living, such as America? Is offshoring really a problem that requires restrictive government actions or are other kinds of policies more appropriate to give Americans or other countries the highest possible living standard?

The term of offshoring refers to the relocation of jobs and production to a foreign country. The relocated jobs and production could be at a foreign office of the same multinational company or at a separate company located abroad. In constrast, the term outsourcing doesn't necessary imply that jobs and production are relocated to another country. The major outsourcing service jobs include human resource, accounting and information technology etc. in-house service jobs in large organizations. However, the loss of service jobs and factory production is caused by offshoring is diffuclt to measure. It is also difficult to determine the impact of offshoring on total services employment in the United States or other countries. International trade in services covers a wide range of industries and activites. For example, travel and transportation includes travel expenditures, passenger fares and frieght and port services, royalties and license fees cover transactions including patents, copyrights, trademarks and other intangible proprietary rights to use, produce or distribute products. Other private services include many of these industries, such as education, financial services insurance, telecommunications and other professional services etc. Some economists indicated that occupational employment statistics for the Unisted States provided additional evidence that past service sector offshoring had been small. About 14 million service jobs were at risk of offshoring in 2000 year, when about 96 million service jobs had a low risk of ofshoring. The decline in the at-risk service occupations from 2000 year to 2002 year was about 218,000 jobs or roughly 109,000 jobs annually, relatively small number that is consistent with the estimates of McCarthy or Zandi. In percentage terms, employment in the at risk occupations fell at a faster rate from 2000 year to 2002 year than in the low risk occupations. This faster decline is consistent with offshoring activity, although the decline is consistent with other explanations as well, such as faster of technological change in industries employing the risk occupations or greater cyclical sensitivity in these industries. Because offshoring was not the only cause of job loss in the risk occupations, the number of jobs moved offshore was undoubtedly less than 109,000 jobs annually. However, the estimates may understate the total impact because domestic companies with expanding worldwide employment may have located may of their newly created jobs abroad even when they didn't reduce their US employment. Some of those foreign jobs might provide services to US customers and potentially foreign jobs might provide service to US . Conversely, the estimates may overstate the total job loss from offshoring of the foreign outsourcing of some support jobs prevents the loss of other domestic jobs by keeping US firms competitive in world markets. For example, cost reductions from offshoring IT jobs might help a US financial services company win foreign contracts, preserving many professionals and support jobs in the US.

Lower production costs in foreign countries are a major cause of service sector offering. Although, the costs of land and other resources may be cheaper abroad, but the main difference betweeb the US and developing countries is labor costs. There is a large gap in computer programmer wages between the US and other countries. Any organizational capital includes both physical capital, such as machinery and computers and human capital , such as skills and knowledge. The cost savings is come from offshoring also might be reduced if the firm needed to pay higher transportation and telecommunication costs or management spends more time on service quality and data security. Still, the much lower levels of wages ans benefits in developing countries suggests that many services can be produced abroad at lower cost. The in-house professional relocation of labor-intensive service activities, such as legal transcription services to countries with lower labor costs is consistent with economists' basic theory of international trade, comparative advantage. So, in-house outsourced professional service will be a corporative advantage, if the country's legal profession is poor level to compare with the another country. e.g. the skill in-house the legal professional labors of the developing country, such as China is poor educational level to compare with the developed country, such as US. So, if China large organizations chose to outsource themselves in-house legal service jobs to outsource offshoring to US legal professional lawyers to do. It can bring comparative advantage to China large outsourced in-house legal service organizations, due to these China outsourced large organizations can reduce to employ to pay too much salaries to these many in-house Chinese domestic lawyers and the US outsourced legal consultants whose can give more professional legal recommendation to serve to the China large organizations.

In conclusion, although offshoring strategy can increase unemployment chance for this disadvantge. But, all of outsourcing benefits weighs are more than the offsourcing disadvantages. However, outsourcing strategy can have these benefits to the outsourced service demanders. Such as outsourcing is no longer just about cost saving, it is also a strategic tool that may power the twenty first century global economy. Moreover, outsourcing can increase productivity and competitiveness, e.g. for every 1000 jobs British Airways sends to India , the airline saves $23 million, companies can devote a portion of their outsourcing savings to helping employees make job transitions, also leader can no longer afford to view outsourcing as a business tactic, it is now essential to remain competitive. On the world stage, workers now compete globally, so individuals must continually learn more to vie successfully with their peers worldwide, the average company only spends about 20% of the value of its outsourcing contracts to manage its relationship with the outsource provider. So, in the positive view point, outsourcing strategy can bring a potential primary driver of the global economy development. Although, outsourcing can also cause the raising of domestic unemployment chance. But companies may soon be more outsourced than in sourced, signifying a fundamental reorganization that will affect employees, managers, customers and executives. Customers' choice will increase product costs will drop and workers' roles will change. Finally, the most important, the developing country will earn comparative advantage from the developed country's employers' offshoring jobs provision. Thus, the developing country's unemployment rate will be reduced, then the global economy will be kept more balance fairly.

Reference
Abrahamson, E., & Rosenkopf., (1993). Institutional and competitive bandwagons: Using mathematical modeling and a tool to explore innovation diffusion.
Academy of management review, 18(3), 487-517.
Hill, C.W.L. & Jones, G.R. 1995. Strategic management, An integrated approach. Boston: Houghtom Mif In.

IV

Internet MULTI-LEVEL SERVICE MARKET

•

What are the differences between multi level
marketing and direct personal sale?

It seems that multi level marketing (MLM), netwrok marketing and direct sellers scheme marketing which are under the pyramid retail sales criterion. It means only third parties with no connection to the selling organizations are considered legitimate "ultimate users". Consequently, it deems the consumption of product by distributors (participants), "internal consumption" to be illegalitimate and simply a cover for fraud.

As multi level marketing or direct sellers from pyramid schemes both marketing which need individual participant or distributor who give money to buy their products to join to whose business to earn commissions. It seems the participant or distributor will be client role more than member or business partnership role. So, it seems MLM or direct sellers from pyramid schemes which main income sources are come from participants or distributors (internal clients). Rather, the key question is to determine whether the purchasers, whoever who may be actually resell or consume their products if the sales transactions are thus reveals to legitimate, as a matter of economic principle. They are also revealised to have increased social welfare. By accepting and adopting without further inquiry the "retail sales criterion", even though it is contrary to basic principles of economics and logic. Consequently, I shall indicate these above proposed test to distinguish legitimate from fraudulent enterprise of legitimacy to multi level marketing or pyramid schemes direct sellers both sale channels.

The reasons of legitimacy to multi level marketing or pyramid schemes direct sellers include which are inappropriately not just the consumer surplus flowing from, but also the profits that the parent firm earns from selling products to dustributors for their internal consumption. This error is caused by asserting that the resulting biased estimates of cash flow are sufficient to indicate that either a pyramid scheme (multi level or direct personal sale) is in progress. These both network sale channels discard all profits earned with internal consumption and because they assume, without the justificaton or validation, that all participants (distributors) in a direct selling enterprise act to as to maximize their cash income. What is the mean of relating high rate at which individuals are to direct selling is sufficient to be defrauded. It is alternative explanations for the rate at which individuals quit direct selling (the "quit rate"), and it provides no economic analysis or inquiry as to the quit rate those distributors might exhibit outside direct selling. It implies the quit rate of distributors in either direct selling or multi level (network) enterprise is pyramid scheme comparable to what one might observe in the counter-factual in which those individuals are employed as wage labour.

As the accounting theory view, pyramid multi level marketing fraud is considered of circumstances unrelated to pyramid fraud, such as calculations of distributors (participants) income whether a parent company's current cash outflows are fully funded by inflows. More direct personal sale or phyramid theme sale business calculations in this regard are biased toward finding fraud because which discard all profits earned with internal consumption and because which assume without theoretical justification or validation that all participants in a direct selling enterprise act as to maximize their cash income. Alternative explanation for the rate at which individuals quite direct selling the quit-rate and provides no economic analysis might exhibit outside direct selling. In fact, a high rate is sufficient to conclude that distributors (participants) were defrauded is apparent upon noting that there are also high quit-rates in other undeniably legitimate businesses. A direct selling (pyramid) of only a few distributors are able to build businesses that six and seven figure annual incomes is similiarly. Chief Executive officer and the distribution of salaries at many commercial entities exhibits a pyramidal form that logic would conclude that all corporations must be considered pyramid fraudsters in the labour market. Even of an economic analysis is well intentioned from direct personal sale market or pyramid enterprises in any countries. The politicies of different countries governments advocated and other misinterpretations, impose costs on consumers, producers and society at large. An objective appraisal of the costs and benefits with using test that are generated false positives represents the first step toward a meaning ful; analysis of the appropriate public policy.

This direct personal sale or pyramid direct sales scheme is concluded by providing an examination of the costs and benefits of regulation and increased enforcement. It seems direct personal sale market has no any legal doctrine support that only sales to third parties constitute legitimate business activity and application of logic and the misinterpretation and misapprehension of prior court rulings that have biased inquiries into the potential to generate false positives. So, some economists have failures of logic and economic that have characterized prior evaluations of public policy low and pyramid schemes or direct sale market.

Our goal is to providing some guiding principles to indicate economically sensible, how a true pyramid scheme or direct personal sale market can be identified and the costs and benefits of different approaches as to how fraud should be detected, with MLM and pyramid direct sale schemes. Otherwise, Multi level market, MLM compensates not only in the form of commissions on sales to distributors (participants), but it also compensate commissions on the sales of it's recurits. The fact, that the share prices of MLM enterprises that have one public have remained positive indicates that the market believes MLM enterprises have value and that this value will be sustained. In constrast, a direct personal sale market enterprise is unsustainable, e.g. a pyramid scheme that will collapse. Or always faces the threat of being shut down as a fraud by regulators, would not be able to sustain positive market value.

It is important to note that legitimate multi level network direct selling benefits not just the parent firm and distributors, but also businesses and society at large. A MLM's products may require its salespeople to invest meaningful time and effort in educating the client as to the benefits of the product, resulting in a long sales cycle before sale is concluded. MLM provides the opportunity to every participant (distributor) to build to personal networks to introduce potential purchases to products. As a matter of economic principle of revealed preference or revealed profitability. Similarly, consumers who choose to purchase from legitimate MLM network direct sellers, they perceive more value in purchasing from a direct seller relative to other alternatives.

Many distributors join the MLM to purchase a preferred product at a lower price. Other distributors find MLM is a convenient way of support their income on their terms and according to their needs, for example by working why reasonaly or part time. Another participants may find that participation in a entry point into a center or business opportunity to invest in their human capital and to acquire a network of business connections. Other participants may find that MLM (network selling) is the perfect match for their talents and skill sets. The goodwill to MLM is needed to concern. Consequently, consumer protection efforts have focused on identifying. Because, same MLM enterprises pretend to be legitimate direct sellers, such as fraudsters' debase the goodwill are trust that legitimate direct selling has established with consumers. Resultly, the direct personal sale enterprises pretend to do legitimate business activities to influence the unhealth or poor economic growth in societies. Otherwise, the Multi level market (MLM) or network market enterprises can do more legitimate business activities to influence the health or poor economic growth in societies.

However, muli level marketing , MLM is as a very popular business model in the Western countries. It is a kind of the method of distribution of products. The method of building a sales network, it is one of the safest carries a very low risks ways of conducting business activity. The enter is to any markets, it is usually with market entry barriers and huge capital needs. Lack of expansion and lack of awareness of common practices. In the traditional business model, the risk of failure is very high. Also, unknown is the uncertain concerning the return on investments. However, despite high level of risk, this is the most popular business model.

So, multi level marketing is also called "network marketing". It is one of the fastest developing and still the least understand methods if introducing products to the market. It is mainly due to poor understanding of the system that multi level marketing is often regarded as network sales, pyramid sales or even pyramid schemes. It is marketing strategy and way of functioning of a company and its partners' independent distributors. Multi level marketing is a branch of direct sale. It involves offering products and services directly to clients on the basis of individual contacts, usually at direct's home, workplace or in other locations outside permanent retail sale branches. It is a form of sale outside, a traditional ship chain. It allows sellers to build personal structures of partners, who provide additional commissions from their sales. Every seller in multi level marketing has an opportunity to build own structure of salesman in which everyone is rewarded based on the marketing plan valid for each company. At the same time, achieving higher earnings, it is as a marketing strategy, way of functioning of a company and a system allowing to build individual network for independent distributors, classifying it has a branch of direct sales is a big mistake.

What is it's differences to pyramid scheme, MLM or network market and direct personal sale method? First, MLM is a retail sale, which is the most basic form of distribution carried out by means of a retail branch, e.g. grocery shop, chemist's shop department store, online auction site. Second, direct personal sale method is covering ususally the sale of insurance, kitchen wave houses etc. products. In this model of distribution commission from sold products goes only to the seller, who can't build network of his distributors. In order to sell products or services offered by a particular company, who has to be employed in the company as a sales representative. This means that who works for the owner of a company, the company's whose employer, thus the sales representative doesn't work for whose own benefit as in case of personal direct sale marketing. Third, direct personal sale marketing is transferring a product or service from the producer of service provider to the consumer. Otherwise, MLM, Multi level marketing is as a system of rewarding people who contribute to sale of products or provision of services. In the multi level marketing method people contributing to sale are those who recommend a purchase directly from a particular company. The employee whose is provided in course of making an order is rewarded for a recommendation resulting in actual sale, as the bonus system is usually multi level and allows generating passive income, income is not the direct effect of the work of recommending person. This works, this way is as every person has the opportunity to build individual consumer distribution structurer. In order words, multi level system rewards for directly recommended persons and recommended directly by direct ones. Fourth, MLM, it means mail order sale, this kind of distribution is characterized by lack of retail points in which products could be exchanged for money. The client makes an order directly in the company after learning about its offer on television, in telephone conversation or from a received catalogue. Finally, direct personal sale method is an illegal organization of sales, which is often mistaken for muti level marketing. One of the main reasons for an illegal organization is presented as a multi level system. The difference that makes pyramids illegal and multi level making legal is the inability to distribute a product or provide service. If there are no sales of a product, it is impossible to take about marketing companies by promising high sales convince participants to pay high one off about of money that allows then to participate in the programme which makes it impossible for participants to generate sales, as all payments go to the account of those organizing the business. Thus, direct personal sale is nothing like multi level marketing or network marketing . MLM, in which sale is always based on a product or service and the commission system rewards participants depending on the contribution, regardless of held position. So, MLM, it is a network created based on contacts and ties between people and the participation of all members of the network in this activity.

-

Whether multi levelmarketing can assist economic growth.

We can view multi level marketing from two perspectives, one of them is the point of view of concept, the producer or the company for which multi level marketing is one of possible ways of introducing a new product to the market bearing huge cost with promotion and without the need to transfer rights to a product to someone. The second perspective is the point of view of an independent distribution for whom multi level marketing is a model of business which doesn't require a concept or bearing the risk with investing capital, as in case of typical business activity or franchising, such an approach makes it possible to define MLM as method of distribution of products, in which costs associated with advertising and marketing are covered at the moment of actual sale. Sales are fueled by clients of the MLM company who use their contacts to recommend the purchase of particular products. The MLM company rewards the recommending person with a commission calculated based on the company's marketing plan for a recommendation ending with actual sale. Any marketing plan creates the possibility to generate unlimited revenues and at the same time eliminate risk with the necessity to invest substantial capital required to launch typical business activity.

How Multi level marketing can assist socio-economic development. For example, insurance business is a kind of MLM business, whether it can assist socio-economic development for long term. In insurance sector, insurance companies are looking for innovative methods to spread the message and maximum business in the short time. Many local MLM companies having quite large spread in the market with leading insurance brands to promote their insurance products along with their own products. Insurance sector makes available long time debt for the economic development of the country. At the same time, the MLM route provides employment opportunities and enhances their social status. The MLM members have opportunity to develop themselves personally. This multipe rise of MLM companies can be looked at as a social contribution and these insurance MLM companies or cooperatives are as a development oriented social movement. How insurance sector can assist the economic and social impact of MLM as a tool which can influence society through employment generation, mobilzing long term funds and improving quality of life of people. There has opportunity to attractive propective candidates to gain network marketing companies. Past studies indicated the fact that a 100 % annual turnover rate among sales personnel in certain network marketing company is not unusual. According to the Direct Selling Association in th United States, it indicated 70% of the revenue from the direct selling industry was generated by network marketing companies and most of this come from the better known companies, such as Amway, was multi level instead of single level compensation plans. Such as India, network marketing was in India during mid 90 year was followed by the establishment of the Indian arm of Amway corporation The total turnover of network marketing companies in India was estimated at $30,104 rising in 2005 year with an annual growth rate of 25%.

It seems Amway can assist USA Government to earn much taxation income and sale income to reduce USA unemployment rate. As, Amway exports to India market. Indian Direct Selling Association (IDSA) facilitates membership to build network marketing companies. So, India is a good network marketing for Amway MLM company. However, consumers often have negative perceptions of direct selling organizations and network marketing organization in particular. The aggressive selling techniques, exaggeration of facts in network marketing organization recruiting and pyramiding scams together toward a basis for this negative perception. Network marketing is a subset of direct selling and is also known as multi level marketing structure marketing or multi level direct selling. Network marketing can best be described as a direct selling channel that focuses heavily on its compensation plan because the distributors (members of the networks) may receive compensation in two fundamental ways. First, sales people (distributors) may earn compensation from their personal sales of products and services to the consumers (non-member of the network). Second, they may earn compensation from sales to purchase from those persons whom who have personally sponsored or recruited into the network (down lines), these down lines continue sponsoring or recruiting to the network sharing the benefits with their sponsors or recruiters (up lines). So, the aim of MLM network market which reward sales agents for buying products and selling products and finding other agents to buy and sell products. In common, the agents (distributors) or participants can earn marketings ranges from 20% to 50% of sales income. In addition, distributors can also receive a monthly commission for their personal volume which is the value of every product who personally buy or sell. Further, the distributors also receive a net commission on the sales of those who recruit into the networks. It seems that the sales developed network marketing are not developed from sales created by retailing, but also developed through recruiting or sponsoring independent distributors. Thus, as distributors continue to recruit or sponsor not distributors to expand whose network, the new distributors will contribute new sales to the network and gain commission in return. This hunge incentive makes the investment in insurance very attractive for a member. For example, coverage margin on first premium for insurance policies can earn the range of 30% to 40%. This given the leverage for structuring the insurance sale through MLM. MLM is a marketing function in which sales people are paid for their personal contribution as well as for the persons who recruit in to the function or process. Employees or sales people who are individual team to work from which who get a reward on the achievement sale force. So, who can sense much ideas to help marketing organizations to raise high demand when demand is too high and the current employees can't meet those are recruits come in the till the position. So, employees are encouraged to bring many employees to the organization.

MLM is also a very important function in providing jobs for the jobless. The recruitment process looks for young jobless people and earns them on income from which who can support themselves. It is happy feeling to know that you are working and at the same time providing opportunities for the loss fortunate to support them. You have chance to increase your paid if you introduce someone to work as participant or recruit or distributer role to any MLM market. It will reduce the numbers of unemployment of the insurance company in society. The idea presents people with great and better learning of the MLM strategy. When people are recruited in to the business, who are trained about its functions. This training acts as a good way of future advancements in the field. It also helps those individuals to use the knowledge to their advantage once who leave to job to enter marketing or sale career.

The job presents flexibility in hours work. Due people can work at any time who feel fits in them schedule. It can also train them to learn how to achieve whose sale target and attempt to do own business and no and captial spending. Is network marketing or multi level selling marketing as it is called all about getting rich quick with minimal effort? Multi level marketing or network marketing means referring products or services directly to consumers within your network. It involves building a network. For each referral is made by the network. The preceding link or upline as those individuals are called in network marketing terms, gets a certain percentage of commission. MLM, network marketing doesn't need you to be a user of the product or service that you would eventally be referring within your network. Network marketing or MLM only need you put ability to put in lots of hard work. In fact, twice as much as in a regular job or business, willingness to learn new diversified skills, ability to discipline your ability to be as network with like minded people who can help you. So, MLM can help unemployment people to find either freelance or temporary or permanent kinds of position choices, such as sales person or distributor role in MLM company. So, network (MLM) marketing can offer various benefits to them like, lower initial costs of setting your business excellent training and product/service knowledge from industry experts, opportunity to earn additional residual income with a greater chance to move into a full time earned income model, flexibility to work at your own pace and time choice of retiring whenever you want.

Network market can be kind of multi level marketing. As network marketing is confronted with a number of issues that include the continuous erosion of campaign effectiveness, the fragmentation of traditional markets, the disappearance of the vendors' information advantage and significant changes in the distribution channel. Based on established building blocks of marketing and social network theory, a conceptual framework called network theory to integrate the two fields in a systematic way.

The networked marketing framework provides a structure for identifying the customer social network's impact on the marketing effectiveness in the different customer lifecycle phases and suggests the use of certain tools to acqire knowledge about the nature and the functional details of the social influence. However, the network marketing framework was tested in a setting on an international sample of a large company's customer database. How customer social network activity with an impact on marketing is the most intense in the purchase phase and the least. Hence, in the awareness phase, as well as the fact, that product and communication are the mix areas most impacted by social networks. For example, health care is an individual necessity and kind of national luxury product of a kind of multi level decision models. Due to health care is neither a necessity or a luxury, it is both since the income elasticity varies with the level of analysis. With insurance, individual income elasticities are typically near zero, when national health expenditure elasticities and commonly greater. It is to expected that measured income elasticities will differ for an individual, a risk-pooling group, or a national health system, just as price elasticities for individual, firm and market demand normally differ from each other. In past, some economists indicate income elasticity of individual, health expenditures under insurance (usually 60% to 95% of total spending) is typically near zero or negative, when the elasticity of national health expenditures with respect to national income is typically greater than 1.0. So, it seems individual income level and health factor has close relationship to decide to buy any health insurance policies.

Whether how multi level decision model quickly resolves to make evident the role of social and private insurance in linking micro and macro analysis in health economics. Within an insurance group, the bulk of the health resources will be allocated to those individuals who are ill and to get benefits from medical care. Individual budget constraints and ability to play concerns are pooled insurance financing. The contrast between the behaviour of the average individual, and the behaviour of the group to buy medical health insurance mean is well illustrated by insurance. However, medical health insurance pools are not only likely to display separation between group and individual behaviour, who are designed to bring about such a separation. The purpose of medical health insurance is to remove the individual budget constraint, and to reduce or eliminate the influence of cost of care on patient's and physician's decisions of how much care to use. If persons are fully insured, correlations with measures of individual income provide no information about income effects per each, e.g. the effect of monetary budget constraints, but instead reflect the influence of other unmeasured variables, cost of time, family resources, education, preferences etc. that are correlated with an individual's income. Hence, it seems that multi level model of determinants of pyramid or network sale method is suitable to sell in health insurance market. In any country's health insurance market, it will have two kind groups of people who will feel who have need to buy health medical insurance product. One group is without purchase any health medical insurance product , and another group owns health medical insurance product . At the macro level, income effects are still strong to influence anyone to decide to buy health medical insurance product, but variation factor due to differences in health status can also influence anyone to decide to buy health medical insurance product . With the country's people who feel need of health medical product, the pooling of funds will remove the insurance market income constraints and tends to strengthen the correlation of individual health status with expenditures. However, individual income effects still dominate the insurance market in the health medical insurance any country. So, it seems that health medical product insurance will have large share to lead to any country's insurance product income among of the travel insurance, accident insurance, life insurance, car insurance, employee welfare insurance etc. different kinds of insurance products market in any country. So, mulit level marketing shall be suitable to enter insurance product sale market.

Direct sale represents a modern product distribution system directly to consumer. Generally, directly to their homes, to their workplace or other places, besides retail shops. Ths best known type of direct sale, the network marketing or multi level marketing implies the existence of a network of distributors which earn income from selling on commission, to which who add the trade marketing. So, insurance, travel agent, share broker, property agent etc. these occupations which can belong to multi level or network marketing.

Following, I shall discuss the another kind of multi level marketing, e.g. franchise business. Franchise means the field of activity in which it was used. It is a license allowing the designee to sell and market a company's products or services in a particular place, using the name or the trade mark of the company, e.g. Mc Donald fast food restaurant. It allows whom to do business for the franchise owner, but not through the franchise owner. From the marketing point of view, franchise represents a distribution system based on the partnership between two parties which are legally independent. Between the franchisor (the proprietary owner, the owner of the trade mark of products and services) and the franchisee. However, developing a franchise using a well known trade mark, so it is a more complex distribution system in multi level marketing view point. Also, franchise business can be sold from internet sale channel in the multi level marketing technological view point.

●

Why the internet has positive influence on direct sale industry in multi level market to assist economic growth.

However, an important factor for increasing the turnover generated by direct sale companies and multi level marketing network represents a structure that is continuously changing. As technological changing, internet invention can raise the MLM sale method of chance. In multi level sale marketing, as house agent or franchise sale agent, insurance agent, share agent etc. these kind of occupations who can expand their businesses market from internet. Some of the trends indicate strong growth multi level products in international market. Also, high participation of women in multi level marketing, women are begining to realize that the internet makes it possible for them to reinvent themselves and begin a multi level business that requires little risk and low start up cost, such as internet sale method, these are no age limit to develop the multi level internet sale channel business and internet sale business can be an important market shares for household products in multi level marketing globally.

Besides these trends, the internet has positive influence on direct sales industry. Internet has had an impact in relations between direct seller and the company and between the direct seller and the consumer. The main multi levels through which the internet helps the development of multi level sale industry. Due to the internet has allowed direct sellers and customers to maintain contact outside the face to face meetings, it also allows direct sellers can use blogs and social media page to sell whose products, direct sellers can use electronic mailings and have online access to products and services brochures, the customers can pay to buy any online products through internet banking conveniently, more and more people were extended his professional activities of direct selling through the use of the internet and social networks, a direct selling activity can be run from home and doesn't require a high investment. Some may even give follow up orders by electronic means.

From the seller's point of view, the major attraction of direct selling is that internet sale channel offers an equal and flexible income opportunity to men and women, across all ages, level of experience and social origins. In the multi level marketing view point, the direct selling industry development trends will be direct influence by maintaining these advantages for the distributors and by using and developing the communicating modern technologies. So internet sale channel will be the potential multi level marketing to influence how to distribute products or service and to through direct sales and mulit level marketing are determined by a set of economic technological and even social factors.

●

Whether multi level marketing can influence economic growth in poverty countries.

I feel that the role of multi level marketing in poverty countries to influence economic growth is important. For example, some businesses who need to manufacture and sell whose products to clients directly. So who need to set up factories and to open shops in local and overseas markets. It seems who need to exploit and save many investors loading more minimal amounts to prepare to sell immediately. It will raise recruiting new downlines and high cost of products as well as who also need to establish production plants in themselves countries or foreign countries to exploit local or overseas economics and to reduce the numbers of unemployment, among many other benefits. It seems the role of multi level marketing can reduce poverty countries unemployment ratio from internet sale channel, e.g. online salesperson , delivered products service and website design technician or computer technician etc. different website related positions will be created to sell to any online buyers conveniently from online sale channel.

Multi level marketing, e.g. online sale channel method can assist any country's businessmen to sell whose products to overseas easily. So, multi level marketing is one global sale market. Such online businesses that empower the people by providing opportunities to the first time businessmen to start businesses to sell their products to overseas market from internet (online sale) channel easily in the beginning. Moreover, multi level marketing has the potential of being a good source for job creation, income generation to sell products to any countries' buyers from online sale channel by websites contact conveniently at their homes.

Whether multi level marketing can solve poverty challenge. If multi level marketing deliberately target the poor as recruits, what role does multi level marketing play in income generation? Is there any relationship between MLM and job creation? Does multi level marketing (MLM) lead to skill and personal development of MM distributors? There are several appraches to poverty challenges. Examining them provides a necessary understanding of the nature of poverty. There are five main approaches to cause poverty challenge: The economic growth, the basic needs of rural development, the target and employment creation approaches. First, the economic growth approach would be leaded to distribution of income by the participation of the poor. In fact, economic growth need long time to develop in any countries. Also, multi level marketing, e.g. online sale channel needs a long time to build online buyer numbers to sell to different countries from distributors' websites globally. It seems this online sale method can assist global economic growth to give benefits to the developing countries to poverty people to solve unemployment challenges during any online businessmen build their websites to sell any products for long term. So, solving poverty challenge is needs long term time to develop any country's economy growth. Multi level marketing can be one of online sale method to solve unemployment challenge to poverty countries globally. Second, the rural development approach recognizes that poverty is multi dimensional. Thus, it aims at providing basic necessities of life, such as food, clean water, shelter, education, health care, and employment to rural dwellers in general. However, the limitation of this approach is that it doesn't directly target the poor. Again, decisions on rural areas to target may be done from political motives. Third, Target approach specifically aims at certain groups in the implementation of poverty programs, e.g. provision of social safety nets, micro credit and school meal programmes etc. Finally, employment creation approach emphasises the need to eliminate unemployment and underemployment. This will be achieved by creating employment from online sale channel.

The whole concept of multi level marketing is relatively new to any European and Western countries where which have existed for long term. For example, the DVD disc is a conglometrate of all firms that distribute to buyer contact in location away from fixed areas, like retail stores particularly at home. It is the locational characteristic that distinguishes it from other forms of personal selling. Multi level marketing is a subset of the DVD disc distributors are used in selling company products and also in recruiting other distributors. As a result, they receive compensation for their sales and from sales of those individuals who recruit. The senior distributors are called uplines when their recruits are called downlines. Other common products sold through multi level marketing include health and fitness product, cosmetics, cleaning agents, electrical appliances and several others which are popular to sell from this MLM marketing either network market or/and online market both methods.

It is very important to influence many multi level marketing companies do not incur any cost on advertisement since who can use internet to advertise whose products in their websites to let global online buyers to discover after they type the seller's website address to enter their websites at home conveniently. The distributors in MLM are usually organized into networks structure connection. Two main types of such structures are the binary and unilevel structure. The former allows just two direct downlines at each level and the other direct recruits are to be placed at different levels in the network of downlines. On the other hand, the unilevel structure permits the recruitment of an unlimited number of downlines. Direct selling firms usually opt between two choices either employees or independent distributors. There are no salaries or other fixed costs associated with recruitment of independent distributors. So a non selective recruitment used with a straight method of compensation often tends to draw poverty people easily earned incomes from only a modest commitment in time and effort. It seems to commission income method. The recruitment of a new distributor allows for only a single connection. However, double registration of a single distribution is not compatible with the MLM compensation plan. A distributor is allowed to participate in three activites of the MLM company's purchase of the products as users, sale to customers and access to mark up profit and recuritment that expansion of the network occurs. The diffusion of the product or service in the market is stimulated strong by the consumption or purchase of the product.

The benefits to MLM offers to distributors include low start cost, distributors can enjoy from the income of others, e.g. the downlines benefit in the distribution network of online sale to different advertisers can help the distributor to advertise whose products to earn commission income from website; online retail group volume and other bonuses and incentives, personal development via training and business support materials to sell from online sale channel, enhanced enterpreneurial spirit to sell products from onlibe channel globally, improved interpersonal skills and increased self confidence and jobs creation from online sale channel.

Nowadays, estimate that 97% of products are purchased and use consumption, which are consistent with legitimate multi level marketing to earn commission income, e.g. a online sale channel is more than a pyramid sale channel. Many of business operations are consistent with the socially beneficial from MLM model and inconsistent with the socially harmful pyramid scheme model. Applying on economic test that requires member performance payment incentives to be primarily funded out of retail based product sales to be classified as a legitimate MLM, based on prior test, at least 62% of total life or eating product purchases would need to be retail based online sale channel. However, multi level marketing is a mulit million dollar global industry. There exists differentiating a valid mulit level marketing scheme and pyramid money circulation scheme. Multi level or network marketing is a form of business that uses independent representatives to sell products or services to family or friends etc. It is a business strategy, which involves participants at various levels, the level above getting returns at the levels below it. Basically, it works on the principle of duplication to increase retail or sale activity. The survival of the system, depends on the chain of earns commissions from retail sales who makes, and also from retail sales made by other people who recruit.

Direct selling organizations can be of various types, multi level format, network hierarchal structure or the organization can be flat. Multi level marketing activity is a method of distributing products or services in which is from distributrs. MLM has these characteristics: the presence of sponsorship lines that create financial rewards between distributors. Suppose x recruits y, x becomes y's sponsor and distributors. Suppose x immediate upline y recruits z, z who as personal recuits of y, and x are y's frontline people (z, t and u) recruited by same sponsor y and on same level and members of the same generation (z, t and u) sponsorship lines seem like family trees. In fact, these sponsors are often called genealogies. Suppose persons s and y are both recruited/sponsored by x. However, y has been more aggressive, heavily recruiting than s. y will become more financially successful than s, even through they are on the same level and had entered the business together. The higher the sales a group generates, the higher would be the amount of commission received by x. There are numerous recognition levels, for example, Amway has various levels of recognition, each with its own unique title and perks. One begins as a basic distributor, works whose way up through the ranks from silver producer to gold distributor to platinum direct distributor to Ruby direct distributors climbing up the ladder to crown direct distributor to crown ambassador direct distributor. But none of the levels and title is authoritative. In MLM schemes, the uplines are paid commissions and bonus on the sales made by their respective downline members. The company using multi level marketing method is a MLM company. The MLM company can be a firm, an individual corporation or other business entity, e.g. Amway, Mark Kay, Modicare etc. MLM entities. It's features include word of mouth sales, means savings on marketing and advertising costs, company can change their similar products in stores, the technique develops loyal customers who enjoy buying from other people who know. It is such a pyramid scheme " which concentrates on the commissions, the participant could earn just for recruiting new distributors" and which generally ignore the marketing and selling of products and services. Pyramid scheme means any sales device or plan under which a person gives consideration to another person in exhange for compensation as the right to receive compensation which is derived primarily from the introduction of other persons into the sale device or plan rather than from the sale of products or services or other property. Pyramid means a multi layered network of subscribers to be a form by subscribers enrolling one or more subscribers in order to receive any money benefits directly or indirectly, as a result of enrollment. It is similar to a continuous chain of participants or investors is recuited, in which each pays a fee to participate and receives money by recruiting others into the system. So each participant can build multi layered network of individuals to have chance to earn more benefit, if who can distribute products to sell successful from whose downline recuriters network.

Finally, the main question is whether this MLM network sale method can assist any country economic growth. I shall analyze what the difference of social effects (influences) are from these kind of sale methods, such as direct personal sale and auto online sale and multi level (network) sale. A phenomenon appears that the distribution companies accept normal direct personal selling method to cause education expenditure to bring loss their bases of values all at once. It comes a lot of direct sellers are lost to any countries. Due to it raise the compensation to the choice of direct personal sale companies. For example, China government achieves laws and policies to stop direct personal sale scheme companies to enter to local market to sell their products. Because China decides to protect its local businesses benefits to let them have ability to sell their products, due to reducing the number of growing foreign direct personal sale scheme companies exist in China itself country. Although, China will reduce GDP income from foreign direct personal import sale. But it can protect its local businessmen benefits to reduce competition. Otherwise, Multi level (network) marketing is a marketing approach that can motivate its participants to promote a certain product among their friends. It can exist in one form before in the internet age began, such as pyramid scheme. Social networks are everywhere, our email and phone address books, our famil relatives etc. Social network has web-based form, as facebook, twitter, linkedin networks made them more tangible. Moreover, internet can be good sale channel for multi level market, it gives the potential to accumulate small rewards from each participant to a sizable sum, as internet channel can allow advertisers to attract early adopters to earn commissions when the advertisers can help any multi level market companies to sell products successfully from internet channel. So, online advertisers and participants or distributors who can earn profit from multi level marketing. It seems Multi level marketing can give chance to let any participants to buid many downline recruiters to assist the team leader to sell many products from internet channel. So, the team leaders and team members do not need capital to set up their businesses and who can do business with the MLM company together easily from internet channel.

MLM or network market is often compared such as direct sales e.g. insurance, franchises etc. In fact, it is in the nature of pyramid schemes for the money to go to the person at the top of a pyramid of participants, with the majority of participants found to be in a losing position at the bottom regardless of when it collapses or is terminated. So, the compensation plan can be considered product-based pyramid schemes or recruiting MLM's because their compensation plan rewards recruiting of distributors through commission from their purchases more than selling direct to consumers. Distributors must not need to purchase products from the MLM in order to participate in the business. These findings raise some important questions: what kind of business has no clients? Only MLM's pretending to be direct sellers. Who is buying the products that can earn income from different countries residents online sale channel. Only MLM's distributors and advertisers are their main customers. If there are no direct sales to speak of, then who is making profits of these supposed sales. Only MLM company founders and officers. Whether multi level marketing can be potential tool for socio-economic development. For example, insurance business is just one among them. Selling insurance policies can operate from internet channel conveniently, traditionally is considered as a job or business. With the competition raises in industry sector, companies are looking for innovative methods to spread the message and maximum business in shorter time. Many local MLM companies have quite large spread in the market, as joining with leading insurance brands to promise life product policy protection to reduce clients' risk loss from internet MLM sale method. So, insurance sector makes online MLM route provides employment opportunities of people and enhances their social status. This multiple role of MLM companies can be looked at as a social contribution and which can develop oriented social movement.

In conclusion, MLM can raise employment generation, mobilizing long term funds and improving quality of life of people. In traditional, successful personal selling based on referrals is the key to ensure regular expansion of client base and building long term client relation. A country like India offers well run MLM online marketing networks to promote consumer products. Conveniently online MLM marketing may become slow or stagnated over a period of time. Online, Multi level marketing may be the tool in such situation, India has many people, so the online multi level businesses can be built to attempt to operate in this country. Concept selling mostly used personal selling as a tool where the sales people depend on referrals. In MLM technically, e.g. online sale, the promotion expenditures on advertisments channel margins etc. is distributed among the participants as individual product distributors or product advertisers , as who can do online business from commission incentives to build businesses from internet. Hence, internet technology can raise MLM to have competitive advantage. For example, it is common knowledge that MLM works on the concept of time leverage. A work to be done by you 100 days can be completed in one day if you have 100 people under you in a chain doing one days work. You can earn a % of incentive for the work done by each of those 100 people under your team downline. Through it is given various names like network marketing, freelance network chain marketing. To conclude, MLM can assist any countries economic growth to compare other kind of sale methods easily in the short time in possible.

V

MTR (UNDERGROUND TRAIN) TRANSPORTATION SERVICE

● Why MTR underground train transportation needs to know passenger behaviour

Understanding individual passenger behaviour is essential for the design MTR transportation, because who can choose to catch bus, taxi, tram, train ferry etc. different kinds of public transportation tools. Individual traveler who decides to catch which kinds of public transportation tools, it depends on whether the public transportation tool can provide real time travel information, liking link travel time schedule. So, MTR underground train needs to understand where it has terminal to give convenience to the local living areas of time travelers to choose to catch MTR easily. Although, MTR ticket fare is one factor to influence any passengers choice. But, those other factors can also influence them to choice. e.g. MTR any terminal location of convenience, short time travelling, none crowding in busy (peak) time, MTR platform waiting arrival time, none sudden MTR engineering machines broken accident events occurrence frequently etc. different factors, any one of these factors which can influence passengers who choose to catch MTR or other kinds of transportation tools.

● Why route choice can influence passenger behavioural choice

Usually, the busy time passengers will regard the route choice as a coordination problem to influence them to choose to catch which kinds of transportation tools. The route choice is as an opportunity costs to influence any busy time passengers to decide to choose to catch which kind of transportation tool which is the best right choice in the right time among of them. In the short time, for example, it seems any busy time passengers will choose to catch bus to substitute MTR underground train transportation tool, due to who feels the bus can arrive any destinations to compare other kinds of transportation tools in the most short time. However even if the MTR can either charge cheaper ticket fare to sell full day or charge discount ticket fare to sell in the busy (peak) time to compare to bus fare. It is possible that the busy time passengers will still choose to catch bus, if between the bus terminal and the another bus terminal that distance is the shorter time route to spend time to arrive destination to compare between the MTR terminal to the another MTR terminal arrival time . Also, although the busy time passengers will feel to enounter traffic jam to influence sitting or waiting bus time to be longer time in possible and who also feel MTR can avoid traffic jam problem. However, usually any busy (peak) time passengers will feel the chance of traffic jam occurrence will be less. So, the short bus route choice is more potential factor to influence the busy (peak) time passengers still to choose bus to catch.

However, if anyone wants to investigate results of day-to-day route choice which can be transferred to more realistic environment. It is necessary to explore individual behaviour in an interactive experimental set up to ensure busy (peak) time passenger transportation behavioural choice. For example, a passenger has a choice between a main road (M) and a side road (S) for travelling from (A) to (B). (M) is faster if (M) and (S) are chose by the same number of passengers. So, this method can be researched whether MTR terminal station is located at the main road (M) or the

"

side road (S) where is more suitable to accept to passengers generally.

● Why trip time reliability and crowding factors can influence MTR passenger choice.

Other problem is MTR busy (peak) time's crowding in public transportation occurrence of MTR underground train transportation tool is becoming a growth to concern as MTR demand growth at a busy (peak) time. To capture the MTR passengers benefits with reduced crowding from improved MTR public transport service and image. It is necessary a identify the relevant dimensions of crowding that are meaningful measures of what crowding means to MTR passengers. Two main influences on MTR model choice that are growing in relevance are trip time reliability and crowding. It represents a benefit-cost framework. In fact, MTR passengers can be willing to pay more expensive ticket fare, it MTR can avoid crowding and short and the accurate arrival trip time between terminals is reliable to occur. How to measure of MTR crowding, e.g. weighting the gap between the busy time, the standard (i.e. objective) and the perceived (i.e. subjective) metrics. We are not in a position to definitely map the two dimensions, which is a crucial requirement for translating objective improvements into equivalent subjective gains that then can be applied, willingness to pay estimates MTR ticket fares to obtain the additional MTR passenger benefits of MTR public transportation investment to any terminal stations. Because MTR crowding has a negative impact on passengers in terms of psychological on emotional distress. MTR passengers are willing to stand for up to 20 minutes of the service is fast and reliable. However crowding outweighed these benefits from a MTR passenger's perpective, experienced crowding leads a increased dissatisfaction. e.g. stress and less privacy during who needs to stand up in MTR. Due to there are no enough places to supply to them to stand up in MTR. If the MTR trip time was longer time between the passenger's terminals, who will feel more dissatisfaction and it will cause who feels whether who ought need to choose to catch other transportation tools to substitute MTR next time. e.g. bus, train, tram, ferry, taxi etc. So, from an operator's perspective, the MTR service frequency or MTR size is significantly influenced by the level of ridership, which sends a signal to respond if the monitored crowding level exceeds the benchmark standard in the busy time. e.g. in the morning time or at the night time, the students or employment people who need to go to schools or offices (working places). The locations of different places between MTR terminals and crowding are regarded as a key service attribute for MTR pubic transportation along with other factors, such as travelling time and reliability, e.g. service quality, none engineering machines are broken to cause MTR stops suddenly.

Given the increasing importance of crowding on both the disutility to existing MTR public transportation users and the influence to it. MTR passenger can choose to use either the MTR public public transportation or other public transportation. It is timely to review the MTR current measures of crowding defined by transportation authorities. MTR operators ought evaluate whether they apporpriately reflect MTR each traveler experiences and perceptions of crowding in busy (peak) time. I suggest that MTR needs to buy other underground trains to supply to the busy (peak) time passengers to let them have enough seats to sit down, so who do not need to stand up in any MTR underground trains when they catch MTR underground trains in busy time. It aims to let who are willingness to pay the estimation of reasonable ticket fares to compare the other kinds of transportation tools in the busy (peak) time.

● What is the crowding difference between train and MTR underground train.

In fact, crowding won't be happened to brother these transportation tools easily in the busy time and non busy time both. e.g. bus, taxi, train, tram, ferry. Because passengers can not choose to stand up in these transportation tools easily, due to these transportation tools have no enough areas (spaces) to let them to stand up easily . So, the crowding will be avoided to occur in these tranportation tools usually. Otherwise, MTR will have many passengers who can choose to stand up because MTR design of length is very long and it has enough areas (places) to let passengers to choose to stand up, even there have none any seats are provided to let them to sit down. So, MTR passengers will feel more dissatisfaction and crowding easily, especial in any peak (busy) time every day.

Comparing to bus, much more diverse crowding measures are defined in the passenger rail industry. For passenger, different specifications for measuring crowding are found across countries and even within a country. For example, rail crowding measures in the UK, the passengers in excess of capacity is crowding measure that applies to all London and South east operators weekday train services at a London terminus during the morning peak from 0700 to 09: 59 , and those departing during the afternoon peak from 16:00 to 18:59 (office of rail regulation 2011 year). The overall PIXC figure is considered the planned standard class capacity of each train service as well as the actual number of standard class passengers on the service at the critical point. i.e. the location on a trains of standard class passengers that surpass the planned capacity as the difference between the number of actual passengers and the capacity of the train divided by the number of passenger is within the capacity . So, it seems train and MTR underground public transportaton tools had been encountering the crowding problems in peak time, the difference in train passengers need to wait next train or more train arrival is who doesn't plan to enter the train, when who discovers the current train has no seats to provide to them to sit down in whose trip. Otherwise, MTR passengers can choose either to stand up within the large areas (places) if who discovered there are no any seats to provide to them to sit down or who can wait the next MTR arrival in order to who can sit down. It seems MTR transportation tool crowding environment includes in waiting platform and inside of the MTR underground train. Otherwise, train transportation tool crowding environment only includes the waiting platform and the passengers will not have crowding feeling inside of the train, due to none of passengers choose to stand up inside any trains because any train inside has no enough places to let them to stand up.

● How MTR can attract many passengers.

On the commuter departure time choice of any reference point researching hand, the departure time decisions of communters are of fundamental importance of peak period MTR traffic congestion. However, whether on the demand side, MTR underground train congestion relief measures, such as MTR ticket fare to every terminal station needs to be charged cheaper fare or discount fare in the peak (busy) time every day. To aim to attract many passengers to choose to catch MTR Underground train public transportation tools, substitute to choose other public transportation tools in the peak time.

Over the past decades, there have been very active research efforts in the departure time problem, both in econometric modeling and dynamic user equilibrium fields. Although, these works provide valuable insights into dynamic commuter decision making, they do not identify the commuters' response to gains and losses related to whole actual arrival time to reference points who may have relative. The appliability of the reference point hypothesis of prospect theory to the commuter's departure time decision making to obtain a better understanding of how departure time choice in MTR platform during their waiting underground train arrival time. However, every MTR underground train actual arrival time and deviation variables related to reference points (gains and losses) are the key factors in the departure time choice model. How the MTR underground train of every communter's daily departure time decision can be modelled when the reference point hypothesis of prospect theory. The MTR underground train's schedule delay is defined as the difference between the preferred arrival time (PAT) and the actual arrival time (AT) for a given MTR commuter. In a daily MTR commute, a commuter in the indifference band actual arrival time is an essential feature of MTR schedule study. Two reference points are the earliest acceptable arrival time and the work starting time for a given MTR platform waiting passengers. In psychological view point, prospect theory proposes that the displeasure of a loss is perceived or greater than the pleasure of a gain of the same attitude and therefore, the value function is stronger for losses than gains.

To conclude, it seems that if MTR waiting passengers need not spend long time to wait underground train arrival in platform and it can provide seats to let them to sit down in the busy (peak) crowding time. It will make them to feel pleasure, even the MTR ticket fare is not fair and reasonable to charge higher fare to compare other kinds of public transportation tools fares. So the peak waiting time factor can influence the passengers to choose other kind of transportation tools to catch easily. Moreover, MTR's two reference points are the earliest role. Similarly a loss is observed when the MTR platform waiting commuter experiences or actual arrival time which is beyond that the MTR schedule time. Due to that a MTR waiting commuter is as an early side arrival of whose actual arrival time is earlier than whose preferred arrival time.

VI

AIRLINE TRANSPORT SERVICE INDUSTRY

● How positive or negative social change can influence any airlines' air ticket prices to be risen or fallen.

We are entering globalization. In Special, airline transportation demands are also increasing, due to many travelers need to catch planes to travel as well as many cargoes need to be carried to planes to transport to different countries to sell. It seems aviation transportation industry is important to influence the health of the global economy growth nowadays. However, ignorance of internal or external market dynamics, catching travelers business can be detrimental to airline profitability more than carrying cargoes business. Because the demands of travelling different countries' travelers' consumption are still more than the demands of businessmen carrying cargoes in any countries every year. So, the global GDP of travelling income sector is still have the important position to any country nowadays.

How can positive or negative social change influence any airlines' air ticket prices to be risen or fallen? In fact, the increase in petroleum price can have chance to affect airlines in a negative manner because increased oil prices have resulted in the reduction of services operations, the number of airline schedules flights, even airline bankruptcies. Whether inflation, terrorism, oil price, bank interest rate etc. external factors which factor has the most influential to cause the bad effects to cause airline industry share price reducing or reducing air ticket price or decreasing traveler numbers. To support this hypotheses, this are my research questions, such as : Does a combination of terrorism and price of petroleum significantly influence airline profit changing mostly? The alternative hypothesis was whether a significant relationship exists between terrorism, price of petroleum and airline profitability more than other factors, such as inflation, bank interest rate or air ticket price changing of these factors influence. I shall indicate that the first assumption was that terrorism has a negative effect on airline profitability and another assumption was that only external factors as oil prices or terrorism affect airline profitability.

● What is the relationship of oil price and terrorism to airline industry?

However the effects of oil price and terrorism on airline profitability was limited to a regional perspective, e.g. the terrorism attack of plane crash event to USA on 11 Sept. After the terrorism attack happened on USA 11 Sept. incident of terrorism attack was restricted to events of skyjacking, attacks on oil production, refinery and distribution. Other types of terrorist activities, such as attacks on financial targets or senior government officials could have an adverse effect on the petroleum and airline industry. I think the disruption of the production or distribution of petroleum because of incidents of terrorism was costly in terms of loss of business and the inflationary effect on fuel dependent products or services. In fact, some airlines have adopted more fuel saving technology, so whose fuel consumption would not use more than other non fuel saving technology airlines. It seems fuel price increasing will not be the only factor to influence the airline industry's traveler numbers decreasing. However, due to some airlines which have fuel saving technology, so which can avoid to use more fuel to provide planes to use and which fuel costs will be reduced, then which can provide cheaper air ticket fare prices to compare the non fuel saving technology airlines. The result will cause some airlines will lose travelling customers in this global airline travelling market, also the non fuel saving technology airlines need to renew their fuel technology if which want to keep their competitive abilities to avoid to close down their businesses.

Also, I shall indicate the financial risk of airline industry evidence from Cathay Pacific airways and China airlines against key determinants of which include interest rate, exchange rate and fuel price risk for the period of January 1996 year to December 2011 year. During this period, these key external factors which were the most serious influence to cause these two airlines choose to change their strategic behaviors. Due to any these financial risks is difficult to predict and it was also changing often, these factors will also affect any airlines stock returns which arise from changing economic conditions, e.g. fuel price movements and fluctuations in exchange rates. These external unpredicted changing factors will attribute to the air tickets cyclical demand, capital investment, fixed costs of labor and landing rights to this global airline industry.

However, the relationship between fuel price and stock prices varies across economies. The effects of oil price changes in sub-sector indices, such as wood, paper and printing, insurance and electricity. In the past, on global stock exchange market was positively significant in 2011 year. Otherwise, with respect to the U.S.A. aviation industry, some economists suggested that global airlines stock returns were negatively to percentage change in fuel prices related to any airline firm value, e.g. Qantas and Air New Zealand were negatively share price growth to fuel price risk in the short term in the 2011 year.

● Why does airline self organization exist in airline industry?

However, there are some airlines which are the characteristic of self organization and they are present in that both of oil fuel production and providing flights service in airline industry. So, these self organization airlines can control the oil fuel price by themselves. However, self organization is also evident in efforts by businesses acts of terrorism against economic targets by adopting proactive steps, such as airline and airport security. So, it seems self organization airline can reduce the risk to avoid oil price raising and terrorism attacks in airline industry risk management sector. Beside, these self organization airlines which have high technology of fuel efficient aircrafts, the use of one aircraft model, the adoption of direct routes versus customer loyalty programs and other operational cost reductions are strategies for increased profitability. To solve oil price, terrorism etc. external risk to airline industry. Instead of high technology of fuel efficient aircrafts and self organization methods can solve terrorism attacks and oil price rising risks. However, I believe that there are other risks are caused to airline industry. The risks include such as user factor, such as culture, tradition, education ; economic factor, such as costs, human resources and macro economic factor, such as political stability, economic development, educational policy, health policy, environmental policy. However, these risks occurrences are resulting in the relationship of cause and effect events. These events are not directly observable. Such as, the complexity of relationship between terrorism and airline profitability. Hence, if global airline industry can predict when those risks occur to do protective strategic behavior. It is possible that which can understand why these risk events will occur and their protective strategic behaviors also influence their outcomes to be positive to avoid any external risk threats on the long term. However, I think hierarchy, airlines self organization efficiency methods which are as possible predictors of user preferences to avoid risk threat events to cause whose airline businesses failure occurrences in airline industry.

● Why tourism and airline industries have close relationship to influence their profitability between of them.

In my study, I suppose terrorism, profitability and the price of petroleum which had properties of distinct and interrelated close relationship. Moreover, these variables (terrorism, profitability and the price of petroleum) displayed differentiation, self replication, efficiency and hierarchy which can cause risk events to airline industry. However, I also think the other internal and external threat factors of airline industry, such as inflation, bank interest rate, business model, service quality, airline fuel or plane engine technology, air ticket pricing, brand loyalty, airline strategic management, government policy and fuel hedging of these factors which can also raise the risks to threaten any airlines existence in airline industry.

There are two basic business models in airline industry. They are network (full service) and low cost (discount) carriers. The network carrier model employs diversification strategy by increased domestic destinations, serving international routes, providing diverse seating arrangements (business, economy and first class), maintaining a complex system of offering high quality service. Otherwise, low cost (discount) airlines focus on lower air fares. To keep operating costs down, discount airlines offer shorter routes and provide point-to-point destinations rather than through sophisticated flights are primarily in domestic destinations. So, discount airlines operate a common model aircraft fleet, offer a single seating arrangement and cheaper flight services offered to compare network airlines. However, these two basic business models have their unique competitive abilities to provide any airlines existence in airline industry nowadays.

In fact, natural resource of oil is decreasing in our earth. But as the same time, human demand is increasing and oil supply is decreasing, so it also causes the oil fuel price is increasing to supply to airline industry. It influences not only to airline industry, it also impacts of higher oil fuel price to tourism, such as expansion of airports are made based on expected demand increase. Tourism has been proven to many adverse events, including terrorism, flight disruptions. Beside, the bad natural climate change influences, such as the volcanic ash cloud event occurred in April 2010 year. So, airline industry need to concern climate change because it will cause high fuel prices indirectly. For example, the event occurred the extreme increase in operating costs for airlines in 2008 year, due to unprecedented prices for aviation fuel also meant, that despite the introduction of fuel charges, so this event causes the global airline industry recorded losses seriously. Even if alternative fuels become commercially available for airlines which are still likely to be more expensive than present aviation fuel.

Higher airfares in the future are likely to lead to reduction in travel and cause tourists to shift from more distant to closer destination. When some of the economic responses to higher oil prices are obvious assessing the overall economic impacts on tourism is difficult. However, long term changes in global oil price rises will be similar to global changes in other commodity prices, exchange rates and income. It is therefore important to consider the impact of high oil prices on tourism from a general equilibrium perspective rather than relying only on bottom partial equilibrium approaches.

However, I believe tourism and airline industries have close relationship, such as tourism and airline industries are likely to suffer in an environment of high oil prices. Given that tourism destinations receive tourists from a range of origins, it would be useful to understand of some countries are increasing oil prices than others. Such as the net oil importing countries are selling higher oil prices than oil exporting countries generally. For example, New Zealand is an oil import country to provide planes for international visitor arrivals, so its oil fuel price is usually higher to charge to NZ airlines because any NZ airlines need to pay to foreign countries to buy any oil more expensive price. So, NZ airlines usually charge higher airfares to its visitors to compare the other exporting oil countries' airlines.

In economic theory, on income effects indicate negative impacts on tourism demand, the exact effects of higher oil fuel prices for specific destinations are far from clear. However, airline industry's different market segments show different sensitivities to air ticket fares changes. On the first hand, if the visitors are long destinations generally wealthier than average and therefore potentially less affected, as energy costs would be a smaller proportion of their income compared will be those from less wealthy groups. On the second hand, oil prices don't translate into higher transport costs especially not on air routes that are highly competitive and that are maintained for strategic reasons. On the third hand, many other factors shape tourists' decision making, including emotion drivers or those related to images, fashions and perceptions. Increasing environmental protection awareness of tourists could also be an important factor to influence tourism consumption, instead of oil fuel price raising causes air ticket fares raising factor to reduce traveler numbers. However, oil price raising reason causes also due to high use of cars, vans and domestic air transport in some countries, e.g. Hong Kong, China countries, there are many people like to buy cars to drive. So, the private driver numbers are increasing demand to cause these countries' oil fuel prices raise in the short time suddenly.

- Why oil fuel raising price factor can cause risk to airline.

In long run, implications of changes to supply and demand side conditions of oil fuel energy may differ qualitatively. For example, due to investment responses of producers, consumers and governments in alternative energy sources and more energy efficient plants, vehicles are supplied in order to achieve oil fuel price can't be risen seriously. However, I believe oil fuel rising charge will be an important factor to influence global airline ticket fares to be also increased. Firstly, on the bank interest changing factor, e.g. bank interest rate rising which only attract more bank saving. But it can not influence the bank savers who choose to reduce relax time to go to other countries travelling. Otherwise, when the bank savers can save more money to earn higher interest in banks, who will prefer to choose to use their saving to consume travelling. Due to who can earn higher interest rate after a period of saving time. So, I believe who behavioral travelling consumption will be raised when the banks will raise interest rate, then the bank savers won't choose to save more money in banks. So it is possible that who will withdraw more money to consume to go to travelling from banks. It seems bank interest rate changing won't influence bank savers' behavioral travelling consumption to be reduced. Secondly, on the exchange rate changing factor, although any country's exchange changing will cause other countries' money value to be fallen down or risen up. However, it won't influence any travelers' behavioral consumption to be reduced seriously. Although, it is possible that the traveler won't spend too much to go to shopping when who travel to the another country and arrive the country. But, it is not possible to influence the traveler decides to reduce consumption to buy any air ticket to go to travelling. Thirdly, any country inflation also can not reduce travelers' travelling consumption easily because inflation can influence consumers who choose to buy cheaper foods and clothing and reduce entertainments in their every day life. But, one country's inflation can not influence it's citizen do not spend much travelling expenditure because travelers only spend one time or two times of travelling every year usually. So, the travelling expenditure rate of any households is not too much to compare daily essential expenditure. So, it seems that bank interest rate and exchange rate changing and inflation won't influence any travelers' travelling consumption of decisions to be reduced easily. Otherwise, if the oil fuel price raises too much, then global airlines' cost will be raised. So, the airlines only choose to increase their air fare prices to aim to avoid loss possibly. It seems that oil fuel price has direct influence airline income.

● Methods to solve rising air fare prices demand.

I. Why will biofuels energy be demanded ?

I suggest these methods how to avoid the oil raising price factor to cause airline air fare prices to be risen to lead the risk of traveler numbers to be reduced. The first method: Whether aviation fuel markets will have what benefits from biofuels supply to planes. I shall refer the scope includes trends in jet fuel price, airline response to fuel price, increases and volatility and environmental goals for aviation. The aviation fuel supply industry includes production, distribution and consumption of aviation fuel and it outlines players in the aviation fuel supply chain. For example, at each airport, fuel supply chain organization and fuel sourcing could differ with regard to the role of oil companies, airlines, airport owners and operators and airport service companies. However, major jet fuel purchasers are airlines, general aviation operators, corporate aviation and the military, with most of the jet fuel in global different countries demanders being used for domestic commercial and civilian flights carrying passengers, cargos or both. Commercial aviation fuel efficiency has improved dramatically over time, largely due to aircraft and engine upgrades and operational and air traffic control improvements. So, it seems that fuel supply factor can influence airline fare prices majorly. However, jet fuel prices generally correlate with prices of crude oil and other refined petroleum products, such as diesel. So, increasing prices and the persistent price volatility of jet fuel markets import airline industry finances in any countries. However, airlines use various strategies to manage aviation fuel price certainty, including financial hedges, increased vertical integration and adjustments in aircraft utilization and size to avoid the jet fuel raising price risk. Investments in alternative aviation fuel could be a mechanism to diversity expose to the price of petroleum. It seems the use of alternative aviation fuel would serve to diversify the fuel mix to reduce the risk of jet fuel monopoly raising price threat. If a diversified fuel mix were to avoid either fuel raising price in short term or to avoid fuel raising price in long term. Potential benefits include reduced actual fuel costs from only choice of jet fuel supply increased price certainty and lessened fuel costs. This diversify could allow airlines to become more consistently profitable and to make other investments in their businesses.

So, biofuels have potential to meet aviation industry needs, possibly including managing risks of upward fuel price trends and fuel price volatility and avoid risks with greenhouse gas emissions. So, the aviation fuels market could use biofuels to reduce greenhouse gas emission and mitigate long-term upward price trends, fuel price volatility or both. What are the challenges of high priced oil for aviation? In fact, nowadays not the resources of oil as such, but much more the insecurity of supply, due to geopolitical instability in combination with a tight oil market makes a scenario with much higher oil prices than the world is currently experiencing not unlikely. Aviation is completely dependent upon oil as its fuel source. Since no practical energy substitute is readily available for commercial aviation, a scarcity of petroleum relative to demand will present a major aviation policy. In addition, efficiency gains, due to operational measures and new aircraft medium term. In particular, it has been demonstrated that the annual reduction rate in fuel consumption traffic unit is not a constant, but is itself also falling, in contrast to past estimates. So, a high-priced oil scenario will have severe consequences for demand, airline revenues, the competitive position of airports and eventually airline networks, strategies and fleet development. In particular, transfer demand, short-haul and leisure traffic can be expected to be heavily affected by high oil prices, due to their relative high price sensitivity. So, different countries' governments or/and airlines are valuable to research another new and potential biofuel energy to substitute oil energy to supply our planes to reduce the threat of oil monopoly supply to influence the cause of air fare raising prices. Because the elasticity is very high to travelers, when the travelers feel air fares are rising high or even low level to influence travelers who will choose not to buy the air tickets to go to travel easily.

Whether will the fuel (oil based inputs) risk be high to compare other costs, e.g. engineering maintenance, employees salaries, general cleaning, security office expenses etc. expenditures to airlines? If the probability-weighted upside effect on firm value when a risk is resolved favorably is greater the risk than the probability-weighted downside effect if the risk is resolved badly, then expected value work not be enhanced by hedging. So, the risk will be resolved badly to any commercial airlines. Airlines are an interesting case because the direct effect of source of risk resides squarely within the no offset in revenue functions (unlike for oil producers, for example), so value effects from costs feed directly into equity value. Most directly, the risk source is fuel costs to commercial airlines. Jet fuel is of course, a mix product of crude oil, so airlines indirectly face oil price risk. There are reasons to expect that airlines' fuel costs might to convex in oil price (i.e. absent any hedging). For example, oil prices, being generally pro-cyclical in recent times, tend to be highest when airline demand is strong. Airlines are therefore apt to use more high priced fuel than low-priced fuel over time. Airlines can raise air fare benefit is limited by the elasticity of demand. Also, cost functions could be influenced from fuel cost corresponds to upturns in economic activity overall (due to demand pressures on oil related prices), so it causes that airline's capacity delivers their services given their level of fixed capital. The essence of airlines basis risk in the case of jet fuel is essentially the time profile of the refining margin between crude and jet fuel, or the time profile of the price differential between other refined distillates and jet fuel. Thus, it is far from clear that risk management with oil is sure to add value to any airlines. It seems the impact of airline energy and any countries' domestic or foreign airline passenger travel numbers which have direct close relationship.

II. Whether the relationship between terrorism and oil prices has close relationship.

Whether the relationship between terrorism and oil prices has close relationship. It needs to judge to determine if a combination of terrorism and the price of petroleum significantly predicted airline profitability and which variable whether the further period was the most significant between the terrorism occurrence and the price of petroleum influence. So, different countries' governments or airlines need to collect samples of financial records from which country's any airline commercial passengers and cargo airlines on costs of fuel and any airline profitability. Also, gathering the terrorism data were comparison of terrorist attacks on petroleum in oil-producing nations, and incidents of high jacking aboard any country's aircraft. When any countries' airlines or governments can judge whether the impact of airline energy and terrorism risk level is high or middle or low level. Then, which can use this sample data to measure how to do positive social change to whether to increase or reduce employment in commercial aviation industry, or ought need to invest other higher commercial activity in tourist and other travel related service businesses and when is the most right time to adopt of green technologies by the civil aviation manufacturing industry after the terrorism attacks occurrence to any country. It seems that any countries' governments or airlines which ought concern that the event of when the terrorism attacks will occur and gather past sample data to predict when the next time terrorism attacks event will be occurred and the risk will be high or middle or low level to influence global airline industry development.

III. What factors will influence airline industry's price elasticity of supply and demand?

In fact, the airline industry is largely dependent on the supply of the oil industry. Otherwise, the oil industry is inelastic. However, the increase or decrease of the price of airfare is directly related to the increase or decrease of the oil's price to fuel the aircrafts because there has no any new energy which can be substituted to oil fuel to airline industry. So, it seems oil fuel producers are monopolies to control its sale price to be raised easily. Another factor that can affect airline industry to be directly targeted by a tragedy brought about by terrorism. The past four years, from 2001 year to 2005 year, there had been at least $40 billion worth of losses in the airline industry because of the September 11 date terrorism attacks in 2000 year. There had been an expected and significant decrease in the demand for the airline industry services because of the attacks that involved planes hijacking and crashing into key locations like the World Trade Center and the Pentagon in USA. Although, terrorism attacks can bring risk to influence fuel price rising in airline industry. However, this risk occurrence to airline industry is only that after the terrorism attacks occurred. It is possible that terrorism attacks won't occur again in the future. Otherwise, our concerning ought be the greenhouse emissions and how it affects global warming. The air quality would be better once this new regulations are adopted. However, it would affect large airlines. So, it would increase the price of airfares because of economic fees that airline companies have to cover. Air pollution can give a negative impact on the domestic or oversea owned airline companies for long term. If airlines' planes can use clean fuel to fly, e.g. biofuel, then it will bring benefits to global airlines for long term. On the positive side, the environment would be healthier as the earth's temperature would rise, and greenhouse effect would be dramatically reduced. This positive effect can come at a cost that is greater than most people perceive. On the psychology view point on travelers, who will be more preferable to catch planes to go to different countries to travel, due to the chance of air pollution and global environmental warm issues will be reduced to low risk to influence our health if planes can use biofuel to be energy to fly in the future one day. It seems that spending expenditure to research other non polluted biofuel new energy is one solvable method to global airline industry in the future. To solve, any airlines or countries' governments or oil producers ought choose to spend more time to research new biofuel. Otherwise, the predicting when terrorism attacks event will be occurred, it is more difficult to predict the time more than researching to produce new biofuel energy method in the future. So, I recommend that researching the new biofuel energy or other kinds of energy to substitute the oil energy is the urgent behavioral economy which the airlines or oil producers or different countries' governments which need to concern nowadays.

VII

DISNEY ENTERTAINMENT THEME PARK INDUSTRY

The Walt Disney Company is one of the largest media and entertainment corporation in the world. Founded on Oct. 16, 1923 by brothers Walt and Roy Disney as a small animation studio. Today, it is one of the largest Hollywood Studios and also owns eleven theme parks, two water parks and several television networks, including the American broadcasting company. Disney entertainment theme park expansion has in recent years focused heavily on Asia, and specifically China, Hong Kong, Japan. For this research, I shall indicate my opinions to explain why Disney won't operate its business successfully in the beginning and how it applied knowledge management strategy . Finally, I shall give evidences to predict why it won't be USA theme park leader to influence USA economic growth and how to solve its problems.

What factors caused Walt Disney strategic and
human resource problems

In the beginning, Disney underestimated and neglected somes strategic and organizational behavior issues which can influence its different departments' operations inefficiently. What factors caused Walt Disney human resource and hotel operational problems? On the human resource problem hand, Bahandin, G et al., (2009) indicated that" errors are made regarding overall operation for Euro Disneyland from its American experience that Disney throughout Monday would be the light day for guests and Friday would be a heavy day to allocate staffs. In fact to this day, it had not enough staff to supply to staffing at a theme park, where the number of visitors per day in the high season can be 10 times the number in the low season ; wrong operational assumption of bus driver, it built the French bus parking space much too small. Bus drivers were unhappy as they had a very difficult time fitting their buses into their designated spots. In addition, Disney provided only 50 restroom facilities for bus drivers and on peak days there would be 2000 drivers ; operational errors are made to computer involved stations at the hotels. It assumed guests would stay at the park for morning spent the day at the park checked into the hotel late that night, and then checked out early the next morning before heading back to the park. Since there were so many guests checking in and checking out, additional computer station had to be installed at the hotels in order to decrease the amount of time the guests stood in line and hotel counter service staff numbers would also need to be increased. "

On the hotel operation problem hand, Dickson et al.,(2005) also indicated that" it had wrong belief that it understood European breakfast taste and Disney was told Europeans didn't eat sit down breakfast. This resulted in Disney downsizing their restaurants before Euro Disneyland opened. In fact, they were trying serve 2500 breakfasts in a 350 seat restaurant at some of the hotels. Further guests wanted bacon and eggs rather than just coffee. Disney reacted quickly with pre-packaged breakfast delivered to rooms and satellite. Thus, it caused resell in Disney downsizing their restaurants."

The reasons showed that French Disney restaurants are caused to fail , such as lacked French cultural characteristics, but only European social and eating pattern ; the non availability of alcohol proved, employees were not expected to be spoken in French language and who also were not fluent in English. Hence, Disney restaurants can not accept French eating style and culture to attract many French visitors to go to Disney restaurants to eat. Due to, USA Disney did not follow French people eating taste and speaking cultural, It must cause its French restaurant operation unsuccessfully before.

In addition, Disney has wrong judgement to operate its business in USA and overseas Disney operation wrongly. Such as Disney estimated the the demand of employee numbers wrongly. It only employed an additional 200 experienced Disney managers were located in the other three centers. In addition, some 4000 employees were unable to find suitable positions. It caused management lacks optimistic assumptions to know who ought to be provided training to its staffing to dealt cultural difference challenges. Moreover, it also had external threats and internal weakness challenges. It included high bank investment interest rates charge , unreasonable working conditions, poor communication and lack of cultural awareness because managers and it caused staff turnover increasing finally. The most failure, before Disney had not carrying on research whether whose visitors feel happy and satisfactory to enjoy its entertainment facilities when who are staying in Disney. Otherwise, who feel unsatisfactory and unhappy , even who need to complaint whose service quality. Hence, Disney numbers of visitors was decreasing before. Such as, visitors felt unhappy because who need to spent much time to queue. It also caused Disney visitor numbers was declining. Thus, Disney will need to consider how to change human resource activities to adapt clients' needs, such as reducing bad emotion to cause visitors who needed to spend much time to queue to wait to play entertainment facilities.

● Knowledge management strategy

As Harriet Griffey (2010) stated that "sometimes, boredom can give disadvantages to reduce staffs' ability to motive to work and reduces positive emotion , such as happiness. Thus, it causes people (staffs) lack motivated reasoning to unconsciously evaluate evidence in ways consistent with whose preferences. This type of bias can hinder a company's ability to learn from mistakes and to build successful strategies." However, Disney needed to implement knowledge management strategy to satisfy visitors demand after who entered .Disney demanded cleaners to repeat to remember any information to prepare to answer visitors' enquiries. It will train every cleaner memory to remember any information to be long term from short term memory successfully and every cleaner won't feel bore to do only cleaning job duty. When every one feel places are clean, who will concentrate on answering any visitors enquiries as the same time. Even, if they can give excellent service performance to serve visitors to let who to know how to go to any places in the short time. It is possible that visitors will appreciate whose service performance to let their manager to know, so that every cleaner will have chance to raise salary. Besides, waiting time and queues are daily problem for Disney theme park. Fast lines or priority queues appear as a solution of efficient queues for clients. Disney understood fast ticket line system affected visitor attendance numbers. Disney entertainment facilities long waits leaded to lower service evaluations and greater customer dissatisfaction. Efficient queue waiting time management can improve Disney visitor satisfaction and the willingness to recommend the service. Disney analysed of theme park visitor behaviour in relation to pay the higher ticket price to select to pay more for fast queuing line ticket than common queuing line ticket. In fact, Disney fast queuing line ticket system choice gave potential queues to any waiting clients . In general, Disney visitors don't like to wait long time in every entertainment facilities queuing line, who will feel a waste of time and waiting can lead to negative emotional response like frustration, impotence, tension or irritation .In fact, Disney amusement theme park needed visitors wait long queues and delays which were a frequent occurrence in every entertainment facilities line. Disney theme park as sets of rides, spectacles and leisure mechanisms are intended to entertainment and spark the imagination of clients, allowing visitors to escape their daily routing. In result, waiting is often a problematic issue that can influence Disney visitor experience and that can appear as one of the principal motives for complaining. As Disney visitor demand fluctuates constantly and demand patterns are often difficult to predict. It caused extra staff needed for the extra line. Finally, priority services such as fast line system facilities segmentation of its amusement park. When Disney offer the possibility of purchases a fast line, which are creating two different group. Disney visitors who are highly sensitive to waiting times are willing to pay to avoid or reduce lines or visitors that are highly sensitive to price that prefer to wait rather than to pay extra money. Also, Disney provides extensive training opportunity for participants through its own Disney university. The question of whether their training opportunity can lead the improve human resource activities. On the third hand problem, Disney are also worried that employees may leave it and join other competitor to serve their parks after training. Disney shows a trend of increasing depending on human capital other than physical capital. It thinks human capital is the knowledge, skills, ideas and commitment of its employees. It explains that investing in training and development is essential to its client service growth. In fact, Disney had owned enough entertainment facilities, restaurants, hotels, shopping centres within theme park, but its visitor numbers are increasing to need to be served satisfactorily. However, it needs to train cleaners, entertainment facilities service staffs, queuing service staffs, hotels, restaurants, shopping centres service staffs, instead of it's entertainment facilities attraction.

Disney observes that spending on training and development is typically regarded as consumption, instead of investment. On job training usually can't be replaced by formal education, therefore Disney chooses to make contribution on providing further training and development to employees. Disney paid salary for staff training, which included classroom, seminars, symposia or conferences; computer based training, on site training, book and periodicals reading, formal mentoring and informal mentoring program opportunities to meet its old staffs and new staffs both needs of motivate factors to achieve advancement , achievement, personal growth responsibility and achievement and recognition to raise its business performance effectively and efficiently. However, Disney's amount of training has a positive influence on intrinsic motivation of its employees. Job satisfaction, salary, working condition, its policies, administration, relationship with supervisors, peers and subordinates are Disney factors to influence it's human resource activities performance. Disney training contents include these functional area: Raising excellent service performance include that hotel food and beverage service delivery, shopping center, merchandise sale, restaurant service, entertainment facilities queuing waiting service, cleaning and enquiring how to go different locations in Disney, cashier service etc. They are very important to influence visitor numbers. Disney implementation of knowledge management solution to improve queuing waiting line process. The use of Disney front line service staffs as human capital combined with knowledge of customer preference has made the fast pass an innovation solution to enhance queuing in the Disney theme parks. Disney ability to capture customers in virtual queues when giving them a pleasurable waiting experience has made them a leader in knowledge management initiatives in the service industry. Disney's emphasis on human capital within their theme parks, combined with traditional queuing theory to create more pleasurable waiting environments. Hence, Disney showed the value of tacit employee knowledge integrated with traditional queuing theory to reduce loss of customer satisfaction to enhance, goodwill and profitability. Knowledge management expresses itself as human action in form of evaluation, attitudes, points of view, commitments, motivation etc. It seemed that Disney agreed that human capital (people, knowledge, ideas, creativity) maybe today's most valuable commodity.

Knowledge Management Strategy was used to queue control from Disney. Disney managers have long understand the pressure of waiting time and revenue; who know that every minutes spent waiting in queuing is a minute that the client is not generating revenue. So, Disney managers have processed with design of a reservation system recognizes that guests can be freed from physically standing in the actually and perception of waiting by allowing guests to engage has arrived. Cope et al., (2008) showed that" the system was first tested at Disney in 1998. Managers assessed the system by surveying guests who used it. Results were positive and indicated that guests spent substantially less time in queuing, spent more per capita, and saw significantly more attractions, satisfaction level sky rocketed.The system was expanded in 1999 to include five of the most popular park attractions and was named FASTPASS. The system has since been expanded to all Disney theme parks worldwide, and is now in use by over 50 million guests per year .That guests have two options .Namely, they can choose to Obtain a FASTPASS ticket and come back a later, designed time or Wait in a traditional queuing. Guests are assisted in making their choice by information regarding estimated waits of both options. Thus, can decide to wait in the traditional queuing, or take a FASTPASS ticket and return it a later time with no further wait. Once an assigned FASTPASS time is generated and provided to a guest, it is valid for the 60 minutes beyond that time, creating a window in which guest can return."

There are numerous benefits in allowing park guests to return to an attraction within a designed time frame. Queue Waits involve managing two major client issues:

1.How long Disney visitors actually wait every time queue.

2.How long Disney visitor think they are waiting by whose psychological feeling every time queue.

Thus, if they feel that who spend much time to queue, it will cause they feel angry and they also feel admission ticket price is paid too high to them unfairly. In general, clients were allowed the ability to see two attractions during the time they would have previously been able to see only one. This can viewed as an implementation of a multi-phased system, depending on the attraction picked, each queuing may be single channel attractions, the guest creates whose own multi phase system. Obvious, results, were that guests were able to engage in more revenue producing activities, saw more of the popular attractions and began to par take care, in other less utilized attractions . Wiig defined(1993)" Knowledge management in different ways and from different perspective. The emphasis is on human know how and how it brings value to an organization. Intangible asset contributes to corporation objective may be immeasurable and isn't simple to evaluate the impacts of knowledge management." However, Knowledge management may not be only factor influencing organizational performance. In fact, Disney refined technology utilization to improve the user design of all human resource related systems, improving timeliness (queue waiting time deduction), setting elapsed time goals and monitor performance towards those standards, considering to use of automated fast queue waiting system, evaluating staffing levels, a close examination of adequacy of current staff level is warranted, beyond to improve visitors satisfaction. Clients holding fast pass tickets may choose to visit a gift shop or any park concessions. Thus, Disney has ability to co-branded products and service. Disney's approach combining queuing and human capital. Dunn, J et al., (2002) showed "The use of fast pass provides an insightful application of the combination of techniques of queuing and human capital to strategically leverage knowledge management principle .When waiting lines are an part of the Disney experience, park guests build magical memories through innovation. It is Disney's recognition of front line service staffs that transforms that employees into knowledge who multi task in their roles.For example, an attraction host or a street sweeper may be a valuable Source knowledge to park guests. In addition to their primary roles, they may have a wealth of information about attractions for guests. They may be able to give directions, provide schedules, and offer helpful suggestions from their daily observation. This is the first stop to increase knowledge management . Next, Disney improves its clients' perception by minimizing the perception of waits. The use of the fast pass enables Disney not only to enhance the psychological aspect of waiting lines, but also to capitalize at the same time." Instead, Disney needed to give people specific tools designed to help them to do their job and solve specific business problems. Thus, after Disney learned how it applied the knowledge management method to solve its challenges, e.g. Human capital and queuing theory provide two very different valuable assets to raise its competitive abililty. Then, its visitor numbers was increasing largely and quickly.

● Whether Disney knowledge management
strategy can influence America tourism
economy growth in the long term.

The development of the travel and tourism
Industry to USA, it changed customer needs and expectation
to cause amusement park industry development
after world war II in USA

The economic activities associated with travel as is measured by the wide variety of current and capital expenditures made by or for the benefit of the traveller before, during and after the trip. Since the Second World War the Travel and Tourism Industry has developed. After Second World War, these main factors that have led to the economic growth and socio-economic circumstances of the Travel and Tourism Industry to cause amusement park industry development indirectly to USA are as below:

Firstly, the greatest single transport factor that has increased for travel and tourism is the car ownership. There was an increase in the number of cars on the road between 1951 and 1970's and an even bigger increase between 1951 and mid 1990's. Also, increased car ownership has now been a major factor of visits to tourist's attractions and leisure facilities nowadays. Then, people now don't have to work as much so more time to have holidays in the USA and abroad to spend whose leisure time. Before second war, the average working week was 50 hours but after second war, the typical hours in a normal working week ranges from 37 – 40 hours in USA. So, nowadays, there are many developed countries people who have more time to go to travel, such as USA, UK, France etc. countries.

Also, after second war, the global employees' salarys are risen largely, who can have afford income to provide to go to travel at least one time every year . It will cause travel industry develops quickly. On the other side, Jet Aircrafts Developed , the breakthrough of the Jet Engine first started after the Second World War. It brought dramatic aeroplances travel between countries, such as France or UK travellers who can catch airplans to travel to visit USA Disney amusement park in the most short time and distance fastly. Then in the 1970s the jet aircraft really started being able to carry more passengers and increased profit and made flights cheaper to attract different countries travellers to go to different conuntries often. The last twenty years tour operators have also created hotel and disney visiting and cheap air ticket price travel packages for the needs to attract to raise further new travellers numbers. Moreover, Many travel retailers use to rely on pen and paper to do the work but attitudes started changing as technology started to improve by the early 1990s. View data was the first industry-wide booking system, first introduced back in the 1980s. View data is more than 20 years old and out of date but still the trade's favourite reservation system. Global distribution systems (GCDs) were known as a computer reservation computer in the late 1980s. These were set up by competing airlines to distribute their fares electronically to business travel agencies. Also now you can book online, over the phone and on teletext. Over the years the technology has improved all through the travel and Tourism industry with better transport, computerised reservation systems at travel agents and airports and better packaged holidays. Evenmore, over the last couple of years the low cost airlines have made a big development in the business. Low cost airlines like Easy jet, Ryan air and BMI Baby make it easy for people to travel to places in Europe for cheap prices, then cheap price travel is popular. Also, long Haul destinations have changed the travel industry a lot most holidays started just to Europe travellers and other travllers like Australia and New Zealand and France and Japan etc. countries doesn't take to long time to travel to USA by air plants very conventiently. This gives people to travel around the whole world and go somewhere different. Moreover, package holidays have made a big improvement in the business. Thus, travel convenicence can cause Disney visitors had been increasing many numbers.

Finally, on the weather and diseases both aspects can cause many overseas travellers like to choose to go to USA to travel. Over the years the weather has been getting warmer so snow will melt in the ski tourist places will start to lose money and tourist because of the weather also some places will have increased tourist for the weather being warmer as well as some countries are also loosing tourist because of diseases like foot and mouth because people don't like to travel to somewhere where they could catch something and can't even go there. For example, Britain lost a lot of tourists a couple of years ago through foot and mouth. After world war II, peoples needs and expectations have changed a lot in recent years. People are now fitter, healthier and more prosperous and are seeking more different and exciting types of leisure and tourism experiences. This, these environment and air ticket and travel package cheap price and warm weather and overseas countries' diseases increasing factors had assisted USA Disney traveller numbers rose.

- The economic and social impacts of America

Theme park Tourism industry

USA People's needs and expectation cause amusement park industry development. Amusement parks respectively theme parks can be met all across United States of America. Those theme parks are tourist attractions as well as recreation areas for the citizens of the Los Angeles area , they enrich the recreational possibilities for the residents. However, USA parks are not homogeneous among themselves; there are different design, composition and in the hierarchy and different dimensions of economic impacts as so following questions as below:

i. How does the establishment of a USA Resort park effect the surrounding region?

ii. Is it advantageous for a region to own a Resort park in USA?

iii. How are parks linked to the rest of the USA region's economy?

iv. How exactly does the park enrich the USA region economically?

In the theme park history, many other companies followed Disney's example and erected large scaled sized theme parks all over the U.S. theme parks of a size like Disneyland, Walt Disney World. Much of the research in tourism is concerned with the economic impact made by tourism on a state, nation, island or community and the arising costs and benefits from tourism are not immediately quantifiable. The costs and benefits of tourism are not evenly distributed. What may be a benefit to one group may cost another group within the same community or area. For example, hotel and restaurant operators may benefit from tourism, but the America permanent residents may suffer in terms of crowding , pollution, noise, and in some cases, a way of life. Sometime, America immigrants must be invited to serve the tourists, which constitutes a costs to the community through the increased use of schools, hospitals, roads, water system etc. Does America tourism introduce costs in the form of reduced quality of life at a destination? I feel the destination is not prepared for such a large number of visitors. As Disney was prepared to a large number of visitors, it won't reduce quality of life at the destination of entertainment. It is important that America visitors are brought into an economy by tourism , the economy gets stimulated-costs of goods and services increase, the price of America land may skyrocket due to Disney was built in the areas. In some areas the economy gets overheated, America Disney Land owners and developers may become rich, but the cost to the average citizen usually multiplies because of the increase. Tourism can have many positive and negative impacts on tourist destinations. However, Disney theme park can bring positive economic benefits, but it can also being negative bad influence to USA economy. It's positive benefits, such as it creates many jobs are made in the tourism business e.g. Disney restaurants, hotels, shopping places etc. Also the owners of the inside Disney or outside Disney shopping places and restaurants make quite a lot of money from tourists visiting and money in the USA country's some Disney regions improves the USA country's appearance because they have the money to improve buildings etc. The more visitors the more well known it gets and people will travel there and is known Disney is as a place to visit. However, it's negative bad influence to USA economy, such as that even though many jobs are produced through the tourism industry most jobs are seasonal so people working in hot summer weather after USA Disney was built in some regions which influnced some travelling jobs were changed to be temporary or part time or seasonal job nature from permanent job nature. e.g. Spain after about October when it's colder and no tourist there's then no work till the summer again. Also for the winter ski holidays. Shops and restaurants also lost business through problems like war and diseases so people didn't travel to dangerous countries so the Spain travelling business owners would lose the money. Another negative impact was how USA country could get destroyed by travellers e.g. Falaraki has had many problems with loads of young people up all night drinking after who travelled to USA to arrive USA some places. Also there have been cases of USA people being arrested and even raped over the last couple of years. Hence, theme park industry can bring these negative cost, such as cost of housing, incidental costs of tourism, life-quality costs, causing traffic congestion ,highway construction and high cost of police services, public transportation, parking facilities, raising crime, vagrancy and homelessness rising emergencies, fire protection, ambulance and police services are needed close to theme parking areas, rising water pollution, increasing water supply and sewage treatment, rising air pollution and public transportation cost, rising noise pollution close to theme park zoning areas, increasing destruction of wildlife Park and recreation facilities development and maintenance, rising forestry protection, fish and hunt regulations, etc. , destruction of scenic beauty Park and recreation facilities, destruction of social/cultural heritage maintenance of museums and historic sites , increasing disease and health conditions hospital facilities, sanitation facilities, food-service regulation and increasing vehicular accidents, police services risk chance. However, in economic terms, the America tourist dollar spent in an area, such as Disney is an export which brings in new money. Lundberg(1995) indicated that "when a fresh dollar enters an economy to America, which in this Disney case is the tourist dollar brought to the America Disney areas destination's economy.Hence, the Disney importance of America tourism to a region and which economic activities are being influenced by hotels, restaurants tourist attractions, retail stores entertainment, housing etc. indirectly." It seemed that USA Disney amusement park can bring USA positive economic benefits, but it also cause negative social challenges in USA.

● The background on how people view the
theme park industry in America

As it is commonly acknowledged, IAAPA (1999) indicated that "Disneyland in Anaheim, California, which opened in 1955 year, is concerned the first real theme park. Since them, the theme park industry in the United States had grown dramatically. The theme park industry is a $4 billion per year business based on an annual attendance of half a million to a million visitors per year add another $600 million revenue. Total revenue for the America park industry is estimated at $4.5 billion, making this a major industry. "

The America theme park industry is by far the largest in the world, and it dominates the world. In respects to scale, product innovating, marketing savvy, and operating knowledge. The theme park industry in the America is mature. ERA(1998) showed "Growth has been about 3 percent over the last 10 years. About half of this growth has come form the addition of new parks and not from attendance increasing in existing parks." Growth in this theme park industry has stabilized and there should not be any huge fluctuations in attendance on development activity. However, there are opportunities for adjusting product to suit changing markets and to effectively compete with other entertainment for consumers' leisure time and expenditures. Now, major corporate owners in the industry control are found: Disney Time, Warne (Six Flags), Universal Studios, Sea World, Paramount Kings entertainment. These major corporations control the dominant share of attendance of revenue in the theme park industry. Re-investment is a key factor in the operation of a park. Several current trends can be seen. The "Arm Race" continues parks must build the biggest , highest, fastest, steepest, most complicated roller coasters. Another factor is the aging of the population which suggests the need and lighter entertainment compared to hard sides. Example of the new entertainment attracts the expansion of the outdoor family entertainment centres being developed in malls, entertainment centres combined with urban mixed use projects, etc.

The final point is that many USA park developer/ owner/markets, including looking at Europe and Asia. Certainly, also looking for opportunities are available for major. The growth of the theme parks in the USA has been followed by the development of the industry elsewhere in particular in Asia and Europe. ERA (1998a)indicated in terms of size, "Europe's theme park industry has grown to approximately $1.5 billion in current revenue coming from approximately 19 major parks . The biggest news in Europe was the opening of Euro Disneyland in Paris, which will entertained approximately 13 million visitors ." Also, IAAPA (1999)indicated "The United States, showed 0.46 theme park visits per capita per year, when in the European community only 0.08 visits per capita were experienced in one year."

The huge scale and board appeal of the Euro Disney land project is likely to create mass market awareness of the theme park product. This awareness is expected to develop theme park in Europe, China, India. This phenomenon has been demonstrated on two continents, and in these locations. In Japan, development interest in theme park projects has been extremely high following the success of Tokyo Disneyland. The experience in France of numerous theme parks preceding a Disney attraction into a new market suggests it may be unwise to reverse the timing of this development process. They all suffer from lacking attendance and some of them were already shut down. The theme park industry in Asia is also in a growth mode. Additional IAAPA (1999) indicated "49 moderate sized parks generate $350 million in annual revenue. The total industry has roughly $1.8 billion in annual revenue. "

Thus, in conclusion, how theme parks industry can impact USA destination tourism, USA economy growth is influenced from theme park industry between before second war and after second war. Having a theme park does not automatically insure an influx of tourism. To impact destination tourism, a theme park must be unique, a must see destination. This can be accomplished though character development (Mickey and his friends), architectural form, natural features, special events and programming (Opryland) or a combination thereof ; Have large scale and a critical mass of attractions. Investment levels to impact international tourism generally must exceed U.S. $150 million ; Combine high technology with human scale and quality service. Investments in the thrill hardware must be combined with a high level of service from the host and hostesses, so that a unique local culture and friendly human contact is balanced to the high technology ; Encourage overnight stays. On the other side, the principal economic benefits of tourism come when overnight stays are generated. Day visitors or tourists who stay with friends and relatives generate only 20% of the economic impact of tourists staying in hotels and motels ($50 versus $250 per day). Thus, in designing a theme park for tourism, a multiple attraction destination (with experiences that can occupy two or three days) is more likely to have the desired impact ; Have complementary destination activities. Tourist- oriented theme parks should be part of a mix of recreation and leisure activities. A true tourist destination would also have supporting recreation uses such as high quality hotels, convention and conference facilities, resorts, recreational shopping and dining experiences, and sports activities including golf, tennis, and water related activities and excursions into nearby local tourism areas ; Support media (TV) coverage and exposure. Like most other things in life, future theme parks must be designed for television . The use of theme parks and resorts as backdrops for variety programs, celebrity games, sports competition and convention / conference broadcasting is increasing rapidly and the resultant TV exposure is very important in creating awareness in tourism markets. Given that these criteria are part of the theme park/ tourist destination program, the results can be dramatic and provide a sustaining economic base. Benesch summarized (1989) that "Walt Disney World, tourism increased from 2.8 million visitors in 1970 year to over 35 million by 1992 year. The increase in the number of air visitors alone was 20 million. This increase in visitation (particularly overnight visitation) spurred the development of over 50,000 hotel rooms and resulted in the direct employment of over 250,000 persons ."

● Characteristics and hierarchy with
respects to economic importance of the theme
parks to the region in USA.

The components to make up the structure of the Travel and Tourism Industry to the theme parks to the regions in USA are: A tourist attraction is the place where tourist would go to visit e.g. Alton Towers theme park. Blackpool Beach ; Transport is then needed for how to reach the tourist attraction e.g. by car, train etc. ; Accommodation is not always needed as some tourist attractions could just to visit for a day but if needed hotels, caravans etc. ; Tour Operators then put a package together using the attraction visiting, the transport and accommodation and then put it in travel agents or a direct sell to the customer and cuts out the travel agent. Travel Agents then sell the holidays to earn commission in many shops all over the USA. Then the Tourism development and promotion section advertise and promote their part of the USA country so more people will visit the area from seeing advertising.

ERA(1998) indicated that" the theme park can divided by these characteristics :Recreation parks are plants whose facilities are used for recreation purposes. Enjoyment parks are all facilities and contribute actively or passively to the enjoyment of these visitors. These facilities don't have a certain foreign in common, neither do they have a teaching, sportive or shopping character.

Urban entertainment centres are mostly indoor built entertainment facilities with a concentration of experience shopping, a theme park entertainment area or a spare time and overnight stay facility. Finally, sport and fun parks, there are zoned areas (in and outdoors) which contain a mixture of several sport or spare time facilities."

● The impact of America Disney tourism
on local government expenditures

On the one hand, USA local policy makers have assumed that economic activities associated with tourism improve the quality of life. As such, much of the analysis of this industry has focused on the positive impacts on employment, income, tax revenue , and local economic growth and development. Generally, such as America Disney tourism, it will influence America government spends expenditures on transportation service aspect. Due to many America residents have no cars to drive to Disney. Hence, America government will improve transportation facilities to benefit local residents who need to catch buses or trains or ships to go to Disney. The general logic behind America local government initiatives to promote its regions as a Disney tourism centre is lying on the assumption that America local residents will benefit from the employment, income and tax revenue generated from Disney tourism. Such as America government permit Disney theme parks were built in some regions. America Disney will assist tourism to facilitate expansion of the property tax base through development, which will facilitate stable or declining tax rates.

On the second hand, a large portion of the tax burden may be exported through the use of Disney admission tickets sales and transient guest taxes paid by Disney visitor tourists. Thus, Disney would seem possible to import visitors to raise economic development. Due to Disney needed land development to build these theme entertainment parks in America's some regions. Land related constraints include limits on the amount of developed land and the need to preserve natural resources such as climate, land-forms, bodies of eater, beaches, natural beauty, and water supply for drinking and sanitation which may form the basis of the attractiveness of the area to Disney tourists. In addition, the use of land for Disney tourist development to build to prevents the use of that land for other purposes. Labour shortages may also limit the America Disney theme entertainment park tourism development. Critics often point out that much of the demand for Disney tourism related employment is seasonal and that low status and low pay characterize much Disney theme park tourism industry employment. As such, a disproportionate concentration of seasonal and low paid employment needed to service the theme park tourism industry can be a threat to the America local employment structure. Hence, in order for major Disney theme park tourism development to take place, adequate streets, highway, and parking facilities; air, water, bus, train, and taxi transportation networks; water and sewer system; utilities; communications networks; parks and recreation; health care facilities; and public safety systems must be established. In addition, private lodging, eating and drinking, and retail facilities must be adequate. Thus, infrastructure planning and development must involve a coordinated and concerted effort on the part of both the public and private sectors.

On the third hand, if a America local airport doesn't have an adequate air terminal or air service, surrounding hotels and attractions may well stand empty. Likewise, adequate streets and highways are needed to allow Disney visitors to get from the airport to their destination. Hence, America government needed to spend expenditure to assist Disney theme park tourism development to aim to attract local and foreign travellers to go to Disney from long distance conveniently as well as America government can reduce unemployment numbers if Disney can operate successfully and Disney surrounding facilities also need to employ many people to work before Disney is built. Hence, Disney development ought increase employment due to America government needed to employ workers to assist this land useful and entertainment facilities development for long term.

Thus, America park and recreation expenditures are affected by Disney tourism because in many jurisdictions park venues such as botanical or zoological parks may be secondary, if not primary, tourist venues. Finally, Disney theme park tourism may have a significant impact on both financial and general America government administration expenditures because of the increased resources necessary to manage capital facilities and infrastructure as well as the America government overhead necessary to deal with demands placed on America local government by Disney theme park tourism. The Los Angeles Area managed this structural change. In a study Friedmann(1999) indicated that" an economic development specialist recently directed for the Los Angeles city authorities, he found that three of the region's fastest growing business sectors (entertainment, textiles and environmental engineering) owed nothing to defence ."

Also The Economist (1997) indicated that "retail sale with America rose 4% in 1994 year after declining for three years in a row. Hotel occupancy rates for the year were up more than 14% and industrial building permits increased up 9%, the first such increase since 1989 year. The construction industry in Los Angeles is now expecting double digit growth this year. If greater Los Angeles were a country, its $380 billion of purchasing power would make it a bigger economy than South Korea . " It implied Los Angeles was a good position for Disney to choose to be built . Barnard (1999) also indicated" France is the world's most popular destination for foreign tourists, attracting 66.8 million visitors in 1997 year compared with the America, in second place with 49 million, Spain, Italy and the United Kingdom occupied the next three place. And despite economic difficulties, western Germans still lead in per capita tourism spending . "

It also seemed Disney would have these foreign countries' travellers who would go to America to travel and visit Disney certainly far from maturing. Hence, the external environment factors can assist Disney success. Such as, Europe's tourism industry is set for faster growth which is caused by the introduction of the single currency, the Euro the spectacular growth of low cost airlines, and the spread of high speed rail links. Barnard (1999a) also showed again that "equally important, Europeans have much more leisure time than Americans or Japanese do most workers have an average five to six weeks annual vacation . It seemed it is right time to Disney developed its theme park entertainment business to foreign overseas markets."

● What is Disney theme entertainment park unique characteristics and image in USA

Disney of the world: A globalisation perspective can include such as, general perspectives are in Disney is as spectacle, theming, as hybrid consumption and perspective on Disney's emotional labour. Traditionally, destination attraction and other types of tourist activities have not been subjects of big attention for economic developers. However, times are changing, economic developers by all means seek job creating opportunities in the service sector of the industry. A major destination where it is located . Foden (1996)showed" the investment in facilities for example, can range from $150 to $300 million and up depending on the size and quality of the attraction itself and on the related investment, such as resort hotels, conference centers. The construction of the attraction and there required from time to time provide employment for the local construction industry." Hence, during Disney construction time, it provided many employment chance to USA job seekers, even USA government needed to build different transportation, shopping centers, public toilets, gardens etc. facilities which located close to Disney to attract and convenient to travellers to visit Disney. In this built period, it provided many employment chance to government labours to participate to develop further economic activities in USA some regions. In amusement park industry grew over the next three decades. The centre of the industry was lonely island in New York, which at its peak was home to three of America's most famous amusement parks along with attractions. Around the world, hundreds of new amusement parks opened, when many early trolley parks expanded by adding new rides and attractions. New innovations provided greater and more intense thrills to the growing crowds. Kyriazi (1997) indicated "that by 1919 year, over 1500 amusement parks were in operation in the United States. Unfortunately, this development did not last for long .The 1929 year, America entered the economic depression and by 1935 year only 400 amusement parks remained. World war II further hurt the industry, when many parks closed and others retrained from adding new attractions due to amusement park industry enjoyed past war prosperity."

Attendance and revenues grew to new records as new parks opened across America. A new concept took advantage of the past war baby boom ,introducing a new generation to the joys of the amusement park in the rapidly growing suburbs .As the 1950 year began, television, urban decay, segregation and suburban growth began in distress as the public turned where for entertainment. Hence, what was needed to be a new concept to Disneyland when Disney first opened in 1955 year, many people needed an amusement park without any of the traditional attracting would succeed. But Disneyland was different. Disneyland offered five distance themed areas, providing "guests" with the fantasy of travel to different lands and times.

● How Disney increases employment chance

Disneyland theme park's influence on the foreign investment urban economy and employment growth in China is more than USA domestic urban and France and Japan etc, countries theme parks after 2016 year, due to China disney theme park is a new amusement theme park and it is very large areas in China disney theme park, so it needs to employ many cleaners, entertainment facilities machine operators, engineers, administrative clerk, performance staffs, queue service staffs, cashiers different kind of positions in China disney theme park. Disney itself is a variety of them park industry, it is a huge impact on the economy and employment in USA before, but it has a more huge impact on the economy and employment in China to compare to USA after it began to invest to develop Disney theme park in China overseas Disney market. What is the direct role in the employment and economic growth of USA and China Disney ? According to macroeconomic theory, a certain amount of investment will lead to several times the national income increase plus, this is become a department of new investment not only increase the income of the department and orders through chain should be cause the other relevant department, higher income, additional new investment for new revenue, promote other departments. Making the national income growth of the total of times the initial investment, public spending and investment will stimulate the effect and the increase of investment will stimulate the economy as a whole have multiplied, called multiplier effect. How Disney promotes job growth. Disney theme park through its own development attracts a large number of travel consumers, thus forming a flow of consumption, also has the strong effect of employment. For example, Disney applicants can apply for construction manager, civil engineers, include senior executive and high administrative management, architectural and design and IT technology etc. full time workers, most of the applicants need have degree requirement. Moreover,the availability of a large pool of part time labour is a real asset for a locality hoping to land a destination attraction. College students, spouses of military personnel, and housewives seeking temporary or part time employment are key sources. location near a college or a military base is particularly desirable. Weather has a direct bearing on the number of days a theme park can operate and, hence, on its potential profitability. Initially theme parks were designed to operate year around, but now many can be successful with 140-150 days of operation. Warm, rain free weather is most desirable, particularly during the period April 1 to November 1. Hence, USA, France, Japan, China and Hong Kong Disney projects will directly add new jobs as a result of its construction and operation. It will also induce new jobs as result of income spent by workers filling these direct jobs, and may, in addition, result in indirect employment, to that extend that direct employment leads to local purchases of materials and services. The additional employment generated by the proposed of these countries' projects is a beneficial impact for job growth in these countries' cities and regions. For examples, Disney hotels, shopping centers, theme parks' entertainment facilities operations in California city in USA. They must need to employ full time and part time and casual workers to assist Disney development. Even, these countries' government will build other transportation and garden facilities to close to Disney. Hence, Disney also bring outside areas close to it to cause employment chance in these countries' cities. Disney had caused the seasonality of employment, an asset in some with large college or military establishment personnel, may be a detriment to some areas, which are seeking permanent, year round employment. Similarly, the lower wages associated with the part time/ temporary employment at most facilities may be undesirable, although in other areas the employment opportunities may represent a real opportunity to meet a need.

● The factors what are contributed to
Disney's successes on its way towards becoming
the world's largest family entertaining company

I shall discuss SWOT strategic analysis to Disney. The first force to be discussed is the threat of new entrants. Since the Disney company has been able to find a very distinctive niche in the industry, the entrance barriers are relatively high. Disney has been able to grow over a long period of time, and has developed from within the departments of Research and developments, marketing and finance. By relying on past experience, Disney officials know to a large extent what the target customer wants. As Disney pretty much dominates the family entertainment market, it will be very difficult for a new organization to develop brand recognition, brand identification and product differentiation . Disney has focused on market diversification for years and Disney covers a wide array of products and service, such as fast pass queue method and Disney mouse animal unique image cards, pens, papers and bags stationery products etc. Being a market leader has made it possible for Disney to practice effective economies of scale in production. For example , over 500,000 copies of the videocassette "Pinocchio" were sold in only two months, and Disney has 40-50 million visitors to its theme parks every year. It required for new entrants into the industry if they want to compete with Disney Corporation. For instance, Disney spent USD$3.6 billion in its European theme park (Euro Disneyland).Only very large companies can meet such large capital requirement to compete Disney in theme park entertainment market. Lastly, the government policy towards the industry appears to be very favourable. The French government invested USD$1.2 billion (40%) in Euro Disneyland, provided public transportation facilities and a large tax relief (from 18.6% to 7%) on the cost of goods sold. The bargaining power of customers is high in the service and in the entertainment industry. Since a large number of customer are needed to make Disney's operations run smoothly, the customers have certain powers. For instance, if the price on a particular home video is too high, customers may be reluctant to spend the money needed to purchase the product. Another example is the entrance fee charged at Disney's theme parks. It is stated in the case that the maximum amount of money that customers are willing to pay is USD$39. Accepting this fact, the entertainment industry is designed in a way that it will make the buyer spend more buy the initial admission fee. A majority of Disney's product mix focuses on intangible returns on the buyer's money. The case that some customers may not realize that they are getting such a return may increase the bargaining power of the customer. The bargaining power of suppliers is moderate. However, Disney is a unique and important customer of many of the suppliers and Disney itself size may certainly be a great advantage for them .By being able to order large volumes of unique products from unique suppliers, a dependency relationship in the industry will be created. The threat to Disney that customers substitute their products or services is moderate to low. Obviously, other cartoon figures, theme parks, and movies can penetrate the market in which Disney is operating in, but this is not necessarily representing a significant threat. The Disney company has already placed price ceilings on many of its product lines and should be able to compete with new competitors. However, Disney threats alone of new entrants into the market and it requires Disney to hedge against such risk by concurrently upgrading products and services. Jockeying among current contestants doesn't play a very important role in Disney's external operational environment. It is true that the company's exit barriers are extremely high (would who buy a huge theme/amusement park?). Furthermore, capacity is augmented by extremely large investments. However, there are no close direct competitors to Disney's operations. Competitors such as "Lonely Tunes" (Time Warner Bros). retail stores don't appear to commit themselves to expensive advertising campaigns to obtain market shares. Moreover, Disney 's products are highly differentiated feature. However, a multinational corporation such as the Disney company faces internal weaknesses and strengths, which can, to a certain extent, be controlled. The external forces such as opportunities and threats are more difficult to control, and Disney has to adopt and take advantage to those forces. I would like to start-up focusing on the internal capabilities of Disney this company. Disney 's main strength is in its resources and in the experience in the business. The company clearly has developed a very strong and well known "brand name" over many years. Disney has also been also to diversify its operations and products to hedge against decreasing sales in product lines. In recent years it has diverted into Home video, film merchandise, radio broadcasting, network television and of course in theme parks. It has also effectively globally diversified its operation from USA to Japan, China, Hong Kong and Europe, such as France countries. The main strengths in internal resources refer to human resources and financial stability. Employees in the Disney studios appear to be extremely innovative and in recent years they have produced several box-office productions, such as knowledge management strategy. A company without new ideas is doomed in today's competitive business environment. Corporations always have internal weaknesses, and in Disney's case they are: A very large work force, Frequent change in top-management, and High overhead expenses. In 1991 year, Disney had 58,000 employees. This fact represents possible communications problems, and a high level of bureaucracy within the corporation. By diversifying into more businesses and niches, it's work force will grow even larger, and the organizational structure has to be able to support an expansion of the work force.

However, Disney also have these internal weakness. The fact that Disney very frequently changes its corporate officers makes the corporate structure even more complicated. There are many positive things that accompany changes, but change is also associated with resistance, and large expenses. Large overhead costs are usually direct effects of large work force and a large number of fixed assets. For instance, ticket prices should not be able to exceed USD$39 for entrance to Disneyland. Customers are not prepared to spend more money than that. Therefore, we can conclude that overhead costs should be closely monitored to match the price that customers are willing to pay for the goods and services offered. Legal and legislative forces are usually identified as being negative external factors to a company. In Disney case, the French government contributed greatly in the Euro Disneyworld project. The French government invested over USD$ 1.2 billion in the project, built communication facilities, and gave Disney tax relieves on cost of products sold accounts as already mentioned. In addition, since the barriers of entry into the highly specialized industry in which Disney is operating, competition will find it difficult to penetrate Disney's high diversified product/service mix. Furthermore, large initial capital investments are required to enter the industry. Also, the external major threats to the Disney Company include the following:

A. Over saturated markets, there are many overseas travellers had visited disney one time or more than one time before. So the traveller numbers had been falling down.

B. Politics and economic aspects from a global perspective, overseas countries' governments achieve close policy or poor economic influence to influence their citizens' travelling needs.

C. Foreign competition is from overseas similar cheap entrance fee amusement theme parks

On the tickets sale hand, Disney had sold reasonable tickets sale prices to let visitors feel more acceptable. The quoted prices are on a daily admission ticket basis. Note that the big parks like Disney offer 3-, 4-, 5- , and 6- day passes as well (on a cheaper per day basis). it attracts attention, that all park share nearly the same admission prices. Foden (1996) already mentioned ,"visitors are not willing to pay more that $39 USD admission fee, so there is no more room for the competing companies. "

Thus , Disney reasonable admission ticket price and queue control service and knowledge cleaners' enquiry etc. human resource change strategy which is these soft factor can cause to attract more visitors to compare to increase new entertainment equipments factor to achieve Disney's success. However, if Disney hope to keep it's leader position to assist USA economic and employment growth in the theme park travel industry. It needs to solve some it's internal weakness in the future.

Conclusion and Recommendation

USA Disney theme park has these weaknesses to influence its operation, if it does not solve its problems, I think it can not assist USA country's employment growth and GDP growth very more. Otherwise, It concentrates on investing to China Disney, I think it can earn more foreign income to assist USA GDP growth. Due to the world tourism organization through the scientific prediction 2020 yr. will become the world's largest tourist destination in China, every year to attract international visitors can reach 140 million people, according to global tourism 8.6 % of total global international tourist. However, if USA Disney still hopes to be the theme park leader to influence USA economic growth in the theme park. It needs have any methods to solve these problems in the future. First problem such as it still have a high employee turnover rate, it will cause high recruitment cost to training and induction cost of new employees, also it was noted that as Disney, all employees are not being given the equal opportunity as employees are routinely assigned to job according to age, appearance, a process which is officially known as casting. Second problem, such as it needs to change its employment culture and it has no age discrimination. The most presentable get the most popular front line jobs and the best shifts, others get the remaining work allocation. e.g. old ladies sell the merchandise, old men work in security, young people work in food service and preparation, American-Americans work as cooks or stewards or food preparation. Disney employees can leave voluntarily, but the average length of service was 15 years essential. When job disappeared, for example, after restructuring, employees were not made redundant but went into a resource centre where other parts of Disney would look first when job vacancies arose. Third problem, such as Disney employees were paid in their resource centre, sometimes for several months and were made offered further training to develop the skills required by this utility. It needs to reduce its training time to let every new employer earn salary early. Fourth problem, such as it lacks good organizational culture includes: Open communication, high absenteeism, bad union relations, and employee relations. It needs relatively small in size, had developed a family culture that helped Disney to improve its performance, despite the relatively large size of Disney and emphasizes its important contribution to Disney's performance. Hence, the role of employees, teamwork, organizational culture, training is also critical achieving on Disney's targeted performance. Fifth problem, such as Disney needs to ensure to employ every right applicant, who are capable of completing those tasks that help it to reach its objectives. Issues, such as the recruitment of staff, the retention of staff, developing staff and succession planning, as well as downsizing and relocation, need to be accommodated in human resource plans. Selection methods and employment sources, newspapers, internet, magazines etc. to produce high performing employees. The final problem , such as Disney human resource in international is different employment methods from its domestic . Changing mix employees for host country and foreign, having to expand one' expertise to include knowledge of foreign country employment law and global organization. Enhanced service performance and improve morale, the ability to determine what Disney can be done in house and what must be outsourced.

In conclusion, Disney ought to have an excellent human resource department to arrange all human resource activities to internal and external departments to achieve overall organization to provide internal staff service between departments and external clients service provision in the best service performance if it wanted to keep visitor numbers rising continually. Thus, an efficient human resource activities will contribute in achieving Disney goals and objectives in an effective manner. At Disney, managing cross cultures is the key factor of human resource activities of the global context. Hence, USA economic growth will also raise from theme park entertainment industry innovation to raise employment chance and visitors numbers in the long term. Hence, I feel if Disney could not change its strategy to be better, I believe that it could not raise USA Disney economy growth and USA Disney income in the future, although it can raise China Disney employment chance and earn China Disney income after 2016 year. However, I believe Disney has ability to manage its business to assist USA economic growth and to raise employment successfully. This is my personal assumption to get this prediction, it is not true to ensure Disney can't assist USA economic growth because Disney is a famous and long time history of entertainment amusement park in the word. Hence, Disney must have ability to assist USA economic growth and to raise its employment at 10 years minimum time in the future.

Bibliography

Bahandin, G. & Guerganna, K.S. United States, (Jan. 2009).Strategic human resource management and global expansion lessons from the Euro Disney challenges in France. International business & economics research journal, vol. 8, no.1.

Barnard, Bruce: Business is booming in the world's biggest tourist market, March 1999, p.22, Journal of Commerce, Brucells.

Barnard, Bruce: Business is booming in the world's biggest tourist market, March 1999a, p.24, Journal of Commerce, Brucells.

Benesch, Dieter, 1989: " Theme parks in Florida-Eine Analyse von Angebot und Nachfrage sowie Regionalwirtschaftfliche Auswirkungen" , Master 's Thesis at the University of Economics and Business Administration, Vienna. AAdvisor: Prof. Dr. Karl Sinnhuber, Library.

Cope, R. R. Cope and H. Davis (2008). Disney's virtual Queues: A strategic opportunity to co-brand services ? Journal of Business & economics research, vol. 6 no10, 13-20.

Dickson, D., R. Ford and B. Laval (2005). Managing real and virtual waits in hospitality and service organizations. Corncell hotel and restaurant administration quarterly, vol. 45 no1, 52-68.

Dunn, J & A Neumsister (2002). Knowledge management in the Information age. E. business review, Fall , 37-45. Jounral of service, spring 2011, vol. 4, no1, De Grovte (2009).

Edinger Tourismberatung GmbH: Study: "Die Entwickling von Freizeitparks in Osterreich, 1998, for: Bundeministerium fur wirtschaftliche Angelegenheiten, wien" Innsbruck.

ERA (Economics Research Associates) 1998: " The Future Role of Theme parks in International Tourism" , Clive B. Jones & John Robinett, Los Angeles, p.5

ERA (Economics Research Associates) 1998a: " The Future Role of Theme parks in International Tourism" , Clive B. Jones & John Robinett, Los Angeles, p.13

Foden, harry G. 1996, " Destination attractions as an economic development generator", Economic Development Review, Fall 1996, 10., American Economic Development council

Friedmann, David:" Status Report of the Los Angeles County Economy", Vol.1, prepared for the "Los Angeles Board of Commerce, 1999.p.78

Harriet Griffey. (2010) The art of concentration, enhance focus, Reduce, stress and achieve move. Macmillan publishers ltd,Basinastoke and Oxford, London UK.

IAAPA: International Accociation of Amusement Parks and Attractions (http://www.iaapa.prg), " Theme Park Industry at-a-a glance" (Brochure), 1999, Atlanta, Georgia.

Kyriazi, Gary, "Amusement Parks: A Pictorial History" Secaucus, NJ: Castle Booka, 1997.

Lundberg, Donals E. (ph.D.):" The Tourist Business", 1995, 5. Edition- Published by Van Nostrand Reinhold Company, New York.

PKF consulting, 1997: " Study of the Projected Future Tax for: The City of Anadheim, the Anaheim Public Financing Authority, Nov. 13, Collections From Designated Sources to be Received by the city of Anaheim", 1997, prepared -1997.

The Economist 1997: "The Los Angeles economy: Bigger than South Korea", Feb, 4. 1997 page 25-26, London.

Wiig, k.(1993). Knowledge management foundations: Thinking About thinking. How people and organizations create, represent and use knowledge vol.1 , of knowledge management series schema press: Arlington, TX.

VIII
SPACE TECHNOLOGICAL INDUSTRY

When discussing the advancement of space science and space technology, most people think about deep space flights, lunar stations, and thrilling outer space adventures. The fact is that the majority of the human technology in space, which consists of interconnected satellites, points towards Earth, and is used to provide services for and fulfil the goals of people on planet Earth. Over the next decade, there will be an increased need for innovative Earth information systems to support the international space community's efforts to provide a robust infrastructure. Space exploration requires vast sums of money. Is the amount of money spent on space research justifiable? Could the money be better spent? There has always been considerable discussion about whether governments should spend tax payers' money on space research. In my view it is impossible to justify the amount of money spent on such projects. Generally speaking, the main reason for this position is that there are several areas in which the money could be invested better. The first point to make is that politicians have a responsibility to spend public money on projects that bring a benefit to the general public. This has not been the case with space research as most developments have been limited to helping astronauts in space or have been very specialised. For example, it is not of great value to the general public that we now have pens and biros that can write upside down. This does not merit the huge amount of money spent. Thus, I feel it is very difficult to justify whether space exploration is value to invest or not at present. We need to wait time to observe whether what the main rewards or benefits to human in the future. However, I shall indicate what benefits human can get from any products or services of space exploration in this book.

A conceptualization of space exploration

Since the early 1970 year, the social sciences concern the process of globalization. Brennan (2011) explained " that globalization means the new international division of labor, changing forms of industrial organization and processes of urban-regional restructuring to transformations in the nature of state power, civil society, citizenship, democracy, nationalism, localities and architectural forms among many others. However, globalization research includes geographical concepts, such as space-time compression, space of flows, space of places, globalization , localization and scape, among many other terms ." Hence, the conceptualization of space exploration can relate to globalization by the channel e.g. the internet, a symbol that we are all connected and nobody is quite in charge as well as everyone in the world is affected, directly or indirectly. Also by this new Global investment in satellite navigation systems was extensive in the 2000 year. The USA with the GPS system. In particular, the space exploration means the space market has expand into new niche sector: Space tourism and travel, mining of resources, manufacturing opportunities , satellite technology all represent a shift toward privatization of the sphere. The new century is an important time in the history of space, not just for science, but in the opportunities it offers for business enterprise and commercialization. Human being are no longer in pursuit of progress and dreams of a high technological, science fiction life, they will use space technology to solve problems on Earth and to improve their quality of life despite limited financial resources.

Again, Brenna (2011) showed "Today, USA, Russia etc. countries are the world's super-powers at the time were engaged in the space race. They believe exploration and application of Earth orbital space become serious resources of national development and real advancement of people's living standards." The present day space industry has evolved from the romanticism of the 1960s and 1970s, when putting a human being on the moon captured the imagination of the world. Now, a multi-pronged approach to space exploration is attempting to address environment issues, advance technology and industry, and cater for the next generation of holiday makers the space tourists. A number of factors have contributed to the globalization of the space industry. Political changes in the 1990s and the end of the space race meant that almost all trading nations, function with market based economies and their trade polices have tended to encourage free market between nations. The globalization of the space industry has been further encouraged by technical standardization between countries. Most governments actively seek to encourage global operators to base themselves in their countries (namely, the USA space infrastructure, Russian know how, Brazilian lower launch costs). Yip (2003) cities "decreasing costs, globalization, scale economies, sourcing efficiencies as offering the potential for competitive advantage to some countries." A recent report from the Futron Corporation (2009) addresses strategic private questions about space power and competitiveness:

- What are the core measure of space competition?
- Is space nationalism on the rise, and if so, what are the implications?
- What are the implications of multi-polar space community?
- What are the economic consequences of a commercial space environment based on multiple international providers of key technologies, systems and services?

Hertzfeld (2007) has described how space power can be viewed from a commercial perspective in two ways. "The first is economic: Encouragement of USA space ventures to be dominant in the world marketplace, either through the creation of a monopoly by market dominance. The second is aggressively denying others access or interfering with the operations of foreign space assets. " Thus, it is possible that space exploration can stimulate the economy via job creation and the possibility of products entering future potential economic aspect of two civilian application of space technologies: communications and meteorology. Another author's opinion, Taraseko (1996) has classified "Russian space systems according to the missions performed. These systems can be sub-divided into space weapons, space surveillance and intelligence systems, support systems and scientific systems ." He implied Russian will concentrate on manufacturing space weapons , then it will also sell space weapons to global finally. I think space exploration will have military and civil two aspects, instead of space tourism. Thus, on space system military aspect, it includes space weapons, space to Earth anti- satellite, early warning. Beside, on space system civil aspect, it includes support and applied communications, navigation, mapping, meteorological remote sensing and scientific research. It implies 'Globalization' will be cooperated by different main space leaders who will be carrying on space exploration activities in the future.

The benefits and Values are managed to international
cooperation in space exploration

The 1960's brought new advancements for all of Earth. Machines and men were sent into space, and this sparked a new government agency, called NASA. Space was a new frontier, and virtually everyone was interested in exploring it. Over the years, the interest in space exploration has weakened, and NASA was almost terminated from existence, although there have been many advancements in it over that time. Space exploration should continue because it could help solve many problems on Earth, such as overpopulation and lack of resources. Exploration of the final frontier must continue in order for human life to continue to international cooperation in space exploration. International cooperation in space exploration has the potential to provide significant benefits to all participants, particularly if managed well. Benefits in the form of monetary efficiency, raising economy development and workforce stability will accrue to those partners who choose to approach space exploration as a mutually beneficial to raise employment.

The first utility benefit, it is common knowledge that international cooperation in space exploration has the potential to reduce a partner's costs by spreading the burden to other nations. Although, additional overhead costs increase the overall cost to among partners. As per-partner cost decreases, pre-partner utility increases. Space exploration has proven to be an expensive activity.

The second goodwill benefit, the more countries participate, the higher will be the utility. As such, Indian, Russia and China countries participation in joint space exploration would send a strong signal to the world of good USA-Indian and Russian and Chinese friendly relations and increases political sustainability. So, these countries space exploration of cooperation which will help them to build friendship of intangible benefits.

The final raising employment benefit, international cooperation can enable workforce stability, one way politicians measure the benefits of a large space exploration program is in terms of the number of jobs and amount of revenue. For example, both the space shuttle and space exploration programs employ workers across the country and serve as a source of revenue to the district of many numbers of congress. The space exploration program also employs enough people to attract the attention of the president. The loss of these jobs and revenue streams would constitute a large loss in utility for both administration and congress. Nevertheless, the aerospace industry must continually engage in advocacy activities to ensure that politicians are made aware of this fact. As such, if either the space shuttle or space exploration programs were to grow to employ more people, an increase in the perceived utility lost in the event of a cancellation of the space exploration program would only result of the growth were significant enough to attract political attention. Thus, positive utility for space exploration programmatic expansion only exists when a supporting coalition may be identified. As such, additional employment doesn't strictly deliver positive utility loss in the event of any space jobs are lost and utility is decreased, there is no additional positive utility to reinstating those jobs. Rather, the threat of the loss of utility inherent in the loss of employment can only serve as a deterrent. Such, employment space exploration programs therefore act in a manner similar to an addiction. Thus on the final employment benefit analysis, international cooperation might seem to decrease employment in the United States, because foreign nations are building components that might otherwise be constructed in the United States. In practice, those who are employed may see more stability in their jobs due to the twin utility losses associated with employment termination. In effect, employment has no impact on utility unless it changes. The stability provided by international cooperation will ensure that the associated utility is at least likely to decrease.

●

The impact of space exploration activities upon society.

As the 21st. century gets further underway, the impact of space activities upon the welfare of humanity will only increase. The period between 1957 yr. and 1991 yr. saw the space age with flights to the planets, footprints on the moon and global communications; even military space exploration. In the not clean solar energy from space powering our industries as well as heating and lighting our homes. Our nuclear waste may be safely and inexpensively disposed of by being carried up a space Elevator and released towards Earth Orbit or on the Moon. We may carry out the development of a multi-planet economy. In addition to the knowledge that space exploration has already delivered , space technologies have become integrated into everyday life so deeply that modern society could not function without them.

Weather, telecommunications, environmental analysis and national security are only the most obvious space technologies that humanity relies on, and transfers from space to non space sectors provide many additional indirect benefits. The basic activities required to develop and maintain the fundamental elements on which a space policy depends for its implementation (access to space, the technology base, industrial capabilities, ground facilities); the activities of sciences and human and robotic exploration ; and utilitarian activities are developing space systems to support public services , such as meteorology, environment, natural disaster prediction management, online education studying, wind, nuclear and water energy and agriculture growing and plant breeding research and commercial offering , such as distance long phone , internet , mobile telecommunications, GPS navigation and imagery for the benefit of the citizen. Thus the impact of space activities upon society has largely been measured I numerical terms. How many spacecraft have been launched by a given country? How many phone calls are made over a satellite? How many lives could be saved by hurricane watching satellites? How much money was spent on space within a given country or by a corporation? The problem with this approach is that generally, the value to humanity is not measured and the value and benefits of such space activities must be justified. For the purposes of such space exploration technologies and researching new materials become cheap enough or feasible enough to do so.

The aims of space exploration include one world perspective, challenges for life , knowledge development, educational stimulation, communications for all revitalization of the human spirit after and contributing ,such as distance learning. On the education hand, the stimulation of education and proactive outreach has been a historic strengths of the space exploration. On the communication hand, communications for all revitalization, such as the space field has matured, the innate human desire to communicate has grown ever more significant. The need to transmit data, information and knowledge. For example, the communication with a spacecraft beyond the solar system or with a friend by mobile phone. Though television, we can watch wars in real time as soldiers and hurt people who are being conducted on the ground, we can witness the sport players at the Olympic Games, we listen to latest news on the radio when driving in our cars. The ability to communicate easily and quickly with ships at seas ,aircrafts in mid-flight or a relative on the other side communications technologies developed for space. On the one world perspective hand, the people of the world saw the blue marble of the Earth as on Earth rise from the window of Apollo 8. The realization is that humanity can view itself in a new light. Humankind has made important in the peaceful exploration if outer space, and this has changed our lives here on Earth for the better new perspective and gain scientific knowledge. Hence, space technology gives benefits that have as to solve social and economic challenges, including poverty, environmental protection and bad weather disaster prediction.

Charles B. (2012) wrote here's an example: in 2012, NASA administrator Charles Bolden published a blog post about the Curiosity Mars rover landing, which was picked up by the White House website. "It's also important to remember that the $2.5 billion investment made in this project was not spent on Mars, but right here on Earth, supporting more than 7,000 jobs in at least 31 states." Another benefit is education, such as NASA's education office has three goals: making the workforce stronger, encouraging students to pursue STEM careers (science, technology, engineering and mathematics), and "engaging Americans in NASA's mission." Other space agencies also have education components to assist with requirements in their own countries. It's also fair to say the public affairs office for NASA and other agencies play roles in education, although they also talk about topics such as missions in progress. But it's hard to figure out how well the education efforts translate into inspiring students, according to a National Research Council report on NASA's primary and secondary education program in 2008. Among other criticisms, the program was cited as unstable (as it needs to change with political priorities) and there was little "rigorous evaluation" of its effectiveness. But NASA's emphasis on science and discovery was also praised. Finally, space industry can bring intangible benefits, such as added to this host of business-like benefits, of course, are the intangibles. What sort of value can you place on better understanding the universe? Think of finding methane on Mars, or discovering a planet, or constructing the International Space Station to do long-term exploration studies. Each has a cost associated with it, but with each also comes a smidgeon of knowledge we can add to the encyclopedia of the human race. Thus, there also are benefits that may be we cannot anticipate ahead of time. The Search for Extraterrestrial Intelligence (SETI) is a network that advocates looking for life around the universe, likely because communicating with beings outside of Earth could bring us some benefit. And perhaps there is another space-related discovery just around the corner that will change our lives drastically. Earth-observation satellites, for example, have been used successfully in Africa, Asia and Latin America to detect the risk of outbreaks of malaria and other infectious diseases. Satellite communications are being used in several developing nations to provide health services and distance learning to rural communities and to relay information for the management of land, ocean and fresh water resources. Space exploration creates space travelling dreams and imagination (particularly in science fiction and the arts) and stimulated research in space , on space and from space. These activities impacted strongly society by providing a key clarification between science, theology and imagination that lead to a better knowledge of the Universe and its evolution and thus of the actual place of humans within it. They discovered that they are all passengers on one complex spaceship that has to be taken care of more seriously, impacting dramatically on their behavior. Space exploration has forces us to recognize how to solve the challenge of how we shall balance population, fossil resources,resources, sustainable resources, even enouraging discover of DNA science research from space alive. Therefore, space activity by itself is impacting society by giving human a different perspective, on giving another 'eye' to look at this world, our culture and everyday life.

The benefits are stemming from space exploration

There are many reasons that space exploration should continue. If Earth ever becomes too overpopulated or over polluted, then perhaps people can move to Mars. The world population in 1970yr. was approximately 4 billion people, and is currently nearly 6 billion people. The world population in 2015yr. is estimated to be 7 billion people. There is a possibility that there are useful resources on Mars. Scientists have found ice and some other clues, such as craters, volcanoes, and valleys, that have led them to believe that there was once life on Mars. However, I shall indicate the technological innovation and cultural and inspiration and new opportunities for job creation and weather prediction and global space economy and global space economy benefits are stemming from space exploration as below:

On technological innovation aspect, there are numerous cases of societal befits linked to new knowledge and technology from space explanation. Space exploration aims to research new outside Earth's useful natural resources to substitute our limited natural resources because our prediction indicates that our limited natural resources, e.g. oil, gas etc. which will be spent to use all none of natural resources remain in our Earth one day in the future. Space exploration has contributed to many diverse aspects of every day life from solar panels to implantable heart monitors, from caner therapy to light-weight materials, and from water purification systems to improved computing systems and to a global search and rescue system, storage and recycling and waste management, advances robotics, health and medicine, transportation, engineering, computing and software, space systems innovaion and service resulting in higher performance and lower costs.

On cultural and inspiration aspect, space exploration it fulfill people;s producing fresh data about the solar system , thus brings us closer to answering profound questions that have asked for: What is the nature of the Universe ? Is there life elsewhere in the Universe? Knowledge derived from space exploration may also contribute to implementing policies for environmentally sustainable development.

On new opportunities for job creation aspect, new opportunities for job creation and economic growth are being created by private enterprises that are increasingly investing in make space exploration and seeking ways to make space exploration more affordable and reliable, profitable , such as medicine, computer science, weather prediction, communication etc. industries. Such as space science discoveries and technology encourages European company to launch a satellite based super fast broadband service serving clients in rural .Telecommunications systems which enables European industry to explore new ideas for satellite communications products and services, such as mobile phones and internet and GPS location search. Thus, telecommunication encourages UK Government to implement digital Britian policy to secure the UK's position as one of the world's leading digital knowledge economies. The most influence indicates space exploration can create many new jobs demand to provide to UK telecommunication industry indiectly and it can assist UK economic growth.

On weather prediction aspect, space based systems have made an impact on how human deal with the environment. Earth observations from space can follow weather pattence. They can provide an understanding of hurricane formation, so that early warning early images from space can show the basing routes for access into areas cut off by flooding and other environmental disaster. Such as weather forecast, advance our understanding of atmospheric dynamic and climate processes, wind speed is one of the biggest unknowns in understanding what influences climate. So studying the climates of our planetary weighbours also help us to better understand the Earth's climate. Such as launched in 2000 numbers uncovered our sister planets, extrordinary atmospheric system, revealing for example, a bizarre giant double hurricane system at the south pole. Venus is extremely hot and suffers from a runway greenhouse effects, so provides an extreme model for studies of global warning. Mars, which is much colder than the Earth is an example of what happens when a planet loses its atmosphere. Mars spacecraft is mapping, the planet and observations indicate that water has once abundant on the Mar surface. Mar could once have harboured life and may do so again if humans decide to colonise it.

On the global space economy aspect, space exploration requires in many different areas to work together to develop new capabilities, that operate reliably in a remote environment. It has advanced telecommunications, medical technology, weather forecasting, navigation, television, radio, computing etc. industries. As a direct result of the innovations, inventions and discoveries that have enabled us to explore space, our daily lives on Earth have changed profoundly. For example, space related products and services is that cost less compared to the convenience, efficiency, information, such as direct to home television and satellite radio m the use of space by broadcast and cable television, satellites also enable truly global internet communication service, long distance telephone service. GPS satellite signals allow users on lands on the see and in the air will inexperience GPS devices to determine their position and aided by computer maps, other satellite capabilities , such as remote sensing, plot a course to their destination. GPS navigation has been so successful and valuable that the europeann space is investing to develop its own GPS satellite, GPS signals also provide precision timing for financial and cell phone networks.

● Summary

The feasibility of promising space product applications include earth insiders and space outsiders both. The earth insiders include distance leaving and telemedicine, electronic commerce entertainment, location-based consumer services, location-based services of traffic management, land cover of precision farming, urban planning, exploration (oil, gas), disaster prevention, meteorology and climate change and monitoring polices etc. aspects. The space outsiders include adventure space tourism, in orbital services, solar or wind energy power satellites technology. It seems space technology invention can solve energy shortage, it can predict weather change to reduce wind or water natural disaster chance occurrence , it can let human to give cheap fares to catch space ships to go to space to travel, it can use satellites to use GPS to assist drivers to find locations to drive different places in the short time or to assist pilots to find locations in sky or to assist ship captains to find location in sea easily, it can use satellites to solve traffic jam to shorten distance leaving on the road, it can encourage to sell medicines or products from internet conveniently. I think space technology can assist other new technology businesses to contribute human need in the future, so I feel that the main country space technology players who are worth to spend time to invest to invent this space technology different businesses in the future.

● Bibliography

Brennan, L. & Vecchi, A., (2011). The Business Of Space, The Next Frontier Of International Competition. Palgrave Macmillan Press: USA, New York.

Charles B. (2012) Curiosity Takes Us Back to Mars the

WHITE HOUSE Available at: Date Of Publication: 6 Aug.

https://www.whitehouse.gov/blog/2012/08/06/curiosity-takes-us-back-mars

Futron Corporation (2009) Resource Centre. Available at:

http://www.futron.com/resource_centre/resource_cemtre.htm.

Hertzfeld, H.R. (2007) Globalization, Commercial Space And Space Power In the USA, Space Policy, Vol.32, no 4. November.

Tarasenko, M.V. (1996) Evolution Of The Soviet Space Industry, Acta Astronautica, Vol. 38, no. 4-8, pp. 667-73.

Yip, GS. (2003) Total Global Strategy II: Updated For The Internet And Service Era (Upper Saddle River, NT: Presentice-Hall).

IX

Facility management how influences airport and logistic employee performance

● Facility management assists employees reduce
maintenance service expenditure

Facility management provides a variety of non core operations and maintenance services to support any organizations' operation. For logistic organization example, it is possible to provide effective maintenance service to warehouse in order to reduce warehouse facilities to be damaged to bring to spend to buy any new equipment facilities expenditure. So, when the logistic company's warehouse facilities can be maintenance to be the best quality. Then, they can be used these warehouses' machines facilities again. Their performance can assist workers to manufacture any products to keep the most efficiently an raising the best production performance in whole manufacturing process. Then, this logistic company's facility management department can bring to avoid purchase any new machine facilities expenditure spending. One to these warehouses' production machine facilities are kept in the best production performance environment even in long term production need.

I shall indicates airport and warehouse facilities how to influence employees performances as below:

(1) How can comfortable warehouse facilities influence workers' efficiencies in logistic industry ?

The logistic industry's facility management department can create cost savings and efficiency of the warehouse's workplaces. It's machines facilities (production machines) are dealt with the maintenance management of the physical assets maintenance service. FM (facilities management) has been being applied to industrial facilities in logistic and warehouse industry long term as well as maintenance plays a significant role to ensure the full service and the warehousing system, including both building components and equipment in warehouse.

Maintenance service is needed to bring a certain level of availability and reliability of a warehouse facilities system and its components and its ability perform to a standard level of quality. So , it seems that logistic industry's warehouse asset cost reducing. It depends on whether it has one facility management department to provide maintenance service to itself warehouse workplace's production machine facilities and warehouse building itself in order to let workers t feel the manufacturing machines can bring good manufacturing performance to assist them to produce any products in one safe warehouse workplace environment. Hence, the performance measurement of warehouse maintenance issue will be valued to be consider to every warehouse manager and facility manager in logistic industry.

In logistic industry, (FM) works at two level on the one hand, it provides a safe and efficient working environment, which is essential to influence warehouse workers whether how they perform to do their manufacturing tasks or logistic goods delivery tasks in warehouse. When they feel the warehouse is safe environment to work. They will not need to consider anywhere has risk to cause they die by accident in warehouse. Hence, they can concentrate on doing their every tasks . On the other hand, it can involve strategic issues, such as property (warehouse workplace and management, strategy property decision and warehouse facility, e.g. manufacturing machine, facility maintenance and checking planning and maintenance planning development.

However, reducing the operating expense issue will be the main aim when the logistic company feels that it has need to set up one in-house facility management department to carry on any maintenance service for its warehouses' any workplace property and manufacturing machines facilities. So, when the logistic company decides to implement one facility management department, it needs to ensure its facility management department can bring the minimum level of keeping manufacturing performance and efficiency to its warehouses' any manufacturing machines and warehouses' property to avoid to be damaged in short term, such as loss of business due to failure in service, provision of project to customer satisfaction, provision of safe environment, effective utilisation of workplace space, e.g. warehouse effectiveness and communication between the workers and the logistic managers in the warehouse workplace , due to the warehouse's space is not enough maintenance service reliability to the logistic company's warehouse, responsiveness of the warehouse's worker individual negative emotion problem, due to he/she often feels need to work in one unsafe warehouse working environment. Hence, it seems that poor or unsafe warehouse working environment can influence workers feel negative emotion to work to bring low efficiency (inefficiency) or under productive performance in warehouse. It has relationship to influence they to bring psychological negative emotion feeling to work when the organization lacks one effective warehouse management repairing service to be provided to the warehouse's facilities and properties' maintenance needs in order to avoid ineffective measurement and misleading of performance.

Hence, the logistic company's facilities management department often needs to be reviewed whether its maintenance service level is passed to achieve the lowest repair (maintenance) service standard to its warehouse itself property and manufacturing machine or warehouse delivery tool facilities or warehouse lamps' light whether is enough to let workers to see anything clearly to avoid accident occurrence or see anything to work clearly or the warehouse space areas are enough to let they can have enough space to walk or communicate to their team supervisors or deliver any goods more easily in the short distance between the worker's sending goods location and the delivering goods destination in order to avoid because the lacking enough space to cause the accident occurrence , due to the space is not enough to let they deliver their goods to any locations in warehouse.

Hence, it seems logistic company's (FM) department can contribute to the organization's mission, such as avoiding warehouse accident occurrence, inefficiency, not enough and unavailability of the facility for future needs when the warehouse lacks enough space areas to bring poor performance of facility and dangerous warehouse itself property in warehouse, e.g. safe and reliable operations of material handling equipment and maintenance of warehouse facilities, grounds, security system, utilities, plumbing, heating , enough lighting system, air conditioning, warming heater, fire protection, security system alarm etc. facilities in warehouse.

Hence, it seems that if the logistic company expected to reduce to spend lot of excessive manufacturing machine purchase expenditure, lose of workers' life or bring workplace accidents , due to poor warehouse workplace environment, even bringing lawsuit compensation claim loss , due to the worker individual accident or death is caused from the poor warehouse facilities, or bring negative emotion to let the workers feel they are working in unsafe warehouse workplace environment. Then, it ought choose to set up on facility management department in order to provide enough maintenance service to its warehouse to avoid these non essential expenditure causing , due to these poor warehouse facilities factors.

Hence any logistic company ought choose to set up one itself in -house facility management department, it be better than outsourcing its all facilities service to one facility management (maintenance service provider) to help it to deal any kinds of maintenance service in warehouse. Because it is long term maintenance need to its warehouse's any machines and warehouse itself properties. If it chose to find one outsourcing facilitiy management maintenance service provider to replace its in-house facility management department to deal all related facilities maintenance tasks in warehouse. Then, it is possible that it needs to pay long time facilities maintenance service fee to its outsourcing facility management maintenance service provider more than itself facility management maintenance service provision department.

(2) Can facility management influence tourism industry's human resource management influence to improve productivity in airline, travel agent, hotel tourism sectors?

In tourism industry, measuring productivity froma HRM prespective is extremely difficult and has proven to be a limitation within the tourism sector. Due to the customers are not tangible. For example, how can the travel agent measure its travel consultant individual service performance to evaluate whether the travelling customer feels or does not feel satisfactory loyalty from his/her service? How can the airline measure its pilot , airline front-line travelling passenger service attendant indiviual service performance to evaluate whether his/her travelling passenger feels or does not feel satisfactory to whose service performance? Whether airport facility management can influence airline counter service staffs performance ?

However, the complaint number whether it is more or less to the airline or travel agent's service behavior , it does not represent whose service attitude or behavior or performance is poor absolutely because there are many travelling consumers whose complaints are unreasonable , although they feel satisfactory to the airline attendent or airline front -line service staffs individual service performance, but if they feel unhappy to be caused by the airline or travel agent service staff. They will still compain their performance. For this suitation example , it is possible that the travelling passenger is delayed to catch the airplance to fly, due to the country's sudden worse weather influnce, he/she will complain the airline fron-line counter travelling customer service staffs, it concerns when the air plane will arrive the airport, if the airline counter service staff's feedback is that the airplane needs long time arrival. Then, the travelling passengers will complain to the airline counter service staffs in angry. But in fact, the air plane delays to arrive the airport, the airline counter service staffs ought not need responsibilitie to explain the reason why they can not assist the delayed air plane to arrive the country in easier. Furthermore, thy will be complained unreasonably. Hence, it is difficult to measure tourism sector's service staffs ' performance, also the complaint exact number is not one judgement factor to measure their service performance absolutely.

I assume any tourism industry's front -line service airline staffs, they must attempt to serve their travelling passenger in positive service attitude and behavior. So, any tourism industy, how to improve their front -line service staff performance in order to let they to know how to deal unreasonable complaints in sudden unpredictive suitation. Their training materials or contents my include: Teaching them how to provide positive feedback to treat any travelling passenger individual difficult problems or unreasonable complaints in order to reduce their psychological pressure to unknown how to treat these passenger individual related problems when they are facing in airports or travelling agent workplaces. The travelling agent or airline travelling service organizations can attempt to collect measures of employee performance from customers , for example, comment cards in hotel rooms, airplane, travel agent's workplace, mystery shoppers etc. more focus shouls be pleased on this form of evaluation. In order to evaluate the actually place value on the customer ratings to every employee. The all every day, the form of evaluation concerning the actually value on the customer ratings , will be gathered to strategic , it has how many customers feel good or bad ratings to every employee individual performance when every one's tasks are finishing. Due to one month, it can make statistic report to calculate how much performance marks to give to every employee in order to evaluate whether every one's performance is satisfactory to be accempted to the lowest level. If the employee's marks rating is low, his/her department manager can arrange a time and day to meet him/her to discuss whether which aspects of problems who feels in order to give recommendation how to improve his/her service attitude to let customer to give higher marks rating to him/her next time.

Hence tourism industry's service sector organizations need to have one training department to arrange courses how to improve employee service performance in order to let customer to give higher marks rating to very one as well as finding methods how to excite every front line service employee individual loyalty , they can increase their confidence to know how to deal sudden unreasonable complaints in effective and efficient positive attitude.

In conclusion, how to improve employee service performance issue will be any tourism service organization's HRM concerning problem. Airports need to arrange how to implement efficient and comfortable and available convenient airport facilities to let any airline service counter staffs feel enjoyable to serve their passengers. They need to know how to find the most effective methods to solve how improvement of front line employee individual performance problem in order to raise the airline or travel agent's quality of service to let itself further customers to feel its service performance is better than others. So, facility management has indirect relationship to influence airport airline service staffs performances.

In conclusion, to decide whether the company ought need or not need facilities maintenance service or either set up in-house facility management department or outsource one facility management maintenance service provider. It depends on whether its organization has how many facilities are used in its workplace, how many staffs are working the workplace, how much size of its workplace, its workplace is office or warehouse or factory, how long time of its facilities' useful time etc. factors , then it can decide whether it needs or does not need one facility maintenance service department or outsourcing facility maintenance service provider to help it to deal any facilities management problem in its organization.

● Facility management role in
organization

When one company feels that it has need facility management service. It can choose to set up either in-house facility management department or seek one outsourcing facility management service provider to help it to arrange any facility management service need. However, this facility management role is only one for the organization. It concerns this question: What facility management maintenance function can bring the benefits to the organization? It can define that all services required for the management of building and real estate to maintain and increase their value, the means of providing maintenance support, project management and user management during the building life cycle, the integration of multi-disciplinary activities within the built environment and the management of their impact upon people and the workplace. In traditional, (FM) services may include building fabric maintenance, decoration and refurbishment, plant, plumbing and drainage maintenance, air conditioning maintenance, lift and escalator maintenance , fire safety alarm and fire fighting system maintenance, minor project management. All these are hard services. Otherwise, cleaning , security, handyman services, waste disposal, recycling, pes control, grounds maintenance, internal plants. All these are soft services. Additional services, might also include: pace planning, things moving management, business risk assessment, business continuity planning, benchmarking, space management, facilities contract outsourcing service arrangement, information systems, telephony, travel booking facility utility management, meeting room arrangement services, catering services, vehicle fleet management, printing service, postal services, archiving , concierge services, reception services, health and safety advice, environmental management.

All of these services will be every organization's in-house facility soft or hard services needs. So, it explains why some large organizations feel need one effective facility management department to help them to arrange how to implement facility services efficiently in order to achieve cost reducing, raising efficiency and performance improvement aims because one effective facility management control system can influence employee individual productive effort to be raised or reduced indirectly.

However, (FM) can be selected either setting up one in-house (FM) department or outsourcing its services to one facility management service provider to help the organization to solve any kinds of facilities maintain service problems. One on-house (FM) department is a team, it needs employees to deliver all (FM) services. Some specialist services are needed to be outsourced, when the service is on expertise in the company. The no expertise services will be outsourced to simple service contracts, e.g. lift and escalator (FM) department will have direct labour, but it can outsource some specialist to help it to do some complex facilities management service. So, the team leader can of can manage whose team staffs, such as maintenance technicians run low risk operations . Otherwise, the outsourcing facility management service provider needs to help it to operate high risk operations or maintenance vital plant facility management service. Anyway, it can set up in-house (FM) department to arrange specialist direct labour and outsourced (FM) services to more than one facility management service providers to do different kinds of (FM) services. One of these outsourcing (FM) service provider, who can arrange sub-contractors to assist it to finish any (FM) services of it's outsourcing (FM) services are more complex to compare the other sub-contractors (third parties).

● What is a facility manager's role to provide quality service to satisfy its user needs?

We need to know how quality can be defined in facility management and why it should be defined by the customer? How facility managers can find out customer (user) needs? What are the difficulties in finding out users' needs and in delivering quality services? Whether improving quality always means requiring higher cost?

In general, facility manager's major responsibilities may include these major functional areas: longer range and annual facility planning, facility financial forecasting, real estate acquisition and/or disposal, work specification, installation and space management, architectural and engineering planning and design, new construction and/ or renovation, maintenance and operations management, maintenance and operation management, telecommunications integration, security and general administrative services. When the facility manager had implemented any one of these FM services for those user. How does he/she provide excellent (FM) service quality ot let whose users to feel satisfactory?

In fact, quality issues can not be considered without customer-oriented perspective service quality involves a comparison of expectation with performance. (FM) service quality is a measure of how well to service level delivered matches customer expectation. So, these issues are (FM) service user's general measurement level requirement. The (FM) manager needs to achieve these the minimum performance measurement level to satisfy whose (FM) user's needs.

However, (FM) service quality has three characteristics: Intangibility, heterogeneity, inseparability. But in fact, (FM) service delivered may be through tangible physical aspects, e.g. factory plant workplace building, machine equipment maintenance, intangible (FM) services, e.g. managing space moving in plant to let staffs to work, managing outsourcing cleaners to clean factory equipment. However, all (FM) service performance often varies, due to the behavior of service personnel. Hence, a well developed job specification and training can help to improve the consistence of services of (FM). Any (FM) production and consumption of many services may are inseparable and they are usually interactions between the (FM) client and the contact person from the service provider.

Hence, it seems that service quality is considered as hard to evaluate. In (FM) service quality, it includes physical quality and interactive non-physical service quality. Physical quality is tangibles: The appearance of the physical facilities, equipment, personnel and communication materials. Non-physical services quality means reliability: The ability to perform the promised service dependably and accurately; responsiveness means the willingness to help customers and provide prompot service to let user to feel; assurance mans the competence of the system in its credibility in providing a courteous and secure service and empathy means the approachability, ease of access and effort taken to understand customers' needs.

Hence, a good performance of (FM) manager , he/she ought satisfy the user's tangible and non-tangible both service quality needs. I recommend that he/she can attempt to predict what are the (FM) customer expects in each (FM) service needs. Then, it can make decision what aspect(s) will be the (FM) users major (FM) service need and what aspect(S) won't be the (FM) users major (FM) service need. Then, he/she can make more accurate decision to arrange time, human resource , cost spending amount arrangement whether when it ought concentrate on finishing the (FM) major service tasks as well as whether how he/she ought finish the major (FM) service tasks to be more easily, e.g. how to arrange staffs number to finish, how many the minimum staffs number is needed to be arrange the major (FM) service tasks, time arrangement is important factor, because it can influence whether he/she ought finish the major (FM) service tasks today or tomorrow or later in order to have enough time to finish other non-major (FM) service tasks. Instead of time management, staff number arrangement is also important factor , if he/she arranged the excessive staffs number to do the (FM) major services tasks, then it is possible that it will have shortage of staffs number to finish the non-major (FM) service tasks on the day. So, avoiding either major or non-major (FM) services can not finish on the day. The (FM) manager needs to predict when the major (FM) services and the non-major (FM) services which are necessary to be finished in order to have enough time and staffs to assist him/her to finish every day major and non-major (FM) service effectively. Then, the achievement of his/her (FM) major and non-major tangible and non-tangible services , it will have more chance to be performed efficiently by his/her managed staffs.

In conclusion, in any organizations , (FM) manager needs have good predictable effort to evaluate whether when his/ her managed team need to finish the major and/or non-major (FM) tasks as well as whether how he/she ought arrange the accurate time and staff number to finish any major and/or non-major (FM) service tasks on the day. Then, his/her leading of (FM) service team can be managed to work more efficiently in order to satisfy her/his (FM) service user's needs.

Facility management how influences
public service transport service performance
● How (FM) space moving management brings employees efficiencies
There are interesting questions: How (FM) can bring value-add to avoid loss or earn more profit to the organization? Can it influence employees to raise performance and improve efficiency ? Some organizations' (FM) service need which is necessary in order to let employees can raise productivity.

It is based on these assumptions: I assume the organizations have completely either outsourced or in-house their (FM) facility management departments will gain more effect on added value than they have no (FM) function as well as organizations have a strong coordination with the (FM) department will gain more added value than organizations with a weak coordination. Organizations in the profit aim can gain more added value than organizations in the not for profit aim sectors.

In fact, any organization is difficult to confirm it has relationship between improving performance, raising efficiency and owning (FM) function in its organization. (FM) could have to do with the attraction of easy but incomplete indicators of efficiency rather than the necessarily and less direct measures if the effectiveness and the relevance of space moving useful management, e.g. whether building has the enough space to let employees to move to work easy in order to raise efficiency, whether the building has excessive furniture and equipment number and they are putted on wrong places to be caused employees move difficulty in the building in order to influence productive performance. However, how to arrange space moving management to equipment, e.g. copying machines, faxes, productive machines, they are putted on the locations where have enough space to let employees to move to another locations. For example, the building floor has more than 50 employees, but its space is not enough to let these 50 employees to move to any locations to let them to feel easily often. Then, it is possible to cause they feel nervous pressure and they can feel difficult to work , when they are working in a small office space or factory space or warehouse space. Then, the consequence will be under-predictive efficiency or poor performance to any one of these 50 employees in this office or factory or warehouse.

" Facility management is responsible for coordinating all efforts related to planning, designing, and managing buildings and their systems, equipment, and furniture to enhance. The organizations abilty to compete successfully in a rapidly changing world." (F.Becker)

The author explains equipment, workplace internal space designing, furniture space putting location arrangement will have possible to influence employee individual productive performance or efficiency to be raised or reduced in the workplace. Hence, it seems that, in the value chain (FM) belongs to the activity part of the firm. To make the facilities cooperation with each office or factory or warehouse using space moving facility management. Facility space moving management must be linked strategically, tactically and operationally to other support activity to add value to the organization's office or factory or warehouse space moving management arrangement more effectively.

Thus, how to arrangement space moving management issue it will have possible to influence the organization's employee individual productive performance and efficiency in whose workplace. It seems that (FM) space moving management arrangement have indirect relationship to influence the organization's employee individual performance and efficiency , due to they need often to work in the workplace, if they feel moving difficulty , or excessive equipment , furniture number is putting into the small office, factory or warehouse locations, or they feel the office or factory or warehouse has excessive (a lot of) staffs number to work in the small space of office or factory or warehouse. Then, they can not concentrate nervous on finishing every tasks in possible. In long term, their efficiencies will be poor or inefficiencies or their performance won't be improved or causing poor performance in possible.

Instead of the not enough space moving and excessive staffs number factor, it will bring another question: Can enough information systems equipment cause a more efficient and improved performance to the organization staffs in the workplace?

I assume that the office has 100 employees and it has only ten copying machines. So it means that ten employees use one copying machine. Hence, it brings this question: Is it enough to provide only ten copying machines to average ten employees to use? It depends on other factors, e.g. whether any one of these 100 employees needs to print how many documents per day , whether the five copying machines' locations are far away to separate different locations or they are stored in one printing room in the office, whether the day has how many staffs are absent, whether the day has how many printing machine(s) is/ are broken to need to be repaired. Hence, these unpredictable external environment factors will influence whether the five copying machines number is enough to let these 100 employees to use in the office every day. Hence, facility manager ought need to spend to observe average their copying behaviors every day in order to make data record. Many employees need to use copy machines to print documents, average how many document's page number, they need to print, how much average time spending to print their documents, average how many staff absent number on the day. Even, if the all five copying machines are stored in the printing room, calculating the staffs number whether how many staffs need more than five minutes to walk to the printing room to print their documents many staffs need to spend five minute to walk to the printing room, and they have other urgent tasks to wait to finish. It is possible to influence their efficiency, due to they often need to spend more than five minutes to walk to the printing room to print documents. If there are many staffs need to often to print documents, but their printing task will have many time, e.g. 20 separate printing tasks. Then, they need to spend at least (20x5) 100 minutes to spend time to walk to the printing room to print their documents. It must influence that they should not finish the other urgent tasks on the day. If there are many staffs to spend much time to walk to the printing room in the least 20 separate printing time or more on that day. All the facility manager needs to evaluate whether all the five copy machines are stored in the printing room whether it is the best location decision or they ought need be separated to put on different office locations in their workplaces, even he/she ought need to evaluate whether it is enough copying machines number, when the office has only 5 copying machines. He/she ought need to buy more copying machines number to satisfy any one of these 100 employee individual copying task need.

In conclusion, effective office or factory or warehouse space moving facility management will be one part task of (FM) function. If the office or factory or warehouse can have accurate equipment, machine , furniture number to avoid excessive or shortage number problem to cause employees often feel moving difficult problem in their workplace when they need to move to another location to work in office or warehouse or factory as well as whether the staff needs often spend time to wait the another employee to use the copying machine to print whose document or fax machine to deliver whose document. Then, it is not that fax or printing machines number is not enough to provide the employees to use in the office or warehouse or factory workplace.

Hence, (FM) includes space moving facility management to equipment , machines, furniture number as well as choosing anywhere is(are) the suitable location (s) arrangement to putting or storing these facilities in workplace as well as decision of the staff number and the workplace area size whether it has excessive staffs number to cause these staffs need to work in the small area size of office or warehouse or factory workplace. So, the organization ought need to decide whether it needs to reduce the office's staffs number to let them to work in another more suitable locations in another workplace. Hence, all these facilities space moving management and staffs and workplace size issues will be (FM) manager's consideration issues, because these external environment factors will influence employee individual efficiency and performance to be poor to cause low valued to its organization in long term in possible .

● Predictive the choosing right
data asset and (FM) analytics
solutions to boost public
transportation service quality

Can gather the choosing right data public transportation lon service station facilities asset and analytics, it can give recommendation to help any organization to boost service quality? (FM) analytics data can be applied to public transportation service industry to be supported how and why the train, train, ferry , ship, air plane, underground train public transportation tools' time arrival and leaving information notice board and automated ticket paying machines facilities are putting on or stored any where locations in order to boost passengers to feel their facilities locations are convenient to let them to buy tickets and see the arrival and leaving time for the next public transportation tool from the information notice electronic board machine. So, it seems that these public transportation tools' station facilities locations can influence passengers to feel the public transportation service company how to consider to its passenger's buying ticket needs and next public transportation tool's arrival and leaving time information needs in order to boost its passengers use service quality and let them to feel better service reliable performance in any train, tram, ferry , ship, underground tram, airplane stations.

As these public transportation service organizations need to learn data analytics represent an opportunity for its ticket paying machine equipment facilities as well as the next transportation tool arrival and leaving time information notice board electronic equipment facilities anywhere the locations are the most suitable to put on or store these equipment to let passengers to walk to the ticket paying machines to buy the ticket to catch the train, tram, underground train, ferry, airplane, taxi, ship more easily. So, they do not need to spend more time to find these facilities locations and spend more time to queue to wait to buy ticket to catch the public transportation tool in stations conveniently. Instead of where is the seeking ticket paying machine location, where is the next public transportation tool arrival and leaving information notice time , these both issues will be any public transportation tool's passenger's main needs.

Hence, how to spend time to seek where the next public transportation tool's arrival and leaving time information electronic notice machine location and where the ticket paying machine location , these both factors will influence any passengers' positive or negative emotion causing. For example, if the passenger feels difficult to find the ticket paying machine in the large area size train station or /and he/she feels difficult to find the train time arrival and leaving information to let him/her to know when the next train will arrive the station. Due to he/she feels difficult to find the train ticket paying machine, he/she needs to spend much time to find any one ticket paying machine in the train station. Then, it will influence him/her to choose another public transportation tool to replace the train public transportation tool, e.g. he/she can choose to catch tram, underground train, taxi, bus, ferry, taxi, ship to replace train. So, it seems ticket paying machine and time arrival and leaving information notice electronic equipment 's location putting or stored choice will be one factor to influence the passenger to choose another kind of public transportation tool to replace train at the moment. When, he/she feels that he/she arrives the destination in the most short time. Then, the public transportation service organization (FM) manager has responsibility to evaluate whether there are enough ticket paying machines number to let passengers do not need to spend more time to queue to buy tickets to catch the public transportation tool in short time as well as there are enough time arrival and leaving for next transportation tool to let passengers to know. It will be their concerning issues when they arrive the public transportation service tool's station.

Hence, predictive passenger individual walking behavior can help the public transportation service organization to choose whether where are the most convenient and attractive locations to let the ticket paying machines and the arrival and leaving time information electronic board machines to be putted on or stored in the suitable station positions in order to let many passengers can find these essential facilities in stations very easily. So, gathering data concerns passenger walking behavior in the public transportation service any stations, which can help the facility manager to make more accurate evaluation to attempt to predict whether where the locations are common places to let passengers to choose to walk daily or where the locations are not common places to let passenger to choose not to walk daily in general. Then, he/she can apply these data of different locations in the stations to evaluate whether anywhere they will have many passengers to choose to walk or whether anywhere they won't have many passengers to choose to walk in order to make more accurate decision whether anywhere are the most suitable locations to let the ticket paying machines and the time arrival and leaving information electronic board equipment to be putter on or stored in order to let them to feel it is so easier to let them to find.

Anyway, calculating each station's passenger number per day issue is important to predict whether where , there are many passengers choose to walk or where, there are not many passengers choose to walk in these different public transportation service stations in order to evaluate whether where the stations' different ought put on paying ticket machines or time arrival and leaving information electronic boards in order to let they feel very easy to buy tickets and seeing the next arrival and leaving time information for the kind of public transportation service tool conveniently in the different stations. Moreover, if the station has no enough ticket paying machines number to be supplied to let passengers need to spend more than ten minute time to wait to buy ticket to catch the kind of public transportation service tool in every queue every day. Then it will cause them to choose another kind of public transportation tool to catch go to working place or entertainment place to replace it to on that day. Then, it will cause these passengers who often do not like to queue in the kind of public transportation service tool's any stations, who will not choose to go to anywhere of this kind of public transportation service tool's any stations again. Hence, in long term this kind of public transportation service tool will lose many passengers. Thus, calculating each station's busy time of passengers number , which can predict when it is the busy time and it can make more accurate decision whether the station has need to increase enough ticket paying machines number in order to bring enough supply number to satisfy passengers' ticket purchase need in the busy time.

In conclusion, gathering above all stations' public transportation service equipment facilities number, storing positions data and every station's passenger walking behavior data, they are necessary to any public transportation tool service industry, because these equipment number and storing locations will influence them to make decisions to choose another kind of public transportation tool to replace it's transportation service if they often feel difficult to find these facilities in its different stations. Thus, it is part of task to facility manager's responsibility if the public transportation service organization expects it won't lose many passengers , due to these external environment factor influence and it also implies cheap ticket price does not guarantee the passengers will choose to catch this kind of public transportation service tool to go to anywhere.

● The relationship between facility
management and productive
efficiency

It is one interesting question: Can facility management function bring benefits to raise productive efficiency to organizations? I shall indicate some cases to attempt to explain this possible occurrence chance as below:

● Facility management benefit to office workplace

In private organizations, when the firm has facility management department, whether it can bring efficient administration to influence clerks to work efficiently in office, e.g. reducing administrative time or shorten time to work in administrative processes, in order to achieve minimizing clerk number labor cost. How to design office facilities to let office staffs to feel comfortable to work and reducing their pressure to work. It seems that office working environment will influence office staff individual performance. If the office working environment could improve efficiency and creativity of services to satisfy office workers' comfortable working environment needs. It will reduce every administration manager's working pressure when he/she needs often to find methods to attempt to encourage whose administrative clerks to avoid to waste working time to do some non-major administration tasks.

Hence, how to design or allocate or arrange office any facilities' stored locations or whether how many equipment number is the enough to store in the locations, which will influence office employees' working attitude in order to raise or reduce their administration tasks efficiency indirectly, e.g. the office is clean or dirty, whether office reception has enough information telephone switchboard operation facilities, whether every clerk's table has enough computers number to supply to every to use, whether internet speed is fast or slow in order to let any employees can send and receive email to communicate or download any document from internet in short time, whether data processing and computer system maintenance service supply is enough to be repaired to employees' computers immediately when their computers are broken to wait repair, whether website editing facilities operation whether is enough to link to office every staffs in order to let any office staffs can apply internet to do their tasks conveniently in short time.

Hence, all of these general office equipment facilities whether they are enough supplied and their stored positions anywhere are the suitable to assist any clerks to work conveniently, they will influence every office employee's administrative and productive efficiency indirectly as well as all faxes, copying machines, computers, whether internet linking maintenance service time is short or long to prepare to any office employees to use conveniently any time, these different issues will also influence every employee individual efficiency in office. Hence, it concludes that office working environment, facilities supply number, facilities maintenance service and facilities location storing both factors will influence employee individual administrative productive efficiency in office.

● facility management benefits to service working environment

Can effective facility management improve service working environment to raise employee individual work performance? It is a concern about the quality of service to its customer question. The term" standards and goals" are often used to measure staff individual service performance whether he/she can serve to customers to let them to feel this staff's service performance or attitude is good or bad.

Is the service workplace working environment facilities enough, it will influence customer service staff individual performance.

For shopping center service industry case example, for this situtation, e.g. shopping center's facilities are enough or are placed to the suitable locations in order to let the shopping center's customers to feel comfortable to shopping when they enter this shopping center as well as whether the shopping center's facilities can influence the customer service staffs to serve whose shopping customers easily or difficult, due to whether the shopping center's facilities whether are adequate supplied or their locations are the best suitable positions to influence their service performance to let them to feel easier or comfortable to serve their customers in any large size shopping centers. For example, whether the lamps' lighting energy is enough to let the shoppers to feel safe to walk to visit any shops when there are many shoppers were walking to cause crowd and they feel difficult to walk to avoid any body contact to any one in busy time when the shopping center has no enough lights to let them to see anywhere in the shopping center's dark environment. Then it will influence customer service staffs to feel difficult to find any shopping center customers, e.g. when two shopping center customers are fighting in one location where is far away to the shopping customer service staffs and securities in the shopping center, because the shopping center is large and it has no enough light to let the customer service staffs and securities to find their frighting location to deal their fighting behavior and other shopping center's shoppers will feel very dangerous to walk their fighting location to avoid to close them. Then, it will has possible to cause death or hurt to any one of these two fighting shoppers ,even other shoppers' life. Because the shopping center's securities and customer service staffs who need to spend much time to find their fighting location, it will delay they can bring the policemen to their fighting location when they arrive this shopping center's destination in short time in order to solve their fighting behavior to influence all shoppers' life in this shopping center. Hence, the shopping center whether it has enough lamps number and the lamps' light whether is enough, these lighting facilities will influence any shopping center customer service staffs and securities who can spend less time to arrive any locations to deal any urgent matters.

For another situation in shopping center, if the shopping center has no enough paying telephone service facilities to supply shoppers to phone to anyone when they feel need to phone to any in the shopping center. Then, it will lead to some shoppers decide to find where the shopping center's reception's telephone to supply to them to phone call to anyone. If they are ten shoppers are waiting to use the shopping center's reception telephone to phone call to their friend or family within one minute. Thus, it will influence the reception customer service staffs feel difficult to arrange how to distribute the only one telephone to these ten shoppers to use to phone call their friend or family when they are queuing within their one minute waiting time in the shopping center's reception. If these ten shoppers can not use the reception telephone to phone call anyone. hen, they will feel dissatisfactory and complain to the reception service staffs politely. So, lacking enough facilities in the shopping center's any where, it will possible to influence their shopping centers' shoppers to feel all shopping center's service staff individual performance to be poor. It means that if the shopping center expects to improve customer satisfaction to its customer service staff's behavioral performance, it meets have enough facilities to be supplied in the shopping center to let its shoppers to feel it is one comfortable and safe shopping center. In conclusion, shopping center's facilities will have possible to influence shoppers' feeling to evaluate its customer service staffs to evaluate whether their service attitudes are good or poor indirectly.

● Can facility management improve productivity

The productivity means resources (input) is therefore the amount of products or services (output), which is produced by them. Hence, higher (improved) productivity means that more is produced with the same expectation of resource, i.e. at the same cost is terms of land materials, machine, time or labor. Alternatively, it means same amount is produced at less labor cost in term of land, material, machine, time for labor that is utilized. So, it brings this question: How can facility management improve productivity? I shall explain as these several aspects, it is possible to be improved productivity from (FM) successfully.

Improved productivity of farm land: If the farming land has better facility management to bring advantages by using better seed, better facilities of cultivation and most fertilizer. It is in the agricultural sense is increased (improved). So, facility management can bring benefits to any land resource to raise productivity in possible. It implies that the productivity of land used for better facility management of industrial purposes is said to have been increased if the output of products or service within that area of industrial land is increased output aim.

Improved productivity of material: If the factory has improved better equipment by facility management method to assist skillful workers to raise the manufacture cloth number, then the productivity of the cloth number is improved by (FM) method.

Improved productivity of labour: When the factory has good manufacturing equipment facilities to be supplied to improve methods of work to product more producing number per hour, then (FM) improved productivity of worker. Hence, in any workplaces, when organization has good facilities, it will influence employees to raise productivities in possible, because they need often to improved equipment facilities manufacture products to achieve higher production number aim.

● Can facility management raise bank employee
productivity

Bank workplace environment is busy, the bank counter service staffs need to contact many bank clients to help them to serve or withdraw money from bank's counters. Whether does the quality of environment in bank workplace will influence the determination level of employee's motivation, subsequent performance productivity in bank working environment. For example, if the bank's staffs need work under inconvenient conditions , it will bring low performance and face occupational health diseases causing high absenteeism and turnover.

In general, bank size is usually small, it will have many bank clients enter bank to contact counter staffs to need them to help them to save or withdraw money. So, it will bring air pollution the crowd queue in every bank counter challenge when the bank has many people are queue waiting in counters to queue. So, bank working condition problem relates to environmental and physical factors which will influence every bank counter staff individual working performance to serve bank clients satisfactory. However, bank staffs need to deal many documents concern every client personal data every day. So, they need to spend much time to use computer and painting machines. This is particularly true for these employees who spend most of the day operating a computer terminal in bank workplace. As more and more computers are being installed in workplaces, an increasing number of business has been adopting designs for bank offices installment. So, bank needs have effective facilities management design because of demand of bank staffs for more human comfort.

An good equipment facility management for bank staffs to use conveniently, it is assumed that better workplace environment can motives bank employees and produces better productivity. Hence, bank office environment can be described in terms of physical and behavioral components to influence bank staffs to work inefficiently. To achieve high level of bank employee productivity, bank organizations must ensure that the physical environment in conductive to bank different department organizational needs, facilitating interaction and privacy, formality and informality, functional and disciplinarily, e.g. house loan or private loan departments, counter service department, visa card application department.

Thus, in a high safe privacy facility management working environment will let different department bank staffs feel safe to worry about privacy loss in possible. So, the improving bank facility to bring safe and high privacy to avoid bank client individual loss in working environment issue, the facility management can be results to bring these benefits, such as in a reduction in a number of complaints and absenteeism and an increase in productivity.

● Can (FM) create value to organization?

(FM) can reduce managing facilities as a strategic resource to add value to the organization and its overall performance, e.g. saving the energy in building and take care of shuttle buses and parking facilities space management for , on economic efficiency and effectiveness, or good price and value for the organization.

If the organization expects to apply (FM) process to save energy, it depends on possible input factors, i.e. interventions in the accommodation facilities services. So, it seems that the organization expects to save its energy consumption in its building. It needs have good space management facilities between parking its shuttle buses in its property's car park.

Why does space facility management is important to influence efficiency and productivity. For one school's building example, when the school decides none of the two gymnasiums student sport entertainment centers to be built in order to reduce financial cost and higher benefits. Remarkably, the use of space with the school overall strategic goals , such as creating spaces that better can support the teaching, motivate students and teachers, attract more students and increase the utilisation of existing space to accommodate an increasing number of students.

If it hopes to make high quality teaching facilities on student's choice where to study. The school will need to choose to build either one comfortable and new design facility teaching accommodation or build two gymnasium sport entertainment centers in its limited land space either for students' learning or sport aim. Due to it feels new teaching accommodation can make more attractive to increase students numbers to choose it to study more than building two new gym sport centers to let them do sport in school.

Hence, space choice (FC) management strategy will be one important considerable issue, when the organization has limited land space resources to make choose to build any constructions in order to increase many clients number. Such as the school organization has limited storage land resource to let it to build either two gymnasium sport entertainment centers or one new teaching accommodation in order to attract many students to choose it to learn. Hence, it needs to gather data to make more accurate evaluation to decide how to apply its space facility to choose to build these both kinds of buildings in order to achieve the attractive student learning choice aim, so whether the two sport entertainment activity centers or one new teaching accommodation choice, it needs to gather information to decide whether the school ought to choose to build which kind of building in order to achieve the increase of student number aim, so space facility management will be this school's land shortage problem.

● The relationship between facility
management and consumer
behavior

How and why shop facility management can influence consumer individual shopping behavior? If it is possible, what shop facility management factors can influence their consumption decision when they enter the shop to plan to buy anything. I shall indicate some shop case studied to explain whether how and why every shop's facility management can influence consumer individual consumption desire when any one consumer enters any shops.

● Shop's low ceiling height location (FM) influence consumer behavior

Can the shop's ceiling height influence shoppers' shopping behavior? Can the shop's variation in ceiling height can influence how consumers process information to decide to make purchase decision in the shops, e.g. for this situation, when the consumer enters the shop, he/she feels the ceiling height is low and it has a lamp will contact his/her head in possible. So, he/she chooses to move far away from the low ceiling location in the shop. It is possible that shop's ceiling low height and the lamp locates at the ceiling low height position will influence many customers' choices to leave the low ceiling height and lamp location, then the shop's low ceiling height will have possible to influenced many customers to choose to find the another shop to buy the similar kind of products , due to the lamp locates in the low ceiling height, so this lamp and low ceiling height will be possible factor to influence any shoppers who won't choose to walk to this dangerous location in the shop. If the shop's all spaces are ceiling height and it has many lamps are located at the low ceiling height spaces. Then, it will be serious to cause many shoppers do not want to spend too much time to choose any products in the shop because they feel dangerous to walk to the any low ceiling height lamps' locations in the shop.

Hence, hoe to design the different concept may be activated by the showroom ceiling if it were relatively high, as it tends to be in mall stores, versus low, as it is in most strip mall shops and outlet centers. Relatively high ceilings may bring safe shopping emotion to let any consumers to feel thoughts related to freedom, whereas lower ceilings may let consumers to feel dangerous to walk the locations in any shops. Hence it seems any shops ought not neglect whether their ceiling height is tall and the lamps ought avoid to locate in any low ceiling height locations in order to influence consumers number to be decreased.

● Can house facility management influence consumer individual purchase intention?

When one new property is built, whether the property consumers will consider how the new property is facility to influence their purchase intention to the property will the new property's (FM) influence buyers in real estate markets' preferences choice and living interest. Any new property's internal characteristics of the house unit itself , such as rooms available, when example, of external are location, accessibility to utilities services and facilities will have possible to influence the property buyer's final property purchase decision, so it seems that even the property price is cheap, it is not represent the property buyer will choose to buy the property, if he/she feels the property's facility management is poorer to compare other similar kinds of properties.

So, it can help real estate analysts better explain and predict the behavior of decision makers in real estate markets. Property consumers will search for property information, concerns the property's quality, price distinctiveness, ability, facility management, service of the property's external environment to decide whether the property is high value to choose to buy to compare other kinds of properties.

However, the external environmental forces, such as limited resources, e.g. time or financial will influence whose property consumption choice and living the property's satisfaction feeling (represent) a feedback from post-property purchase reflection used to inform subsequent decisions. The process of the property buyer's leaving experience will serve to influence the extent to which the property consumer how to consider future next time property purchases decision and new information methods. Hence, when one property consumer chooses to buy a house, it refers house features are house internal attributes , such as quality of building, the design as well as internal and external design, which are important factors for a property consumer when he/she needs to select and purchases one house.

The other (FM) factors which can influence the property consumers' needs, include living space as features, such as the size of kitchen, bathroom, bedroom, living bath and other rooms available in the house. The environment of housing area is also important factor, e.g. the condition of the hood, attractiveness of the area, quality of houses, type of houses, type of houses, density of housing, wooded area or free coverage, slope of the attractive views, open space, non-residential uses in the areas vacant sites, traffic noise, level of owner-occupation in , level of education in level of income in, security from crime, quality of schools, religious of , transportation , shopping center, sport entertainment can be supplied to close to the house area. All these human related issue of the property's location will also influence the property buyer's living location selection. Hence, above (FM) influence property consumer purchase behavior, it is based on the relationship behavior. The consumer's house purchase intention and house features, living space, environment and distance to recreation center, supermarket, library etc. public facilities variable (FM) factors.

In conclusion, the house internal space facility management and external environment facility management factors will influence property consumer individual house purchase intention.

● The effects of in-store shelf design facility management factor influences consumer behavior

Can every store retailer's shelf design influence supermarket and large retail stores shoppers' behaviors when they visit the stores? However, currently many stores tend to build on traditional and repetitive design for their store shelf layout, it brings results in outdated store layouts.

Another important store shelf layout design aspect, retailer should consider carefully is the allocation of products on shelves. So, it seems that efficient shelf space allocation management does not only minimize the economic threats of empty product shelves, it can also lead to higher consumer satisfaction, a better customer relationship.

Why does supermarket shelves design is important? Any retail tore will sell product category within a shelf. They can use the same nominal category , e.g. crisps next to light crisps, same food product shelf. Anyway, a goal-based shelf display can contain several product, that determine a common consumer goal, e.g. fair trade. Hence, these two categorical product structuring methods are also described in terms of how to put product, or food on shelf benefit and attribute -based product categories.

These shelf design food or product storing method will have more influence consumers to choose to buy the supermarket or retail store food or products more easily , due to products, or food put on their shelf very convenient and systematic to attract consumers' shopping consideration to the supermarket or retail store.

● Music (FM) environment influence consumer consumption desire

Is it possible that shop music (FM) environment can raise consumer purchase desire? In one shop or supermarket, it can provide soft music (FM) equipment to let consumers can listen soft music or songs in the supermarket or retail shop when the are staying to spend more time shopping and whether soft music facility can be expected to raise customer individual value-added options to the music facility shop in the supermarket or retail shop.

Can the music facilities prolong consumers to stay in the store? It is possible that tempo soft music can influence consumers to stay longer time in restaurants and supermarkets and retail shops. It is possible that the different types of music (FM) in any supermarket, restaurant, retail shop owning music listening facility shopping environment. It will have possible to influence consumers to prolong staying in their shops. For example, one wine selling retail shop has classical music (FM) listening equipment to let consumers to listen when they enter the wine shop, it is possible to cause consumers to choose to buy more expensive wine products. Some researchers indicate when the wine shop owns classical music facility to let all consumers can list classical music when they walk in the wine ship, it can evoke the wine consumers to choose to buy purchasing higher prices wine products in the long term classical music listening environment. Otherwise, in a fitness sport center, musical fir and excite or popular music (FM) environment can attract fitness sport players' emotion to play and kind of fitness sport facility longer time. Also, in one supermarket, the soft music facilities listening environment can persuade or attract food consumers to spend more time in the mall consuming food or beverage also purchase other products more easily, due to they will listen soft music to be influenced to choose to prolong staying time in the supermarket. It seems that it has relationship between retail shop's music facility environment and consumer's emotion will be influenced by these different kinds of soft music or songs to raise consumption desire in the supermarket, if some consumers like to prolong to stay longer consuming time in the owning music facility environment's retail shop.

In fact, some researchers indicate the owning background music facility selling environment's ship , it can affect consumer decision making, memory, concentration consumption desire. So, classical , jazz soft music facility ought be installed in restaurants, retail shops, restaurants' environment. Otherwise, popular , exciting, noise, pop music facility ought be installed in fitness sport centers, theme park entertainment parks business places in order to influence fitness sport players or theme park entertainers to prolong playing or entertaining time to feel real sport or entertainment theme park playing machine facility's entertainment enjoyable feeling as well as attracting restaurant or supermarket or retail shop's consumers to prolong their staying time to make consumption decisions. Hence, it seems that music facility environment can raise consumers' consumption desire in possible.

● University bookstore atmospheric factors how to influence student's purchase book behavior?

Any university bookstore how to do international control and structuring of book internal environment to raise students' purchase book desires in university itself school's bookstore, it will be one popular question to any universities. Hence, whether the university bookstore internal (FM) factors include: lighting, music, colors, scents, temperature, layout and general cleanliness as well as university external factors include: the university bookstore shape/size, windows, university parking facility for students availability and location, which can play an influential role of the university bookstore image in order to influence the university itself students to choose to buy books from themselves bookstore or university outside bookstores.

Whether the university student needs to spend how long individual learning time and how much learning nervous to spend time to choose any kinds of book in the universiity bookstore or outside bookstores, this issue , he/she will consider. Because he/she does want to expect spend much time and nervous to choose to buy books in any bookstore. If the university's bookstore physical location and internal (FM) image can let its target student customers to feel it's all book products are stored in any attractive internal book shelves places, e.g. the cheapest and the most expensive different subjects of text books are stored in one system method to bring the positive image of value and quality in order to let university target student customers can find their books' choice location to spend less time to search any books to read in the unviersiity bookstore easily.

However, due to learning time is shortage to every university student of the university's book shelves can display all text books in the attractive right locations in the university bookstore as well as the university's bookstore ought has an adequate space to let university students to walk to anywhere and find any subjects of text books and compare their book sale prices in the bookstore's any shelves' locations easily when they walk to the subject of book shelf location, then they can make accurate decision either to buy the right kind of subject book or not buy it to read in the short time. They will feel their book choice purchase decision making process won't influence their learning time in themselves universiity. Then, the university students will be influenced by themselves university's bookstore's attractive external university facilities in the university's any teaching places and the university's bookstore internal attractive environment facility image which can influence the students to make final choices to buy their liking books to read from their university's itself bookstore. Hence, the university's bookstore internal and external building environment (FM) design factors will influence its students whether choose to buy from themselves bookstore or another outside general bookstore.

● How and why does retail atmospheric environment influence consumers behavior in retail shop?

Any shop's internal facility management design can influence atmospheric environment to influence consumer individual shopping desire, e.g. colour, lighting, music, crowding, design and layout factors, which internal shop (FM) environment can influence the first time shopping visiting client ' cognitive process how to feel the shop store image. Such as if the store's (FM) environment can bring enjoyable and fun and happy image to let them to feel shopping's enjoyment.

In conclusion, when consumers will like to stay longer time in the store. Due to the store's internal (FM) atmospheric environment can attract them to stay longer time in the store. Then, the customer's shopping value will raise and it can bring purchasing intention and shopping satisfaction. How can (FM) influence retail atmospheric physical (FM) environment ? Can (FM) bring indirect relationship to influence how the consumer individual causes positive or negative purchase intention when he/she has influence to prolong staying desire in the store, when the shop has good (FM) , it will bring long time to make consumption chance in the shop.

● Facility management influences
consumer satisfactory service
level

Can facility management (FM) quality influence consumer satisfactory service feeling? Any organization's facility management can improve the effectiveness of the maintenance organization. It can provide improved operational and maintenance functions to maintain the physical environment to support the overall mission. However, any organization will consider whether it improves its facilities, it will raise consumer satisfactory feeling when it provides the service to them, e.g. education service industry, when students need to often to attend any school's classrooms or lecture halls, computer rooms, libraries, all these facilities will be student's learning environment. If these school facilities can be maintenance to let students to feel comfortable to enjoy to study in their schools' any learning locations. Then, it has possible that to bring their enjoyable learning feeling in theirs schools.

● How school's facility management influences student's learning satisfactory feeling.

However, in education industry case, the school's facility management has those criteria can be used to measure effectiveness. Student individual response time between the student's request for computer use service in school computer rooms, library reading service in school library , classroom computer facilities and tables, chairs etc. furniture supplies service and the facility management supply number and available to useful time. If the student believes that the response time is too long when he/she feels need to use any school facilities, the actual number of seconds or minutes, he/she needs to wait how long time to queue to use his/her school's any facilities in library, classroom, computer room. So, the student's queue waiting time to use any his/her school's facilities, it can measure the school's facility management effectiveness.

● Scheduling of preventive maintenance activities.

It schedules of any maintenance activities are not arranged effectively to the school. Then, it will influence students' poor learning facility service to their school. For their situation, when the school's first floor has two men toilets are damaged. They are needed to be required. However, it is one week period, the first floor 100 students can not use the first floor men toilets. Hence, in this week, all 100 students need to go to other floors toilets to often use. They will feel busy and time is not enough when they need to attend to any classrooms to listen the first floor classrooms teachers' lesson. If he/she arrives the first floor classroom too late, due to he/she needs to go to another floor male toilets to queue to use. Then, he/she will feel angry and worries about whose absent or late attending classroom behavior when the lesson's teacher has attended early in the first floor classroom , and he teacher will need him/her to explain why he/she will go to this classroom lately, if his/her explanation won't be accepted to attend to the first floor classroom too late in the week. So, arrangement maintenance schedule to any school's facilities issue is importnt to influence student's satisfactory feeling to the school. Also, lacking of preventive maintenance activities will bring results in unscheduled shutdown of critical equipment can have an unrecoverable impact on the school's good learning environment providing to student's mission.

In fact, however in any organizations, such as school, ship, office etc. organizations, achieving balance of effectiveness and efficient difficulties and takes time and effort on the part of management and staff. It is not enough to establish an optimal relationship between these two parts. It has another factor that organizations need to consider costs. In today's budget tightening environment, decreasing expenses requires accepting a lower level of efficiency and effectiveness. The goal is to determine the point at which decreasing efficiency and effectiveness is no longer acceptable before that point is reached.

It brings this question : How to apply facility management knowledge to rise efficiency and effectiveness in order to improve quality standard of service to satisfy consumers' needs in short time? Such as school's facilities service case. What factors can influence student's level of satisfaction with regards to higher educational facilities services? It seems that any school's facilities will influence its students how to satisfy its education service indirectly. Because they need often to go to school to learn. So, any school's facilities, e.g. classrooms, computer rooms, libraries, toilets, lecture halls, canteens, sport and entertainment centers, research laboratories, school car parks, student enquiry counters, all these places to the school's any students will attend. So, how raise schools' facilities improvement to satisfy students' learning needs in the school's any locations which will have help to influence it student individual satisfaction level to the school's service, instead of every teacher individual teaching performance service to the school's students.

For any service organizations , such as hotels, restaurant, financial institutions, retail stores and hospitals etc. The physical environment can influence how customers' evaluation of their service. Due to service has intangible nature, so customers will rely on evaluate service quality.

Any higher education institutions are education service providing organizations. They need have comfortable and enjoyable educational environment to be provided to the students to attend the school's any places in order to meet whose learning expectations and studying experience needs. So, the school's facility management will be one factor to influence student's learning satisfaction when they expect to attend the school's any locations or places to let them to feel the school's learning environment have good facility management feeling.

In fact, if the school has comfortable classrooms or lecture halls educational environment to let its students to feel, it will bring assistance to raise their learning satisfactory feeling. So, comfortable learning facility management environment is one kind of school's facility service characteristics, it includes intangibility, perishability, inseparability and variability. So, they are every student individual learning feeling when they are attending to the school's any learning locations. So, school's facility management service feeling will influence whether they expect to choose this school to study. If the school's facility management learning environment is more comfortable and teaching facilities are better to compare other schools' facilities. Then, it will have possible to attract many students to choose this school to study. Such as any educational organizations, instead of the teachers (lecturers and professors) whose educational level is influence students number. The university's building environment will influence students' learning feeling, when they attend in the university. The facilities include laboratories, lecture theatres an offices, but also residential accommodations, catering facilities, sports and recreations centers because university students need have university life feeling to let them to fell the university can give welfare services , e.g. medical services, career guidance, sport entertainment, residential accommodation etc. service, instead of educational learning service in classrooms and lecture theatres. Hence, university's diversification facilities services are needed to satisfy university students to choose it to study, instead of university teacher's educational performance.

When one student can enroll the university to study from secondary education institution. The admitted student will usually consider two aspects to decide to choose the university to study. One aspect is the academic programs, of sequence of courses choices and the another aspect is the university's facilities whether they can satisfy their university life need, e.g. library, dorms, bookstore, food canteen , gym's sport entertainment, education technological facilities in the classrooms and lecture theatres to let the students to feel the university's teaching facilities are achieved his/her learning demand.

So, these two factors (teaching and learning and facilities) are linked to each other to influence student's total school learning experience and attitude towards a particular institution and this is termed as value chain in the student's learning process in the university. Hence, student individual evaluation variables will include teaching staff, teaching method, enrolment and facility enough supply actual service need.

However, the university's facilities, such as any residential accommodation, canteen, library , classroom, lecture theatre, sport gym, entertainment center will be their useful facilities need to satisfy their learning, entertainment and eating ,even living need in residential accommodation in the school's learning life experience every day. If one student chooses to live in the university residential accommodation . All of his/her learning and eating and living time and spending will be calculated to the university's any facilities to let him/her to feel it can provide enough facilities to let him/her to enjoy.

Hence, the facility management factor, such as overall campus environment, library, laboratory, classroom, lecturer theatre size and facility supply of on campus accommodation, welfare right service, parking areas, cafeteria , sport center etc. They will be every students facilities service needs from the university supplies choice. So, any university ought not neglect how to improve itself university's space area facilities to achieve satisfy their needs after they choose this university to study. Hence, any university's facility management will influence how the student's satisfactory learning service feeling when he/she chooses the university to study.

In conclusion, better facility management will attract more students to choose the university to study. Otherwise, worse facility management will not attract more students to choose to study the school. Hence, it seems that the school's facility management factor has relationship to influence student's satisfactory feeling, instead of teacher individual teaching performance factor to the school.

● Property facility management influences householder buying behavior

One new property's low price is attractive factor to influence property buyer individual preference choice. Does the new individual's facility management factor influence the property buyer's preference choice decision, if the property buyer feels its facility management is better than other similar properties, even it's price is higher than other properties. I shall indicate some cases to analyze this possibility as below:

Some properties' facility management service quality has possible to create true value for any property buyers when they consider the calculation ingredients to make decision whether to new property has higher value to choose to buy. The factors may include: price, natural environment, transportation tools convenient available, shopping centers supplies, the neighour quality, and the property's internal facility management etc. factors.

In fact, car or house purchase buyers, they have similar behaviors. It is that car's buyers will consider the car's machines whether they are safe to drive on roads, instead price, manufacture loyalty factors. It is possible that the car's machines quality factor will be preference to any car buyers when they make preference decisions to choose which brand its cars are the suitable. However, if the car's brand is famous and its appearance beautiful and price is cheap. But the car consumer feels its machine qualities are unsafe to let the driver to drive on road. Then, the car's poor machine quality factor will influence the car buyer's decisions to choose to buy this car. It can influence the car buyer individual car purchase decision.

The car buyer's behavior is similar to property buyer's behavior. Although, the new property price is cheap, good neigh ours are living near to the new property's location, shopping centers and transportation tools are available to near to this new property's area. But if the property buyers' feels its facility management is poor quality to compare other similar properties. Then, the poor quality of facility management factor will have possible to influence the property buyers whose final buying decision to choose to buy this new property. It brings this question: How and why can the facility management poor quality factor influence property consumers' preference choice?

In general, all property consumers won't know whether the new property's facility management is good or bad quality , they need to spend time to visit to the new property in order to observe whether its internal facility is satisfactory to his/her acceptable level. In simple, their purchase decision will regard to how to allocate household budget, how the household's economic resources are influenced, e.g. for travelling, visits to restaurants, comparing the different similar types of property product groups, e.g. apartments or houses or houses of a givn size data. For example, if one property's room(s) size is (re) small to compare other kind similar product type of room(s) size. Although the prior property's price is cheaper to compare to the later properties. But, if some property buyers hoped the property has large room(s) size, then the later larger room(s) size which will be possible to some property buyer's preference choice. Even, their property price is more expensive to compare the smaller room(s) size of properties. Thus, the property's room size which will be one major factor to influence property buyers' purchase decision. room's size had relationship to facility management issue. Moreover, if the room's quality and design is attractive, then it will bring more attractive to persuade some property buyers to choose to buy them to live in preference.

Hence, whether the new property is good durable product feeling which will influence householder's choice. If the householder feels the new property has long term durable life to avoid to spend much maintenance expense when they have been living in the new property for a long term period. They will believe it has better facility management, quality to let them to live longer time and the most importance is that they do not need to spend any maintenance expense , due to the property 's any internal facilities are damaged easily.

The external factors may include: culture, reference groups, family, social class and demography of lifestyle as well as internal factors may include: feelings, past property buying and living experience , property knowledge, motivation of the property buyer individual psychology. These both factors can influence any property buyer individual decision making process to do final house purchase behavior. However, internal factors, such as: property knowledge of facility management and property living experience, e.g. how to evaluate to choose to buy the property , due to the property buyer's past living experience for the past property's facilities whether its facilities can satisfy its property buyers' comfortable living needs. This internal factor will be more important to influence any property buyer's property purchase final decision. If he/she feels whose prior old property's facilities are satisfactory. Then, he/she will compare this new property and old property's facilities to decide whether this new property is value to buy. So, the old property's facility will be the measurement standard to compare his/her next new property purchase choice. So, the property purchaser will compare these new and old property's property facilities product knowledge to similarities among property alternative which will influence his/her final decision to choose to buy the new property to live.

It seems that property low price factor must not guarantee to attractive many property buyers' choice. Otherwise, it is assumed that many property buyers like rent or buy to live the property for themselves for long term intention. There are less property buyers expect to sell the first property to earn profit intention. So, they will usually consider whether the property is long term durable product to avoid to pay maintenance expense when they had been living in the property in long term.

Some factors that taking consideration are proximity to the specific location, housing prices, developer's brand, the payment scheme, reference group, which are not the main factors to influence any property buyer individual choice. Because property buyer's need is that the property has good facilities to supply to them to live, e.g. good heater equipment can provide hot water to them to bath in winter or good air conditioners can provide cold temperature to let them to feel cool comfortable feeling in summer in their homes. Good electric tools facilities , when they have need to use electricity in safe environment at home, e.g. car park accessibility facility , level of security facility , surface area facility and housing types, bedroom, bathroom facilities, quality of housing manufacturing raw material, house design , house durable guarantee, speed of complaint responsiveness, specification accuracy, confirmation of building plan service, showing legal file property purchase process service, finance instalments process assistance, speed of responsiveness, officers' skills of presentation. All of above these concern property facility management issues will influence any property buyers' final choice to decide whether the property is value to buy. So, facility management will influence property purchaser individual final decision in possible.

● Hotel facilities influence hotel consumer choice

Travellers choose hotel to live. They will consider price, room comfortable feeling, hotel location , gum sport or entertainment service facility supplies , hotel room booking service etc. factors to decide whether the hotel can achieve every traveller individual minimum living need. However, whether hotel facilities factor will be the main factor to influence travellers' living needs. How and why do travellers consider hotel facilities whether are enough supply or facilities of quality to satisfy their demand to cause their living choice to the hotel final decision.

Usually, hotel's customers won't plan to live too long time, e.g. more than three months in the hotel. Because they are travelling aim. It will bring this question: Does hotel facilities quality consider to influence their hotel living choice if the traveller is short-term traveller to the country? However , some travellers who have effort to spend money to live high class hotels, even their journey is short trip. Hence it seems that short trip , hotel living reason can not influence the high class hotel travellers' living comfortable demand to the high class hotel room. Hence , the high class hotel room's facility management quality is also needed high performance. Even, when they need to eat breakfast, lunch , dinner in the high class hotel canteens or playing any sport equipment, or gum equipment or wathching movie in the hotel's small cinema room . They must need high class hotel can supply more entertainment, restaurant , sport facilities to satisfy their comfortable needs in the high class hotel. Moreover, they must consider safety issue when they are living in the high class hotel. So, thy must demand the hotel have enough five fright equipment in their rooms, or corridors and the stairs to let them can leave the dangerous locations to arrive the most safe locations immediately when the hotel has fire accident occurrence in any where . So, it ensures that the high class hotel's customers must ensure the high class hotel's facilities can satisfy their any one of above these needs before they decide to live this high class hotel.

In fact, high class hotel's room price must be more expensive to compare the low class hotel. So, it explains why high class hotel's consumers will need the hotel has safe and good quality of facilities to let them to feel it is one reasonable price, safe , good service and good facilities' high class hotel to live. Usually, when the traveller arrives the country to travel, the travelers chooses the hotel to live, it is whose first time visit in common. So, he/she ought consider that the hotel environment seems it is good or bad to let the traveller to select to live. If the hotel's facility environment is new and beauty and design colorful to let the first time travellers to feel. Then, it is possible that good facilities environment can influence the first time travellers to select to live, even the hotel's room price is more expensive to compare other similar hotels in the travelling living places. Hence, it explains why hotel facilities can influence traveller individual room booking choice. When he/she is the first time to visit the hotel to select whether to live or not.

● How and why facility management can influence workplace productivity to bring customer satisfaction

Facility management is one part of manufacturers or retailers as their productivity in workplace as their input and functionalistics within physical environment. In fact, facility management in workplace may include: site selection, property disposal, site acquisition, workplace space allocation, space inventory, space forecasting facility management, interior furniture change planning, interior furniture installation, moving maintenance, inventory, design evaluation, employment satisfaction evaluation plan, external maintenance and breakdown maintenance, preventive maintenance, landscape maintenance, energy space facility management, hazardous waste disposal, capital , operating furniture budgeting. So, it seems that one workplace considered whether the workplace's facility is enough to let employees to work in order to raise efficiency and improve productive performance more easily. Then, it will bring this question:

● How and why workplace facility management can influence consumer individual satisfaction?

Strategic FM delivery is essential for business survival. I shall explain why for delivery is important to influence customer satisfaction. In business process view point, an effective and meaningful service to their customer , i.e. the user. For logistic industry, the product's delivery time will influence when the product can be sent to the user's arrival destination. If the product is delayed to sent to the user's home or office or any location destination. The reason is because the logistic product sender has no efficient facility management (FM) arrangement in its warehouse . Then, its warehouse lacks efficient (FM), which will cause users to feel its delivery service is poor and they will complain its delivery service staffs. Then, they will find another delivery service company to replace its service. So, it explains that logistic industry's warehouse (FM) service arrangement can raise efficient time to send any products to their customers in order to let they feel satisfactory service. For example, Amazon online logistic company's warehouse has applied artificial intelligence robotic tools to assist warehouse workers to arrange the different kinds of products to deliver to the right shelves . Then, the warehouse robotics will follow their right product shelves locations to follow the right products to deliver to US domestic or overseas product buyers in the short time and it can avoid the wrong products to deliver to the wrong buyers' risk. Also, the (AI) delivery tools can raise time efficiency to assist Amazon warehouse workers to reduce their work load, and tried to work in large warehouse environment. Although, its warehouse's area is large, the (AI) tools facility can help them to deliver the different products to different shelves in the right locations , e.g. exact product number and the kinds of product to be delivered to the right country' client's shelf location in the warehouse. Also, it implies FM is very important to influence Amazon warehouse delivery efficiency and avoiding delivery wrong occurrence chance. For example, the shelf location belongs to US domestic customers, or the shelf location belongs to Japan customers, or the shelf location belongs to Hong Kong customers, or any other Asia or Western countries' different customers' locations. The warehouse's facility needs have different countries' shelves enough space to put and it also need enough space to let the (AI) tools, robotic delivery workers and human workers both to walk to different shelves locations easily and the different countries' shelves number needs to be calculated accurate. For example, it has how many client number will buy Amazon's the kind product per day. If it has above 5,000 to 10,000 China clients to buy the kind of product. Then, it will need to make judgement how many shelves are placed in the warehouse. So, it can avoid to lack enough shelves to put any different kinds of products to prepare to delivery to China clients in efficient time and it won't avoid to delay to deliver to their homes or offices or any locations in China.

Hence, such as Amazon logistic case, it explains why warehouse's space shelves number and area or locations facility management can influence workers or (AI) delivery tools how to move convenient and avoiding the delivery to the customer's wrong destination chance occurrence and shortening time to deliver products to its clients efficiently. Then, due to the delivering time is shorten and the wrong delivery destination's occurrence chance is also reduced , even it can avoid to deliver the product to wrong client's destination occurrence. Then, the logistic firm's clients will feel more satisfactory to its product sale delivery service and their complaints will be avoided. Hence, it explains effective warehouse (FM) space management service arrangement is essential to any logistic businesses nowadays.

● Facility management brings departmental benefits

Why do organizations need have facility management (FM) service? As above examples indicate that (FM) can improve workplace environment facilities, e.g. warehouse environment to let workers to raise efficiencies or improve performances, even it can influence consumers to raise satisfactory to it's services indirectly, also it can help organizations' equipment to be used long term to cause old and are needed to spend expenditure to maintenance or change new equipment in order to improve better quality . So , it can assist organizations to avoid to spend more expenditure for new equipment purchase or maintenance. All these issues will be facility management service's benefits to an organizations, which can concern raising customers' service satisfaction, raising efficiency or improving productive performance, raising productivity, reducing equipment or property maintenance or new alternation much of expenditure spending, office or warehouse or any workplace space planning arrangement .

However, every organization will need a facility manager or manage whose team effectively . When a facility manager begins to apply FM techniques to solve business problems. The case for FM is made. It is a simple matter of demonstrating a qualified return on the investment required. Every organization's success, FM operation of three key activities: they include: needing a proper understanding of the organization's needs, wants, drivers and goals and knowing when needs to review its changing circumstances, developing an effective facilities solution o support the organization's needs, wants , property drives and contribute to achieve its goals both short term and long term, achievement of reliable delivery of that solution in a managed, measured manner.

So, it bring one question: What are the influential factors to be followed the right direction to FM manager's strategic FM operational decision? The influencing factors may include: ownership, governance sector, complexity and perhaps of most significant, the size of the organization's property portfolio.

In fact, major occupiers feel FM service need, they are large corporate organizations and public service organizations. Their aims usually are to raise. The most marginal improvement in efficiency or effectiveness, these aims are the great significance. Major property occupiers will already have a facilities department or individuals performing the FM function with another department like property, finance or human resource, sale and marketing's facilities.

Usually these FM need occupiers who will encounter this problem: How can apply FM service systems and processes to be developed to improve reliable service delivery making use of the economies of scale, not suffering because of the size of the problem. This question will be facility manager individual concerning question: How to apply (FM) technique to solve the improvement reliable service delivery making use of the economics of scale problem for whose organization?

In reality much of external facilities management benefits to organizations, instead of raising efficiency, improving performance, raising productivity, reducing maintenance expenditure, e.g. energy saving, reducing natural resource waste, increasing local employment, improving supply chain management are all elements of the FM contribution to every organization's need. Hence are the work life balance argument and provision of an effective and safe working environment that supports why some organizations feel need (FM) service to support their organizational development.

Moreover, on cost benefit of space saving efficient view point, space service cost reduction is a key driver for all organizations and the medium, or large sized players will benefit directly from a well coordinated facilities strategy. For example, application FM technique to help warehouse or office space area to save 50% space vacancy to let employees can move easily or putting enough furniture or equipment or many stocks can be putted in warehouses . So, paying more rent expenditure to rent or purchasing another new warehouse or office to satisfy workers or employees' working environment to be better need. If the organization has effective (FM) technique, then it has enough space vacancy to supply to the increase stocks number to be putted inside in warehouse and it can let workers to move safety in available to let staffs to move easily and equipment have enough space to be stored in the limited warehouse space problem.

For greater space savings benefits will bring either long term renting or buying of increasing offices or warehouse number expenditure problem to any organizations, when the organizations' cost or renting or buying accommodation probably accounting for 60 to 70% of total occupancy cost . So a strategic program to release space or the prevent the acquisition of moves can be the most significant consideration to any facility manager, with between 40% and 60% of the workplaces are unoccupied in most offices or warehouses at any given moment in time.

Hence, how to apply (FM) technique to save space occupied areas for employment moving or stocks or equipment saving need in offices or warehouses. This issue will be any facility managers' seeking methods to solve problem. However, the important major advantage of facility management to organizations is that the application of management principle to keep the organization's property assets with the aim of maximizing their potentials. Thus, any organizations' facilities have become important, due to the property facilities' worth will increase if the organization's facility management technique can protect the organization's facilities have good performance. Then, the organization's maintenance expenditure will reduce and it won't need to spend expenditure to buy any new facilities to replace old facilities , due to they often damage factor when they are used old.

In conclusion, it explains why effective FM combines resources and activities can raise work environment improvement, which is essential to the raising employee performance aim. For hotel living service case example, this industry must need have good facility management service because hotels must need to fully equipped in term and facilities for effectiveness to satisfy hotel living clients' demand , hotels ought need good facilities asset management style lead to effectiveness in service delivery, there are benefit derivable from the adoption of facilities management from which other hotels can learn from for their effective operations. Hence, it explains why effective FM can bring benefits to hotels' properties to be more comfortable, beautiful appearances to attract many hotel customers to choose to live the hotel. Because hotel's building industrial kitchens, rooms facilities, equipment , halls of categories, restaurant facilities, gum sport entertainment centers' facilities, fans, elevators, lifts, electrical installation, escalators, baking equipment, recreational facilities, including golf courses which will be important factors to influence hotel clients' comfortable living feeling, if the hotel can keep its all facilities in the best living environment often. Then, it can raise chance to attract many hotel customers to choose it to live. So , hotel industry has absolute need to implement effective FM strategy to keep its properties more attractive to satisfy its clients' living needs.

Instead of hotel industry, logistic transportation industry also needs effective facilities management in warehouse, because of the logistic company's warehouse 's facilities are good, then it will assist to raise employee individual efficiency in the safe and system shelve stored facilities in workplace environment and improving performance. Consequently, it will bring the shorten time to deliver any products to clients to avoide the delaying time delivery in order to let customers to feel more satisfactory to their services. In simple, it seems that some industries need have effective facilities management techniques to help them to bring long term customer satisfactory feeling, worker individual efficiency raising and performance improvement benefits. Hence, it seems facility management techniques' demand will be increased to some industries in popular in the future because it has help to raise employee individual efficiency , productive performance and client individual satisfactory level consequently.

Facility management how influences employee Psychology to raise productive efficiency

● How to impact of workplace
management on well-being and
productivity

In facility management strategy, design can lead promotion, the value of offices that are enriched, particularly including warehouses, shopping centers to raise their market value. Moreover, effective organizations, such as raising powering workers when giving the effective design of office space. I assume that a good design of an interior office workspace environment seems a psychological department to influence staff individual emotion to bring positive power in order to raising productive efficient influence, such as in a commercial city office. So, it brings this question: How workspace management strategy can impact on staff's working behaviors in office.

In fact, office tasks general include various forms of productivity, e.g. information processing, information management and any clerical tasks by computerization. Hence, office productivity concerns how to influence each office white color worker applies computers to work in office. The office space can impact on white color workers' performances in these several aspects: feeling of psychological comfort, organizational physical comfort and job satisfaction and productivity, efficiency. So, it seems that office workspace design strategy can influence white color workers' working behavior and attitude and performance indirectly.

The office space management includes: how to removal from the workspace of everything except the materials required to do the job at hand, how tight managerial control of the workspace, and how to implement standardization of managerial practice and workspace design. So, these key ideas will influence how each white color worker's efficiency and productivity in office working environment.

For this office space design situation, a large unseparated small space size's space design can accommodate more people and so brings itself to economies of scale. As a result, space occupancy can be centrally managed with minimal disruptive interference from office workers. Indeed, many businesses now adopt a clean and fresh air office working policy because they have more employees than they have spaces at which they can work. This desks are either taken on a first -come first -served basis. (hot desking) or can be booked in advance. So , when a company has many employees need to work in a small space working environment. It must concern how to let staffs to feel more comfortable in order to reduce high psychological pressure to work in this uncomfortable working environment. Hence, it explains why workspace design can impact on office workers' performance in some offices. All these issues are assumed that empowering workers to manage and have input into the design of their own workspace, then the effective office or any working places space management will enhance wellbeing to bring workers' positive emotions and improving productivity. I also assume the space working environment design have relationship of these depend variable factors to influence office worker individual productive efficiency. The variable factors may include psychological comfort, organizational comfortable, job satisfaction, physical comfort and productivity.

However, office furniture , facilities will influence office white color workers' performance ,e.g. the room size whether is big or small for manage office worker, a high backed, comfortable leather chair is needed for office staffs to sit down to let more comfortable, the door and most of the walls need glass, the office room environment needs have sea-grass rug beneath the desk covering the immediate working area, the office also needs have plants and pictures, mail boxes, telephone and computer facility is needed. When one staff needs to send email or phone call or send letters or deliver documents conveniently. These office elements are essential in order to increase physical well-being and feeling of satisfaction to white-color workers. Hence, geren office and office working space design management is needed in order to influence white color workers' productive efficiency in long term.

● Effective workspace design can influence communication to raise productivity

Office white-color workers often need communication between their managers, supervisors, and themselves. Office communication extends from the way that a user experiences a service. An effective office communication can bring these benefits; Providing positive influence on decision making by presenting a strong point of view and developing mutual understanding, delivering efficient decisions and solutions by providing accurate , timely and relevant information, enabling mutually benefit solutions, building health relationships by encouraging trust and understanding between the high level, middle level and low level staffs.

Effective office communication needs to clearly communicate its nature and purpose. Good communication ensures that all service staffs are sending out the same messages. Communication is also important for ensuring the service understands what users requires and why he/she talks about understanding users' needs and communication receiver can have effective communication skill to understand what he/she needs the another to do and the another knows he/she ought how to work by his/her task demand. Then, it will shorten much time. If the office has 100 staffs need to often communicate. However, if the office has good space management arrangement to let every staff can communicate easily and walks to anywhere to find the right staff to communicate conveniently. Then, they can spend less time to waste on communication issue. Then, their productive efficiency will be also influence to raise.

● Health and safe work environment influences productivity

Is a health and safe work environment can raise employees' work productive efficiencies indirectly? How and why it can influence employees' productive performance? Some occupations' working environments are easier to occur occupational accidents and diseases risks when the workers are working in the high health and safe risk's working environment. Hence, health and safety issues at these high life risk workplaces can be considered as a key to influence employees' overall performance. The idea that health and safety management program have positive impacts on productivity.

When one worker needs to work in this high risk of health and safe workplace. He/she will consider whether how his/her work behavior will bring suffer serious injuries for shorter or longer time from work related causes in possible. So, he/she will work carefully in order to avoid injuries occurrence chance. It is possible to influence whose work performance, low productive efficiency in order to avoid any occupational accident occurrences in the dangerous workplace.

If the employee feels danger when he/she needs to stay in the warehouses stable location to work often. Then his/her absenteeism day number will have increase, due to he/she feels that workplace accidents and occupational illnesses and can lead to permanent occupational disability, when he/she needs to attend the stable dangerous workplace to work in the warehouse. Hence, he/she will choose to apply holiday often in order to avoid injuries chance increasing when he/she needs to stay in the stable workplace location in the warehouse. It explains why companies increase need qualified, motivated and efficient workers who are able willing to contribute activity to technical and organizational innovations. So, healthy workers working in healthy working conditions are thus an important precondition for organization to work smoothly and productively. Hence, a health and safety workplace environment can bring these benefits to organizations as below:

It can prevent among workers of learning work, due to health problems caused by their working conditions, the protection of workers in their employment from risks resulting from factors adverse to health. The placing and maintenance of the worker in an occupational, environment adapted to his/her physiological and psychological, capabilities, mental , physical and social conditions of workplace and adequacy of health and safety measures are needed to any employees in order to bring positive impact not only on safety and health performance, but also productivity. However, identifying and quantifying these effects will difficult to be measured as well as the quality of a working environment has a strong influence on productive efficiency.

For one aviation air plane manufacturing factory, where workplace can environment will have high risk to occur occupational related accidents to cause employees' injuries. Hence, employees will be consider themselves safety when they need to work in high accident occurrence workplace. The bad consequence will influence such as absenteeism day number increases, leaving this kind of aviation air plane job of employees number increases, low productive efficiencies, due to there are many proficient experienced employees who choose leave this kind of high accident risk occupation.

Consequently, any high accident occurrence risk workplace environment, employers need have good safe and health strategy to let their employees have confidence to work in this kind of high risk accident occurrence workplace if they expect low productive efficiencies effect is caused by high accident occurrence risk workplace factor.

● Employee personal
empowerment factor influences
performance

Is empowerment one good method to raise employee himself/herself effort in order to improve productive efficiency in organizations. Empowerment often consists of support groups, e.g. management's effective leading or trainer's training, course educational opportunities. Employee self-management education may impact to improve himself/herself job performance, e.g. increased self-empowerment, self-management skills and job treatment satisfaction.

Only organization's empowerment strategy can lead every employee to through improvements in the employee individual decision making efficacy, improvement task performance behavior by reviewing whether what are the employee himself/herself errors when he/she encounters any job difficulties, after he/she reviewed his/her task error and his/her manager feels his/her performance can be improved. Then, it can enhance satisfaction with the employee and his/her manage relationship and better access and raising efficient performance in possible . Hence, empowerment can let every employee to discover whether what task related difficulties he/she faces or encounters every day. When his/her manager give ideas to let him/her to know how he/she ought review his/her task error in a supportive education working environment, it aims to let the low performance or low inefficient employees to increase confidence to continue work in the organization. So, the employee turnover number will decrease , if the inefficient employees can feel that they can attempt to solve their task-related difficulties successfully by themselves. So, empowerment can increase social support, leadership and advocacy development , it has resulted in greater employee individual performance psychological empowerment, autonomy and authority to let every employee to feel to achieve to improve themselves efficiencies more effectively in any organizations.

For hospital organizational efficiency measurement empowerment influence case, how empowerment can influence hospital's efficiency raising? Efficiency is one of the most important indicators of hospital performance evaluation. Why do some hospitals' efficiencies poor? It is possible that mis management of resources, lacking health plan packages, e.g. coverage of basic health insurance, poor quality of care service, more payment demand for out-of pocket payment , quality of primary healthcare , healthcare providers neglect to concern potentially about service efficiency issues.

In fact, low hospital efficiency is the major problem to influence patients number to choose the hospital's medical service, e.g. when the hospital often needs patients to queue to wait for doctor's care medical service. They need to wait on hour at least or more when the hospital has many patients are waiting for its medical service. Then, it will influence them to choose another hospital to replace it , if the hospital 's medical fee is cheaper and it does not need patients to spend long time to queue to wait its medical service. So, service efficiency is important to influence patients consumers' positive or negative feeling to choose the hospital's medical service. Even, the hospital's doctors are famous or they own many medical working experience, if patients often need long time to queue to wait its medical service . Then, it will cause its patients number to be reduced .

These are variable factors to influence the hospital's inefficiency. They may include old speed hospital information system and medical record documents based on inefficient input and output variables. Input variables may include the number of hospital admissions, the number of nurses and the number of available beds. The output variable may include average of length of stay and bed turnover interval inefficient paper document record in the patient record administrative department.

However, to evaluate the hospital efficiency indicators may include technical, scale and managerial efficiency the out-based data development analysis approach and the variable returns to scales assumption was used. Based on the out-input based approach (maximizing the factors of medical service production), to increase efficiency the organization should be increased outputs.

Hence, when the hospital has good efficient evaluation method to measure every staff's performance , e.g. ward administrative clerk, patient registration clerk etc. Then, it can base on an put-put based approach and assuming a variable return to scale, there is capacity to improve technical efficiency and managerial efficiency in these any hospital different administrative units without an increase in costs and use of same amount of resources in relation to technical efficiency and managerial efficiency and scale efficiency of hospital's administrative labour individual task.

In conclusion, factors, such as modification of managerial practices, use of modern technologies tailored to the cultural, political and formulation of clinical guidelines to standardize the medical processes in order to reduce medical errors and increase the empowerment of health care buyers (insurance organizations), length of stay, management hospitals by specialist managers, administrative requirement, full time hospital physicians, limiting the authority of decision makers in relation to the recruitment of staff in accordance with the needs of the hospital and optimal allocation of beds, conducting economic evaluations and the type of hospitals ownership had an impact on the hospital efficiency significantly. By increasing the number of beds the hospitals efficiency decreases. Otherwise, optimizing the bed size can increase hospital efficiency.

However, the important factor to raise hospital overall staffs efficiencies empowerment is needed to let every hospital staff to review whether why and how himself/herself error is caused and he/she needs to review his/her errors to avoid to be caused from any negligence again in order to avoid patients' complaints again or reduce the patients' complaint number aims. So, empowerment of staff himself/herself error review factor is one major raising efficient good method.

● How organizational facility environment factor influences new and old employees long term performance

In psychological view ,in any organization's environments, they depend on the types of social and physical environment factors to influence employee personal behavior how to be caused. How and why does the employee select to do whose behavior? If the organization's physical and social environment is better, then it may influence its employees select to work hard. It is possible to bring productive efficient raising consequence.

In fact, when one new employee enters the new organization to work, he/she needs to learn how to adapt to cooperate with the organization's old employees to work together. So, it explains how and why organization's physical and social environment can influence the new employee individual motivation of behavior to work. In regarding new employee individual behavior by new employer's culture expectations as well as new employees need to adapt of actions that are likely to productive positive outcomes and generally discard those that bring unrewarding or puniishing outcomes by new employer's treatment.

However, anticipated material and organization environment co-operation outcomes between the new employee and the organization old employees' cooperation, which are not the only kind of incentives that influence the new employee behavior of the new employee actions were performed only on behalf of anticipated external rewards and punishment from the new employer. In actuality, the new employee concerns considerable self-direction in the face of the new employer's organization's old employees competing influences. However, when the new employee has adopted an intension and an action plan. When, he/she works in the new organization for a period, he/she can't simply not back and visit for the appropriate performances to appear.

The new employee's new job goal will be motivated by enlisting self-evaluative engagement in activities rather than directly. By making self-evaluation conditional on matching personal new job standards, the new employee will give direction to his/her new job pursuits and create self-inventions to sustain his/her efforts for new job goal attainment. The new employee will select to do new task behavior to give him/her self-satisfaction and a sense of pride and self worth for the new job chance.

Efficacy beliefs also play a key role in shaping the new employees' behavior to do their tasks by influencing the types of new organization's activities and working environments, the new employees choose to set into any factor that influences the employee's choice behavior can affect the direction of employee personal career development in the new organization. This is because the organizational working environment influences operating in the employee how to select working environments continue to work. Thus, by choosing and shaping the new organization's working environments, new employee can have a hand in what they expect.

In conclusion , when a new employee chooses the new organization to work. He/she must need to adapt the organization's new working environment. If he/she feels difficult to adapt or accept to the organization's new working environment, then he/she will be influenced to work inefficient or poor productive performance , due to he/she feels unhappy to work the new organization's working environment and the new organization's manager will dissatisfy his/her performance and complain or give verbal warning to dismiss him/her. Then, it will bring the poor consequence to let the organization's inefficient productive performance effect. If many new employees feel difficult to adapt to work in the new organization. Then, inefficient productive performance will be influenced to keep a long term. So, it implies that the organization will need to change its organizational culture in order to let many new employees can adapt and accept this new organizational culture to work happily if the organization expects new employees work to raise productive efficiency successfully.

● Raising efficient and effective
interview psychological methods

In human resource department, interviewing and selecting the most right applicants to do different kinds of positions, it is one part of HRM function. If the interviewer need to spend more time to interview to decide whom is the most right applicant to do the position in one day, e.g. 50 at least , even more applicants number as well as he/she can also make the more accurate personal selection decision to choose the most right applicant to do the position after the interview day. Then, the interviewing process needs to be avoided to spend more time to choose the most suitable applicant to do the position within the day. It is difficult to judge whether whom ought be the most right applicant to do the position, if there are more than 50 applicants , they are needed to be interview in the day. The consequence will bring HR department can spend extra time to do the interview task, but it can have enough staffs and time and resource to do other urgent or important task at the interview day. It will bring this question: How to apply psychological method to raise interviewer's efficiency to shorten to spend extra time to do interviewing tasks ? I shall explain some psychological methods to attempt to let interviewers have more confidence to select the most right applicant in short time as below:

1. Behavioral interview skill

The interviewer can apply the actual behavioral interview method to let the interviewee to answer how he/she deals the matters, he/she feels that it is the best decision in order to judge and analyze whether whom applicant is the most suitable to be selected, e.g. describing the situation, he/she needs or the task that he/she needs to accomplish. The situation may be from a previous job, any relevant event, describing the action he/she took and be sure to keep the focus on him/her , e.g. discussing a group project or effort in the team; explaining what results he/she achieved, what happen? How did the event and what dis the applicant accomplishes? What did the applicant learn?

In the behavioral-based interview. the interviewer can need the applicant to attempt to explain examples clearly in order to judge whose analytical skill whether he/she is the suitable applicant to do the position. The interviewer may ask the applicant to identify some examples from whose post experience where he/she demonstrated top behaviors and skills that employers typically seek. To judge whether his/her examples should be totally positive, such as accomplishments or meeting goals, the other half should be situations that started at negatively , but either ended positively or he/she made the best of the outcome.

This behavioral interview test aims to review whether the applicant's every example answer, he/she can provide an appropriate description of how he/she demonstrated the desired behaviors. In the behavioral interview, the interviewer can attempt to judge whether the applicant has good imagine effort to mind any relatively small set of examples to respond to a number of different behavioral questions to satisfy the right example are applied to the right situations in the limited interview time. Hence, behavioral interview can let the interviewer to make more accurate analysis to judge whether whom applicant(s) has (have) good analytical effort to solve any work-related situational problems in the most reasonable way or attitude in order to select whom is the most right applicant to do the position.

2. E-mail interviewing in qualitative research

E-mail interviewing is another good interview method to select right applicant to do the managerial level position. E-mail interviewing can be in many cases a viable alternative to face-to-face telephone interviewing. Internet-based qualitative research methods may include online personal interview and virtual focus groups. However, it brings two questions: What opportunities and challenges does online in depth interviewing present for collectively qualitative data? How can in depth e-mail interviews be conducted effectively?

The applicant targets may be the top-level manager, advertising executive , sales manager, human resource manager etc. management position applicants. They need to answer any complex or difficult interviewing question by email in the limited time, e.g. how to solve one case study problem , how to give recommendation to solve the situation problem. The interview participants may be recruited by tool/method of psychological test questions, the interview questions may be interview guide in a single e-mail and follow yp, length of email data collection period may be up to 10 weeks, the number of e-mail or follow up exchanges may be several number. The electronic formal and require little editing or formation before the applicants are processed for analysis all e-mail interviewing questions. So, they need to answer any managerial case study problem in limited time.

It is one good managerial interview test method to evaluate whether whom applicant has the best analysis effort in order to the managerial position, because they need to find the best solutions to give recommendations to attempt to solve any situational problems in any un predictive case study problems. For example, when the applicant or a focus group of discussion applicants whom need to spend the maximum half hours to give recommendations to discuss to solve one complex or difficult case study problem either between the interviewer and the another interviewee applicant or between the group of five to ten interviewees (job applicants) themselves. Thus, after the interviewer sent the one case study question to let the applicants to know by every email channel. The interviewer needs to judger whether whom one applicant or one of the focus group applicants their recommendations are the most reasonable to solve the case study managerial situational problem within half hour to one hour. Then, the interviewer can make more accurate judgement to select whether whom has the best analytical effort to do the managerial position.

3. The effectiveness of motivational interviewing for young or older adult applicants selection process

How can apply case management skills to be effective to prepare any interview motivation? How to do the most effective and efficient to meet the objectives of the interview? Some interview techniques used may vary the based on the individuals involved in the interview. For an interview with the young age applicant more require a different approach than an interview with a senior adult applicant. The following are one pointers to assist with preparing for the interview as below:

Knowing the purpose of the interview and what needs to be accomplished . What is the expected outcome? Gathering all forms that need to be completed or signed having the interview and making list of questions that need to be asked, knowing the key facts and topics to be discussed, during the interview. Gathering factual information that may be helpful. Opening mind is needed in the whole interview process. Making an appointment for the interview and arranging sufficient time to set fully participate in the interview. Taking notes during the interview, let the participants know in general terms the reason notes are being made and how they will be used, opening ended questions invite the applicant to provide more information usually begin with other words who, what, where, how, asking one question at a time and keeping wording simple and specific, defining any terms that may be unfamiliar to the applicant , giving the interviewing participants in the interview an opportunity to ask their one questions or to clarify anything that was discussed, closing the interview with a review of the information discussed and facts gathered, reviewing any follow-up that is to be done by the case manager or others involved in the interview.

In an efficient and effective interview, the interviewer needs have good body and spoken word communication to the interviewee or the position applicant. Because a good communication can reduce waste time or avoid the extended longer interview time if the interviewer can make good communication to impact good message to let the applicant to understand what is the mean to his/her interview question. What he/she wants to know, the total impact of a message includes ,e.g. 7 % verbal (words), 38% vocal /volume, pitch, rhythm etc. and 55% body movements (mostly facial expression). The interviewer's body and verbal behavior can make more clear message to let the interviewee(job applicant) to understand what answers are he/she wants to know mostly. Hence, an efficient and effective interview can let the interviewer to control and manage the whole interview to evaluate whether whom the applicants' answers or feedbacks are more reasonable to be acceptable to be better to compare other applicants to apply the position more accurately.

● What is efficient achievement of technological inputs factor in construction industry

What is organizational efficient raising actual mean? I shall indicate construction industry case to explain technological factor is the major factor to assist construction organization to raise efficiency. For construction industry example, improved productivity could be attributed to advances in and increased usage of information technologies, increased competition, due to globalization and changes in workplace and organizational structures.

For construction efficiency, the construction process can reduce waste in coordinating labor and in managing, moving and installing materials, loss avoidance. It can achieve efficient aim. The construction productive efficient concept can be defined efficiency improvements as ways to cut waste and labor. So, one construction organizational efficient achievement means that it implemented through the capital facilities sector, these activities would significantly advance construction efficiency and improve the quality, timeliness, cost effectiveness of projects in construction processes.

On construction industry technological factor influence hand, it can influence that construction productivity how well, how quality, and at what cost buildings and infrastructure can be constructured, directly affects prices for homes and consumer products and the robustness of the national economy. Construction productivity will also affect the outcomes of national efforts to renew existing infrastructure systems; to build new infrastructure for power from renewable to renew existing infrastructure systems; to build new infrastructure for power from renewable resources to develop high-performance " green building" and to remain competitive in the global market. If the construction organization expected to achieve effficient aim. It ought consider how to change in building design, construction and renovation and in building materials and materials recycling, will be essential to the success of national efforts to minimize environmental impacts, reduce overall energy use, and reduce greenhouse gas emissions.

However, construction industry analysts differ on whether construction industry productivity is improved by efficiency outcome. They indicate construction efficiency needs to reduce 25-50 percent waste in coordinating labour and in managing, moving and installing materials. This is the most minimum standard efficient achievement level to any construction organizations.

What are the factors influence efficiency to any construction organizations? An efficient construction task process is made possible by a range of information technological tools and applications, including computer-aided design and drafting, three and four dimensional visualization and modeling programs, laser scanning, cost-estimating and scheduling tools and materials tracking. So, high technological tool will assist to raise efficient construction process to any construction organizations. It can help them to shorten time and avoid materials waste and control cost effective estimation for any construction projects.

Effective use of interoperate technologies requires effective team cooperative processes and effective planning up front and this it can help overcome obstacles to efficiency created by process fragmentation. Interoperable technologies can also help to improve the quality and speed of any construction project related decision making, integrate processes, managing supply chains, sequence work flows, improve data accuracy and reduce the time spent on data entry, reduce design and engineering conflicts and the subsequent need for rework, improve the life-cycle management of buildings and infrastructure.

All of these factors will influence whether the construction organization can implement efficiency in success. For example, interoperable techcholgies include legal issues, data-storage capacities and the need for " intelligent " search applications to sort quickly through thousands of data elements and make real-time information available for on-site decision making. How to improve job-site efficiency through more effective interfacing of people, processes, materials ,equipment, and information. The job site for a large construction project is a dynamic place, involving numerous contractors, subcontractors, trades people and labors, all of whom must require equipment, materials and supplies to complete their tasks. So, they need to know how to manage activities and demands to achieve the maximum efficiency from the limited available resources. Time, money, and resources will have possible to be wasted when projects are poorly managed, causing workers to have to wait around for tools and work crews are not on-site at appropriate time or when supplies and equipment are stored in complexity or difficulty, requiring that they can be moved multiple time (time waste).

How to improve job site safety and improve the quality of projects, significantly cut waste? The use of automated equipment, e.g. for excavation and earthmoving operations, pip installation, concrete placement, and information technologies, e.g. radio-frequency identification tags for tracking materials personal digital assistants for capturing field data. These high technological tool can help any construction projects to raise efficiency to process improvements and the provision for real -time information for improved management at the job site.

Moreover, on mannal research and development tools hand, instead of data technological tools hand, any construction organizations also need to consider how to take a variety of forms: How to test field on a job site? How to arrange lecture shows in efficient way, seminrs, training and conference, and scientific laboratories time, human resource available arrangement, spending expenditure budget to finish. Moreover, effective performance mearements are enablers of innovation and of corrective actions throughout a construction project's life cycle. They can help any construction companies or organizations understand how processes led to success or failure, improvements or inefficiencies and how to use that knowledge to improve construction products , processes and outcomes of active projects.

The nature of construction projects, the industry itself, any construction organizations ought consider the construction working environment how to influence construction workers' emotions. For example, when the construction site is high levels, of noise, dust and airborne particles, adverse weather conditions,and other factors that can cause injuries and thereby reduce efficiency and productivity. New types of equipment can make an active physically easier to perform, easier to control, move precise , and safer for construction workers. Similarly, changes in materials can reduce the weight of construction components, make them easier to handle, move and install. Manufacturing building components off-site providers need more control conditions and allow for improved quality and precision in the fabrication of the component, One study that examined the relationship between changes in material technology and construction productivity based on 100 construction a related tasks, the study found that labor productivity for the same activity increased by 30 % at least when higher materials were used and labour productivity also improved when construction activites were performed using materials that were easier to install or were pre-fabricated. So, it seems material heavy can influence construction worker individual productive efficiency in site, if the material is higher , then the construction worker's productivity will be influenced to improve (Goodrum et al. 2009).

Thus, the factors influence construction organization's efficiency. It focuses on whether the construction firm applies how advanced construction technologies to assist its construction workers to work as well as whether its construction environment can let workers to feel safe to avoid life danger or accident occurrence. When the workers do not worry about whose life safety as well as they can apply advanced construction technology to assist them to work. Then, their productive efficiencies ought need to be improved easily. Thus, facility management and advanced technology will be the main factor to raise construction workers' efficiencies.

X

Psychosocial and medical interventions for mental and physical health facility management strategy

The business case for implementation science is clear: As healthcare systems work under increasingly dynamic and resource-constrained conditions, evidence-based strategies are essential in order to ensure that research investments maximize healthcare value and improve public health. Implementation science plays a critical role in supporting these efforts. This case concerns how management scinece solves psychosocial and medical interventions for mental and physical health facilities management challenges.

Implementation science is "the scientific study of methods to promote the systematic uptake of research findings and other EBPs into routine practice, and, hence, to improve the quality and effectiveness of health services." Implementation science is distinct from, but shares characteristics with, both quality improvement and dissemination methods. Implementation studies can be either assess naturalistic variability or measure change in response to planned intervention. Implementation studies typically employ mixed quantitative-qualitative designs, identifying factors that impact uptake across multiple levels, including patient, provider, clinic, facility, organization, and often the broader community and policy environment. Accordingly, implementation science requires a solid grounding in theory and the involvement of trans-disciplinary research teams.

Facility management, or FM, is a broad discipline that includes a variety of industries, from food to technology, manufacturing to e-commerce and beyond. But, though the core of each business may be completely different from even its closest competition, successful facility management practices are easily interchangeable from enterprise to enterprise. As a matter of fact, it is one of the only job titles that can be found in, basically, any small to large organizations, including public entities, like schools and hospitals, to private buBut, reciprocal tendencies aside, facility management procedures and techniques must be highly-specialized for the business in which they are being used. Because the discipline covers complex specifics, including business continuity planning and even fire safety, it's key that your organization offers a holistic outlook on its facility management procedures.sinesses, like those that manage their inventory in warehouses.

The discipline of facility management encompasses – and why poor management could easily lead to an organization's demise:

Safety – It's the facility management team's job to ensure the safety of all of the employees and customers occupying the property. This responsibility spans all possible environmental health and safety issues, particularly ones that concern the building and its equipment, specifically. Failure to do so can mean serious business in the form of fines, lost business, or even prosecution if it was deemed that the manager or business' negligence caused casualties or permanent environmental damage. Fire, for example, is usually right at the top of the radars of facility managers because it's a preventable tragedy that, when prepared for sufficiently, can save lives and valuable inventory. A thorough facility management team can protect its company best by guaranteeing that all parts of the facility are up-to-code, its employees are trained well, and all permits and certificates are completely valid. This function entails everything from safe and efficient lighting to flooring choices.

Security – In regards to importance, second to safety is facility security, yet another important piece of the puzzle in which the facility management team must answer to. Though larger companies or ones with particularly pricey inventory or equipment might make the wise choice to outsource its security needs in the form of a private firm, it's still the role of the facility manager to ensure that the firm performs competently. Technology advancements like biometrics and wearables are making it possible to maintain strict access control for high-security areas, but it's up to facility managers to stay on top of these developments and make smart security technology investments. In addition to general safety, it's also important that the facility management team has the technological know-how to safeguard and maintain its priciest hardware. This role is a key one as it doubly affirms that assets are protected just as closely as the safety of the community.

Maintenance and Inspections – No matter the focus of the organization, one of the most heedless things that a facility management team can do is slack off on its building maintenance duties. Every part of the building, including installed machinery such as HVAC systems, must be maintained by the facility management team. Because some facilities contain countless elements that need regular maintenance, establishing and following strict maintenance schedules helps to ensure that all moving and permanent parts of the facility stay up-to-date and working well into the future. Along with general maintenance, inspections are also something that facility management teams must always be ready for. They can prepare the business by conducting internal inspections, as needed, for the many formal regulatory inspections they might incur annually. Of course, the team must also take into account any time the facility undergoes a major change in hardware, level of inventory, or capacity – and, they must also keep their eyes on all changes in laws that could affect their current procedures.

Business Continuity Planning – Part of leading an effective facility management team means planning for "worst case scenarios." This means that each team must sit down with the powers that be to come up with a plan in case disaster strikes and the business can't afford to shut down operations. For example, let's say that a community college endures a major fire and the authorities have deemed the entire main building a total loss. The community college is currently in the middle of a semester which it can't cut short – this is a situation where prior business continuity planning is key. If this were done in the aforementioned scenario, the facility management team would have already come up with alternate locations to hold classes and operate the organization's administrative duties. In addition to the new venue, the team would have already made a solid plan for the temporary facility's security, maintenance, and hardware needs.

Daily Operational Duties – In addition to serving as the safety and security liaisons for the facility, it's also important that facility management teams are organized to handle the inherent day-to-day challenges that might arise. Depending on how the given organization is structured, this can mean anything from mending a leaky roof in the women's restroom to even fixing a jammed fax machine.

I shall discuss how to apply facilities management strategy to assist hospial organization how to raise its medical health care service to let patients to feel more comfortable and care for medical care in any hospitals as below:

Hospitals and health systems that engage in cost management are looking to reshape and reduce costs, and there are eight main strategies that can lead to effective cost management opportunities, cost management, at its core, involves two components: improving the planning and execution of current operations and attacking overhead costs and other costs that are "flying below the radar." Here are the eight strategies to reduce hosptial cost as below:

1. Understand the organization's readiness for cost management. Conducting a cost management assessment that details a hospital system's thinking, alignment, operational planning, overhead management and other moving parts could determine if a hospital is actually ready to begin a large cost management initiative.

2. Define cost-reduction goals based on the organization's capital shortfall. Revenue streams are not what they used to be for hospitals and health systems, and all cost-reduction goals should aim to close the capital shortfall as much as possible. "The goals quantify the performance levels necessary to fund the organization's strategies and maintain its competitive financial performance," according to the report.

3. Use internal and external benchmarks to identify possible sources of savings. Reviewing historical trends and applying global and departmental benchmarks and peer department comparisons can give a clearer picture of where possible savings could be.

4. Supplement benchmark data with other data analytics. Benchmarking data, while necessary and helpful, cannot map a cost management strategy alone. Using several data analyses, with input from medical staff and department managers, can hone in on cost-reduction opportunities.

5. Understand and focus on the key drivers of staffing and productivity problems. Inadequate plans, poor execution of staffing plans, unclear staffing roles, use of overtime and other staffing and productivity issues drive higher labor costs, which generally constitute more than half of a hospital or health system's operating expenses.

6. Drill down on staffing methods. Changing staffing methods could certainly keep costs in check, but it could also enhance the relationship between staff members and patient demand. For example, improved staffing in the operating room or emergency department will account for variations in patient volume but will still keep a strong semblance of patient contact.

7. Streamline overhead functions. Eliminating redundancies in human resources, accounting, revenue cycle, information technology, marketing, legal, materials management and other hospital functions can both improve operational flow and "yield large savings," according to the report.

8. Ensure cost-reduction targets are integrated with organizational plans and budgets. Inserting the cost management initiatives into the hospital's strategic financial plan, annual budget and operating plan can allow management to monitor progress and report results to the entire organization.

However, above these cost management is accounting method to reduce cost in hospital organization human resource side, such as reducing staffs or staff number, reducing electricity fee. But, it does not represent the actual successful to implement the actual cost reducing, but it won't influence the patients' comfortable and enjoyable feeling. So, how to implement facility managment to bring actual cost reduce and avoid patients feel medical services are worse and lack of enough nurses or doctors number care need. I shall explain how to implement the new kind of facility management strategy to reduce cost and raise patients comfortable and care feeling in the same time to medical organizations as below:

● What is the new model of healthcare facility management

A growing number of healthcare organizations are moving to an integrated real estate model in an effort to better manage costs, respond to regulatory requirements, and support changes in patient care delivery. As healthcare organizations seek solutions to the challenges presented by today's evolving marketplace, it's clear that the cost and performance of their facilities will have a significant impact. Whether it's the need to drive cost reduction, respond to regulatory requirements or support changes in patient care delivery models, the effectiveness of an organization's facilities management program plays a critical role in their ability to provide high-quality, cost-effective patient care. As healthcare leaders realize the importance of an effective real estate platform, many are finding that transformative changes are needed in order to realize outcomes that cannot be achieved under traditional facility management models.

● What is the tradition facilities management model to hospitals

Historically, facility management services have been provided on a campus by campus basis or separated into acute care and outpatient programs. In many cases, these programs have been limited to plant operations, which are segregated as an individual support service and function in a silo environment. Due primarily to organic growth or mergers and acquisitions, healthcare systems often find themselves managing their facilities in a bifurcated manner, with individual hospitals operating more or less autonomously. While many organizations have identified the goal of standardizing real estate operations across their system, it's common to find that these initiatives have been in the planning stage for some time. As a result, the inability to proactively manage facility costs and performance at the system level continues to be an obstacle to progress. Although facility management teams may have a "best-in-class" process at an individual hospital, a lack of resources or resistance to change may prevent that process from being consistently implemented across the system. As each individual campus makes incremental process improvements, they move further and further away from a comprehensive real estate solution. Recognizing that future success will require a systemwide approach to facilities management, continuing with the status quo model increases the cost of change in the future and forfeits the savings that can only be achieved through a centralized real estate platform.

The lack of a comprehensive real estate delivery model also inhibits an organization's ability to effectively develop essential programs at the system level. Services which are critical for long-term success, such as work order management, energy management, benchmarking, and standardization, are often pursued on a campus by campus basis. These initiatives require the dedication of significant time and resources to collect and reconcile data before creating and implementing the new program. So, successful facility management to any health care or hospital organizations. It must help them to bring cost reducing benefits.

With disparate facilities management systems at each campus, the process must then be repeated across the system. When evaluating the benefits to be gained through individual campus initiatives, consideration must be given to the cost of replicating the process as compared to the cost and time to market to create one process for the entire real estate portfolio. The lack of a consistent facilities management program also creates challenges related to business planning at the system level. A common example may be seen in the capital planning process, as the prioritization of projects breaks down due to a lack of reliable comparison data and the absence of analytics based on performance and cost projections. The process then becomes politically driven, rather than following a disciplined approach based on projected need and justified by consistent business case analyses.

A similar result is frequently displayed when organizations attempt to implement segregated processes related to space allocation to any hospitals or medical care organizations. The practice of assigning space based on availability is common, but it creates higher occupancy costs and difficulties in forecasting future demand and associated expenses. This reduces the accuracy of the business cases that drive the decision making process. Hence, one excellent facility management medical organization , it ought can reduce cost , but it can also let patients feel more large area occupancy patients rooms or any occupancy area to toilets, bath rooms , cooking rooms in any hospitals locations. It aims to let patients to feel comfortable and enjoy to live in the hospital. Without a comprehensive approach to facilities management, the space allocation process becomes reactive and can lead to the unnecessary construction of new space, when the reality may be that a solution is achievable within the organization's existing real estate.

● Approach to reducing costs

The challenges caused by the lack of a systemwide facility management platform are exacerbated by the traditional approach to reducing costs, which is to cut staffing levels. In the absence of a comprehensive facility management program, these staffing cuts are often a reactive response to an immediate need to reduce costs rather than a component of a long term plan. As the ability to focus on preventive maintenance decreases, the organization's risk increases and employee satisfaction and performance decreases. At some point, doing more with less is counterproductive and a new approach is needed. In order to achieve significant improvement, the status quo model must be transformed as part of a centralized delivery model to optimize the performance of facilities and create financially sustainable real estate practices. A comprehensive facility management plan will provide alternative paths to achieving cost reductions, as well as processes to ensure the continued support of patient care.

● The path to a solution

In order to achieve lasting results, healthcare organizations should embark on a process to consolidate their existing facility management services into a systemwide, best-in-class real estate platform. With the volume of changes impacting the healthcare market, having best-in-class facility management will be critical to long-term success. All aspects of facility services should be included as a baseline delivery model, with adjustments made in policies and processes to address different facility types. This system-based approach to planning and analytics provides a substantial competitive advantage. Given the time involved in developing and fully implementing real estate plans, organizations that pursue integrated facility management models will have an advantage over their competitors who continue operating as they have in the past.

A systemwide real estate program, including facility management, project management, facility activation services, property management, strategic real estate planning, real estate accounting and market-based transaction management allows organizations to successfully implement proactive initiatives such as ambulatory prototyping, site selection, labor analytics and workplace environment optimization. Once the assessment is complete, it will be possible to produce a gap analysis to identify opportunities to reduce costs and improve processes and performance. These opportunities can then be evaluated by weighing the cost to implement new system based programs against the expected savings or operational benefits. Each opportunity should be validated as part of a consistent decision process, allowing prioritization based on an organization's overall business plan and appetite for change.

Once the facility management program is on its way to best-in-class status, it should be integrated with all other real estate services to fully optimize performance. Ideally, this transformational process will follow concurrent and coordinated schedules across all real estate services, with the objective of developing supportive and complimentary processes among all teams. As the delivery of patient care evolves, the delivery of real estate services must transform to keep pace. The solution is to transition to an integrated systemwide real estate model, drawing on examples of successful platforms and driving improvements based on quantifiable data and objectives.

As part of an integrated platform, these programs allow organizations to fundamentally change the way real estate is managed, dramatically reducing year over year expenses and enabling the accurate prediction of future space requirements and the reliable forecasting of associated long term financial obligations. When truly integrated, the real estate platform will provide cost-effective management of assets and contribute significant value to many internal departments, including strategy and business development, clinic systems, finance, compliance, and procurement. The benefits of an integrated real estate platform cannot be achieved without completing a comprehensive transformation of the traditional model.

On conclusion, in order to achieve that goal, healthcare organizations should pursue the transformation of their real estate platform by taking the first steps towards a best-in-class facility management program. Successful healthcare organizations of the future will have integrated real estate services, with facilities that operate at peak efficiency and are proactively managed to respond to and support changes in the delivery of patient care.

Reference

Becker, F. (1990). " Facility management : a cutting edge field?" property management 8 (2): 25-28.

Bernard, M.B. & Bruce, J. A. (1994) Improving organizational effectiveness through transformational leadership: US. Sage publications, Inc. pp. 11-13.

Fiona, M.W. (2004). organizational behavior and work , a critical introduction, 2 ed. : New York, US, Oxford university press, pp.79 .

Jac, F.E.& John , R.M. (2014) predictive analytics for HRM:US Pearson Education pp.13-16

Stephen, P.R. & Timothy, A.J. (2018). Essentials of organizational behavior, 14 ed.: US. Pearson Education, Inc. pp.108-110.

XI
Strategy Plan Implement

● Economy and management factors
    Economic factors influence
to meet strategic management?

What economic factors will influence any organizations to achieve their strategic plans successfully? Why does one firm cut prices when another firm buys out competitors? Why does one firm diversify into new industries, when another firm spins off subsidiaries to focus on its core ? Why do some strategic rise when others all? These organizations' activities will be influenced to choose to implement by economic factor influences.

These are central concern of both strategic management theorists and strategic management draw on diverse ideas as well as which have relationship to be influenced by unpredictable economic factors . So, organizations need to concern what external environment economic situation is. Such as development or decline (recession), then to decide how to adopt the most effective strategic plan to achieve the aim of effectiveness and efficiency more successfully. So, it seems that external economic environment factors can influence why organizations need an efficient and effective strategic plan to do more better.

Firstly, In organizational internal need hand , strategic management theorists need to view whose firm from different standpoints. Each strategist explores efficiency from the perspective of whose firm, developing theories of why one strategy is more successful then another, given product, service and industry characteristics.

Sociologists focus on efficiency from the perspective of the corporate environment itself, who neglect the exernal economic environment factor can influence the organization leaders how to implement their strategic plans. Developing theories about the context in which one strategy becomes defined as efficiency an effectiveness.

Secondly, In economic factor influences organizational strategic plan hand. Strategic management theorists need to begin with very different methodological imperatives. Strategists seek to develop adequate theories of why certain strategies are optional or at least efficient, based typically on insights from successful firms. Sociologists seek to explain variance in behavior across large populations of firms and over time, to research why potential causes for any economic situation.

These differences derive in part from their different goals, strategic management is oriented to develop concepts for cooperate leaders, whereas, economic sociology is oriented to explain the trends why to cause corporate behavior. For example, why does IKEA furniture business need to let any visitors who attempt to sit down to have comfortable feeling? Why does Apple brand computer business need to design and innovate any new model of notebooks and mobile computers.

In external economic environment influence, strategic theorists presume that firm behavior is driven principally by competitive pressure and quest for effectiveness and efficiency. Analysts tend to give great power to market factors and little power to historical, political and social factors. So, organization leaders need to concern how competitive pressures may lead whose firms to alter whose strategies, but the new strategies who choose are shaped by public policy, limitation, power and historical happen.

I shall indicate this question concerns why organizations need strategy plans. Why do firms diversify? In another view point to ask this question. Why is it efficient for some firms to diversify, and for which firms to diversify and for which firms is efficient and effective? Why do firms choose diversification? Why does a particular firm choose at a particular time? Economic sociologists usually ask this management challenges, who find organization challenges to give solution in economic view point. But for strategic management theorists, this problem concerns an argument based in efficiency. Question is such as: Can organizations make diversification efficient if which lack one efficent and effective strategy plan?

For economic sociologists, this problem is to explain the social processes behind the rise of a new business practice. Does it ensure to need diversification tend if the organization lacks an efficient and effective strategic plan to evaluate ? It's possible that diversification strategy can let multi-product firms are more profitable to campaign single product firms.

In the past, the diversification trend is during the 1980 year. What does cause this? On economic first view point, Davis et al. (1991) cite the inefficiencies inherent in diversification. Can strategy plan cause efficiency effect? On economic second view point , Davis also showed most firms make a mix of good and bad decisions, such that a disastrous strategy in product, which may be altered by a good one in marketing, or in human resources. On economic third view point, he also indicated firms seek to copy their profitable pears may have difficulty figuring out what to copy and may have difficulty copying it. However, sociologists certainly see managers as striving for efficiency . But managerial decisions , which are focus on how sociological processes to led managers to choose from an alternatives.

How to feel strategic thinking? Strategy took on a military significance and represented the action of commanding or leading armies in times of war, i.e. a military campaign. It meant a way of prevailing over the adversary, a tool of victory in war and why was it applied to other contexts and fields of human relationships: Political, economics, business, among others.

Into a field of knowledge in management, strategic management, with content, concepts and practice reasoning can be applied to any businesses. Management uses this old military concept to associate the activities of an organization's manager. Since it represents an important tools for business management in a competitive marketplace. The main objective of strategy involves preparing the organization to deploy the skills qualifications and internal resources of the enterprise.

So, it seems that strategic plan is similar to military campaign. If one country's soldier team lacks one efficient and effective military strategic plan to prepare to war, it is possible that the soldier team will fail, due to the soldier team lack one team leaders who can lead them how to organize whose team to co-operate efficiently. So, one organization will be failure to compete its competitors if which lacks one efficient strategic plan to prepare to organize which teams to co-operate to work from top level to middle level and down level in its organizational structure.

According to Obembe (2010) indicated knowledge management in an organization is begun by identifying the knowledge that individuals bring in from outside the company. In this case, the development of organizational strategy depends on understanding the perceptions of their managers on what strategy and strategic management actually is. The identification of perceptions of future managers on the concept is used in contributing significantly to organizational management practice. This enables the organizational knowledge on the field of strategy can hardly be managed should each manager understand the concept differently. So, if organization can have one efficient strategic plan, then it will raise ability to learn knowledge management skill to solve any human resource, strategic management etc. challenges more easily.

For example, Walt Disney entertainment theme park, which had innovated one efficient knowledge management strategy to reduce visitors' complains and dissatisfaction, such as designing fast ticket queue system, which can reduce visitors' queue time. Although, admission fee is more expensive to compare to normal ticket buyers. But who can choose not to need to wait long time to queue to play more than one kind entertainment facility to play. If who can come back the prior entertainment facility queue within one hour, who do not need to queue again to play the prior entertainment facility. So, who can reduce queue time to chose to play any prior queue entertainment facilities within one hour coming back, who will feel more satisfactory to spend loss queue working time to play different entertainment facilities. Also, when any visitors feel need to enquire how to go to anywhere , who can find cleaners to enquire how to go anywhere conveniently and easily. Because the cleaners will give map to indicate any location to let who to know. So, any visitors do not need to spend much to find to any visible map noticeboard to find location. Cleaners can tell to them how to go to any anywhere to let them know more clearly. So, knowledge management is one kind of strategic thinking to solve customer individual psychological dissatisfactory feeling. The Disney leaders need to continue to discover to seek any weakness points to solve customer psychological satisfactory feeling or need from daily observation in Disney entertainment park.

Strategy is a business logic, rational and sequential to the most dynamic that understand this process as associated with culture and learning factors, political and power relations. Thus, there are two major problems affecting the understanding of what the concept of strategy really means that confusion is between strategy and effectiveness tools as well as confusion is between strategy and strategic planning. The rook of the problem seems to be the lack of a full understanding as to what strategy really is.

Organizational strategy can mean different in scale and complexity, which can mean policies, objectives, tactics, goals, programs, among others. However, the concept of strategy has been used indiscriminately in the field of management, meaning anything from a precisely formulated course of action, a positioning in a particular environment, through to the entire personality and existential rational behind a company's existence. Strategy is not only one way of dealing in a competitive environment or market, as treated by much of the literature and its popular use, as it can't only summarize the ideas, proposals, guidelines. This fact has an explanation. Strategy in organizations , as a field of study is much newer than its current practice, and its knowledge remains under construction.

Some strategic professionals think strategy is such as: what matters are for the effectiveness of the organization, the external point of view, which stresses the relevance of the objectives against the environment, in terms of internal stresses, balanced communication between members of the organization and a willingness to contribute towards actions and the achievement of common objectives, analyzing the present situation and changing at whenever necessary to find what one's resources are or what which should be.

It is the determinant of the basic long-term goals of a firm and the allocation of resources necessary for carrying out these goals, it is a rule for making decision to be determined by product/market scope growth, competitive advantage and synergy. So, it is a thinking to any leaders to be prepared to make any decisions and develops the learning process in organization as well as it is the pattern of objectives, purposes or goals and major policies and plans to achieve missions for any organization within a limited time prediction or expectation.

All business organizations are concerned with low which will survive and prosper in the future. A business strategy is often thought of as a plan or set of intentions that will set the long term direction of the actions. However, how organizational plans or how intent , an organization's strategy can only become a meaning reality to achieve include corporate, business and function three levels.

The top corporate level key issues concern that what businesses shall be in , acquire or divest, how allocate resources what the relationship businesses and center is . The middle business level key issues concern that how businesses compete, what the mission is, what the strategic objectives are. The low function level key issues concern that how the function contribute to the business strategy, what the strategic objectives are managed in the function, what technology is used in the function, what skills are required by workers in the function.

Organizations need to concern these questions. Is the strategy consistent between the organization's strategy and business strategy, between operation strategy and the other functional strategy, between the different decision areas of operation strategy? Does the strategy contribute to competitive advantage? Enabling operations to set priorities that enhance competitive advantage, high opportunities for operations to complement the business strategies, making operations strategy clear to the rest of the organization, providing the operating capabilities that will be required in the future.

Organizations need have operations performance objectives to measure which performance. It is a criterion against which to evaluate the performance of operations. There are considered to be five possible operations performance objectives, cost , quality, speed, dependability and flexibility. Such as, the ability to produce at low cost, the ability to produce with specification and without error, the ability to do things quality in response to customer demands and offer short lead times between a client orders and a product or service and when who receive it, the ability to deliver products and services with promises made to clients, e.g. in a quotation or other published information, the ability to change operations. Flexibility includes the ability to change the volume of production, to change the time taken to product, to change the mix of different products or services produced , to innovate and introduce new products and services. Thus, these are basic organization structure of strategic management.

How to apply strategic planning and management in public and private sector organizations and what are their differences?

Management issues can be divided in two groups: governmental or public, with its specific aims, methods and challenges, and private sector responsible for economical results, competitiveness and state revenues. How can strategic planning, management and leadership of public and private sectors identify opportunities to improve performance with differences? Concerning this research, some strategic management professional had attempted to do research to conclude that in public sector there is great emphasis on strategic planning part of management process, but implementing plan to clear activities delays or is even misled. In private sector enterprises tend to look short term. Otherwise, thus gaining results in small every day actions , but looking greater sight to future and therefore to get chance of greater growth . Government should implement more client-oriented approach using best example from entrepreneurial world. Private sector should learn how to generate concrete long term plans, delegate duties and not to mix responsibilities in enterprise for greater result. So , who concluded that strategic plan is considered that private sector prevails over the public sector in efficiency and result oriented actions. Although, this assumption reasoned with lots of practical examples and arguments and efficiency's prevalence of private sector over the public administration was proved.

Considering the public administration strategic plan, the strategic management professionals argument do not encourage public administration to work in its own self-interest, but who discovered more efficient environment where to find the best management practices, in stance in field of customer care, that can be adopted in a legal and rational way.

Public sector is advocated that intellectual work is more hierarchical , within the team work more knowledgeable team member for a special task will already to be an informal interim leader, regardless of the structure of hierarchy, to compare to private sector hierarchical structure. They showed that are subordinated hierarchically to the long term development planning documents. The short term development planning documents are subordinated hierarchically to the median term developed planning documents. According to the updated system all public administration situation should develop the action strategy from the period of three years that serves for the budget planning and allocation to compare to provide sector. Otherwise, strategic planning in private enterprises come within strategic management and contributes as part of it. Strategic management is focused defining of business mission, the company's development direction, objectives and the resources and long-term management decision -making for implementing the strategy .

Why is middle management important in strategic organizational chart structure? Middle level managers, their role no longer entails issuing orders to subordinates. In fact, middle level managers in flat organizations may have very few direct reports. The most successful middle managers must rely on strong influencing skills and the ability to a complex network of resources critical role in the ultimate ability of a company to achieve its strategic goals. For example, marketing managers and engineering directors, there are the middle level managers who are being asked to do more with fewer resources. They are being held responsible have no direct organizational authority. They are being asked to influence partners, drive into unfamiliar channels, and motivate complex networks of global resources to get results .

So, employers or top managers, leaders need to concern whether who have worked relative pressure from worked relative causes. And yet ongoing restructuring, the dissolution of the career ladder, and persistent job insecurity have eroded middle level managers' sense at loyalty, frequently leaving them feeling demoralized and disenfranchised. Because it has chance, these middle level managers who are at risk of leaving your organization, unless you provide the proper support and development to perform their new responsibilities. Higher turnover among this crucial middle manager group , risks undermining company performance and diminishing the vital connection between strategy and execution. With more pressure , greater responsibilities , less training and fewer resources at the command. IS it any wonder that many middle level managers are suffering from increasing levels of stress?

Companies recognize that such high turnover rates will significantly to implement to middle level management to hope them to achieve strategic objectives. So, it seems , instead of top and low levels management, middle level management ought to be the most important role in any organizations. Because these middle level managers are such as middle communication staffs , who need to listen top level management to let the top level managements to know how to do whose job duties in most efficient methods and effective final results to achieve organization's expectation. So, any strategic plan implement must need whose assistance to finish plan more easily.

● Management factors influence organizational strategic plans

Nowadays, many countries public institutions had implemented total quality management. For example, in the United States, strategic planning was introduced after the 1900 year with much of the early literature focusing on local government applications (Poister and Streib, 2005;45). The emphasis in strategic management approaches to be more in focused on a future time horizon. Ideally, strategic management attempts to achieve future goals by liking strategic initiatives to operational process. When total quality management is also forced looking and seeks long-range improvements, applications also emphasize attention to current quality and citizen satisfaction concerns.

So, strategy means the determination of the basic long-term goals and objectives of an enterprise, and the adoption of actions and the allocation of resources how to carrying and these goals. It is the pattern of decisions in a company that determines and reveals its objectives, purposes or goals, produces the principal policies and plant for achieving those goals, and defines the range of business, the company is to purpose, the kind of economic and human organization , it is or intends to be , and the nature of the economic and non-economic contribution , it intends to make to its shareholders, employees, customers and societies.

Is strategy implementation suitable to apply the public sector? It depends on whether perceived service is affective, efficient and equity to department departments. A logical incremental and mostly rational style of implementation are associated with better effectiveness, efficiency and equity, with the absence of an implementation style associated with worse performance.

Nowadays, strategy management tools and ideas been brought into play by governments across the world to enhance capacities and performance standards in the force of in face of increasingly challenging. In response, researchers have begun to investigate whether management can be applied to strategic public organizations. What are the relationship between different strategy implementation styles and the effectiveness and efficiency? Is a rational strategy implementation styles associated with good organizational performance? Does an incremental strategy implementation style have a stronger or weaker relationship with performance or weaker relationship with performance than a rational one? Does some combination of the two styles result in the best performance outcomes? What is relationship between strategy implementation styles and the perceived effectiveness, efficiency and equity to public sector?

To answer above questions. It is important to know that the actual content of those strategies and the way in which were initially formulated to public sector if any public organizational departments want staffs work efficient and effective and equity. The introduction of new public service delivery models, monitoring the effectiveness of how public departments operational evaluation system and culture requires to fit a distinction between more or less planned styles of implementation tends to be top-down and hierarchical, involving the use of prepared action plans, performance monitoring, and review processes to any government departments.

In theory, private and public organizations may adopt different implementation styles for different purpose, for example, using a highly formal process for introducing an efficiency, focused strategy, when adopting an incremental approach to the explanatory search for innovative solutions to service delivery problems to public needs for any public sector departments. An emphasis on a rational implementation style is thought to result in better public sector and department organizational performance because the goal clarity on which it facilities the on-going inter-department coordination of internal and external activities between public sector's different departments.

Overall, the evidence from the private sector suggests that a rational strategy implementation style is associated with better organizational performance. However, decisions from private and public organizations are found that strategic planning has a stronger positive influence on the success of implementation than a more ad-hoc approach in which decisions are made on an incremental basis as situations. For example, Hickson et al (2003) study exploring implementation style and performance in a sample of public and private organizations finds that a dual approach combination elements of both planned and adoptive implementation has a stronger positive association with organizational performance than an emphasis on either planning or adaptation. Thus, it beings this hypothesis, such as a logical incremental strategy implementation style will have a stronger positive relationship with organizational performance then either a rational or incremental implementation style.

Due to public organization is a hierarchical structure. I suggest that a logical incremental and a mostly rational implementation style are associated with higher levels of effectiveness, efficiency and equity than other implementation styles, with no clear approach associated with the lowest level of performance to any public departments. Strategic decision theory is an important school of thought in management studies. So, policy markers need to seek how to improve the effectiveness, efficiency, effectiveness and equity of local public services should therefore consider the extent to which it is possible to encourage incremental adaption of strategies.

● Organization strategic plan challenges

School strategic plan challenges

In researching this question how to achieve the greatest level of effectiveness to school organizations. This can be measured through a conceptualization process of the S.W.O.T. (strengths, weaknesses, opportunities, threats) environmental analysis, clearly defined mission statement, goals and objectives, specific strategy formulation outline, implementation of the strategies and control of the strategic plan. This conceptualization control process is the action that will link the independent variable of efficient strategic plans, through the original measurements of the steps of those plans.

Why do school organizations need an efficient strategic plan? School strategic plan is thinking and responding satisfy social education to adopt student and school cultural, and to adopt economic influence threat factors. Strategic planning is needed at the point when priorities begin to compete with another one school. It is necessary to have specific goals for any activities or decision to measure school effectiveness in addition to thinking strategically for long term education success.

There are many different dimensions to school planning classified according to :(i) the time involvement of the school plan, (ii) the school organizational level performing the plan, e.g. classroom control performing, teaching performance etc. (iii) the activities involved in the school plans, e.g. what is the standard (criteria) to decide school fee charge amount, each course of student maximum numbers per year, how to design each course content and (iv) the general characteristics of purpose of the school plans , e.g. mission, education development long term plan.

The criteria of school effectiveness include such as, significant relational student groups to foster a sense of close relationship between teachers and students, providing opportunities of each student group for learning sharing, each student personal psychological caring and belonging, strong teaching leadership resources that are characterized by the presence of a key teaching groups of strong experienced teaching leaders, that compliment the leading the lack experiences teachers, and who how a set of strategic educational objectives outlining what who are to accomplish each course teaching structure, participatory decision-making, characterized by ownership and openness to diverse beliefs and opinions between experienced teachers and lack experienced teachers, classroom space and teaching facilities that will provide flexibility as well as classroom to growth and expansion for the needs (demands) of student numbers increasing.

So, it seems an effective school strategic plan is broad in scope and identifies how a school organization will commit its resources over a pre-selected period. It is a long term plan analyzing and creating objectives to reach a specific set of education goals. When the school strategic plan is incorporated, it involves dividing and assigning the responsibilities of each education task with specified resources and completion target dates. The advantages of planning help schools adapt to changing education environments and specifies to whom the responsibilities belong. It gives a sense of direction for assessing the education market position and establishing education objectives, priorities and strategies to accomplish the education goals with motivation.

For educational strategic planning has these basic steps processes including: the external educational environment analysis internal and external analysis, a clearly defined education mission statement with educational goals and objectives, education formulation and implementation and control. The first stage of development, an education strategic plan is an analysis of the external educational environmental opportunities and threats of an educational organization, (strengths, weaknesses, opportunities, threats) analysis. This external overview includes analysis of the macro environmental forces, educational industry environment and trends. Macro environmental forces including: the political and legal , economic , technological and social forces. For example, school organizations can evaluate which countries economic situation to predict student family financial afford, if the country unemployment ratio is high, it is possible that students need more student loans in the year, if the country technological production industry 's need is much, then it is possible that engineering , computer subjects demand will increase, if the country's political and legal system is stable, it is possible that the low and policy subjects demand will increase. So, schools need to concern whether what external environment is occurring to predict what kinds of demands (needs) of including a schools' resources, mission statement and goals. It also entails the sustained competitive advantage, which is the structure of human (staffs), e.g. teachers, clerks, computer technicians etc. as well as school organizational and physical resources, e.g. classroom facilities, school library, classrooms and offices furniture and computer facilities etc.

The mission statement is the reason for the existence of the organization. Such as school organization mission statement can be providing professional knowledge to prepare students career development, providing reasonable school fees to educate poor students. To be the top university at school world rank, providing high educational quality service to let students to study in an enjoyable environment. Following, schools need to know or plan what which short term plan educational goals and objectives are. For example, goals and objectives will be increased double student number in the end of this year or will be increased double school fee income more than 30% each course and it has no influence to reduce student current enrolling number in the end of year. For long term plan example, goals and objectives will be raised famous and loyal university rank within the 100 rank from world university rank between five and ten years. Finally, the most important reason why any school needs an effective strategic plan. Any school can revise what challenges which will encounter and which can find the reasons why which can not achieve to implement whose original educational goals and objectives and to attempt to find the methods to solve these challenges to achieve which objectives and goals more easily. Even, if the school ensures to achieve its goals and objectives. Strategic plan can let which to find what needs to be improved to adopt to satisfy which potential student needs. Thus, an effective strategic plan can let any school to achieve its objectives and goals more easier as well as to revise and either to find reasons why which can not achieve which objectives and goals or to measure what which needs to do to improve its strategic plan more effective when the school has achieve its objectives and goals ensure. Thus, it seems the school can achieve its objectives and goals more easier in a effective and logic attitude if the school can have an effective strategic plan to predict what challenges it will encounter during its strategic plan achievement process.

● Service organizationsveffectiveness
and efficiency challenges
The service concept plays role in service design and new service development in service or manufacturing industry. The service concept indicates the how and the what of service design and helps mediate between customer needs and an organization's strategic intent.

A service organization can only delivers a service after outsourcing investments in numerous assets, processes, people and materials. Much like manufacturing a product composed of components, services similarly consist of components. However, unlike a product, service components are often not physical entitles, but rather are a combination of processes, people skills and materials that must be appropriately planned or designed service. In designing a new service of redesigning can existing service, service managers must make decisions about each component of the service, from major decisions like facility location to seemingly minor decisions like supervising workers. For even a relatively simple service, numerous decisions are made in taking a new or redesigning service from the idea stage.

In many cases, these processes are ongoing as service organization continue to invest in their physical assets , these processes are of their workforce as well as make changes and improvements. The strategic level to the operational and service encounter levels. A major challenge for service organization is ensuring that decisions each of these levels are made consistently, focused on delivering the reasonable or satisfactory service performance to targeted customers. Any services include physical and non-physical components both. Or do customers need a service as a singular outcome who are seeking when who obtain or purchase the service? e.g. restaurant waiter service, cinema ticket sale service and cinema seat seeking helper etc. Similarly how do service providers (i.e. service employee) provide excellent service attitude to satisfy customer expectation successful, such as one satisfy customer expectation successful, such as one package of restaurant or cinema watching movie of service. Customers have a preconceived notion of what a service is, even who have not experienced it previously (Johnston and Clack, 2001). So, service providers need to provide excellent service performance or attitude to satisfy any customers' real preconceived psychological needs if who hope customers must choose to consume whose service again, e.g. restaurant or cinema service etc. any shopping service consumption choices.

Before, during and after service delivery, service organizations need to arrange excellent service to satisfy consumer's needs or expectations. These expectations relate to the nature of the nature of the service package, as well as to the nature of service, during the service encounters. So, to ensure the service package and service encounter to satisfy the customer's needs and service organization, itself must focus on the design and delivery of whose service concept. Some psychologists indicate service concept has three levels. First, the service concept is how it drives design decisions for new and redesigned services. An organization's definition of its service concept is necessary at the strategic level of planning. Second, who describe how the service concept is useful at the operational level during service concept is useful at the operational level during service design planning, particularly in service strategy into the service delivery system and in determining appropriate performance measures for evaluating service design. Third, who indicate service recovery, one component of service design it used to show the usefulness of applying the service concept in designing and enhancing service encounter interactions. They propose that it is critical to clearly define the service concept before and during the design and development of services. The service concept then serves as a driver of the many decisions made during the design of service delivery systems and service encounters.

Johnston and Clark (2001) further defined the service concept as: service operation is the way in which the service is delivered; service experience is the customer's direct experience of the service; service outcome is the benefits and results of the service for the customer ; and the value of the service is the benefits to the customer perceives as inherent in the service weighed against the cost of the service. So, service concept includes operation, experience, outcome and value four aspects. The service concept is not only defined the how and the what of service design, but also ensures integration between the low and the what. Furthermore, the service concept can also help mediate between customer needs and the organization's strategic intent. One reason for poorly perceived service is the mismatch between what the organization intends to provide (its strategic intent) and what its customers may require to expect (customer needs).

Without a clear and shared understanding of the nature of service to be provided, i.e. the service concept, how can an service manager expect to design a successful service? For example, a car salesperson needs to explain the characteristics and quality and speed and safety issues to let the customer to understand what the functions are for the car. The car salesperson needs to know how to give the excellent customer feedback service to persuade the customer to choose to buy the car easily. So, the role of car salesperson (service provider) who needs to know what the car manufacturing technology, car engines physical facilities and equipment to prepare to give enough information of the car to let the customer to know. Then, the chance of successful sale will be increased.

In conclude, service concept includes these steps: The first step is service strategy, which includes inputs elements, such as staffs, technology, processes, physical facilities and equipment. Next step is service delivery system, which indicates how staffs perform whose service. The, the step is outputs, which include service outcomes and service experience. Finally, the step is performance, whether the performance is efficient and effective as well as how the service provider will measure and will give feedback to its performance. So, service concept is one system process and it is a cycle process.

● Electronic health record system

to health care organization challanges

Why strategic management concept (planning) is needed to apply to any hospital organizations , when which needs to apply electronic health record system to serve client records for administration. Nowadays, these factors have been facilities to new model of health care delivery to hospitals, such as electronic health record (EHR) system. Electronic health records care professionals, health care systems and governments. The use of EHR is growing rapidly in various countries including the UK, the USA, and Australia. Each country has developed its own methods of design, adoption and implementation. However, they face many challenges, particularly relating to interoperability, privacy and security. Thus, health care organizations need have good strategic plan to meet the electronic health record system chance needs to satisfy customer needs for excellent health care service. The strategic plan includes how to describe the definition and features of primary health care service, such as what is the health care service, such as what is the health care organization's core value(s), principle(s), objective(s), and elements of a primary health care system, how to arrange the primary health care team and how to give the benefits and how to solve the challenges of primary health care teams in the health care service organization.

Healthcare is influenced by a range of factors, like new technology, advances in medicine and society expectations. A healthcare delivery system is a way of organizing health services. It is finite resources. So, as patient's expectations grow, it has to be managed effectively and efficiently by government throughout the world. Primarily, healthcare is delivered through primary care centers, which deal with patients whose healthcare can be managed outside of the hospital. Secondary, healthcare is managed in hospital. Tertiary care providers more sophisticated care in specialist medical centers. So, health care strategic plan is needed to designed to follow who will manage it, such as government or hospital or medical centers. For example, to develop the electronic health record system, each health care service organization needs to concern how to apply the electronic health record system to provide the most fast speedy, the most safe and the most excellent quality care to serve patients satisfactory. Health was once defined and thought to be influenced by people's habit relating to lifestyle, exercise, the environment and food (Stanhope & Lancaster, 2000). Later, health was seen only as the freedom from disease (physical or mental). So, patient service is related to physical or mental needs in any health care service organizations usually.

In the future, because electronic health record (EHR) system will be popular to be used to serve patients for any health care service organization, such as clinics, hospitals, medical centers, psychological illness health care clinics etc. It is therefore suggested that political leaders at the Ministry of health need to establish a broad vision for how EHR will be developed in the future. This vision must be influenced by all the main stakeholders. By consulting with these stakeholders and thus involving them in defining the EHRs, it development and maintenance of the EHRs. To ensure that the adoption process runs smooths and never loses direction. It is proposed that government staff should prepare a strategic roadmap, which will enable resources and actions to be prioritized to ensure effectiveness and efficiency. The strategic plan " tool" has become increasingly important in dealing with the continually changing environment of the health care setting. So, it is well placed to monitor the health system for any potential threats or challenges from encountering patients' needs immediately in any hospitals, clinics or medical centers. So, the strategic plan can also be used to coordinate stakeholder involvement, monitor and utilize policy changes, coordinate the involvement of potential users in the design and implementation of potential users in the design and implementation of the electronic health record system, assess and priorities finances and coordinate human resources. So, this health electronic record system will be a popular tool to sustain direction and action for any health care service organization in the future. Hence, any health care service organization need to use electronic health care system to adopt to the new change needs for patient service. As the same time, any health care service organizations' strategic plan ought to follow how to design its health care system to implement its strategic plan, then those health care service organizations will be more easy to achieve whose objectives or goals or missions. So, it means that how to design the health care service organization's electronic health record system. Then, it will know how to implement its strategic plan more easy.

● Benefits of rationalization from strategic plans

Reducing costs and improving service for strategic plan to service organizations

In general, organizations throughout the public and private sectors face to improve support for operations, reduce costs, and improve efficiency. In most, organizations, the costs for operating and managing applications makes up from 75 % to 80% percent of the budget. The emphasis on ongoing portfolio governance, system that cost reduction strategic plan for operational plans to any departments. Application rationalization means : selecting organizational application based on business and prioritizing related actions (choosing what the business will to and what which won't do), effectively managing the value of both existing and proposed applications, monitoring changing priorities and application value in real time, continually reviewing and adjusting as necessary, application inventory is the process of rationalizing the business applications begins with capturing in inventory of all applications currently in use.

One element that characterizes these efforts is that which one usually one-time events marked by a statistic method to collect application data, which results in a new statistic information that is probably different from and unrelated to the one collected 18 months earlier. Some painful meaning analysis is done on the collected data, and a few actions might be taken. The rationalization questions may include: How does the application fit with technical standards? Does staff have the necessary skills set to use it to best advantage? Are users satisfied with its performance and benefits? Are there better alternatives? What are the maintenance costs? Mergers and acquisitions, application rationalization can be performed before and after mergers and acquisitions to assess the best strategic fit. The value and impact to apply rationalization strategic plan method to reduce cost and improve service benefits for operational plans to any departments.

Business process management, application rationalization can provide insights into gaps or redundancies in the current application portfolio, enhancing an application's ability to finish any business process more efficiently. In doing so, the business can introduce innovation products, provide customer service, and manager risk more efficiently and effectively compliance management. Organizations need to know of their application rationalization at its every department from an aggregate compliance score perspective, how to manager the application investment from a lifecycle management perspective.

By consolidation technical strategic plan, organizations are able to reduce the costs of different departments. They provides cost reduction to overall business expenditures which enables new products and technologies that drive the bottom line. For example, vendor price reduction management rationalization can apply efficient management for vendor negotiations by giving them the advantage of a detailed application, e.g. inventory numbers. The risks associated with it, and its business value. Once on an even playing field, the organization can negotiate wisely and put terms into on agreement that place demands back on the vendor to reduce risk or add business value, going way part pursuing price reductions. For another example, prior to outsourcing strategy , experts say organizations should have a good sense of the value of investments, which have already made, the value and risks of outsourcing and specifically what whose money is accomplishing through their outsourcing negotiation. Knowing what assets are in their application portfolio and what services which need to acquire will ensure that business set up the right outsourcing agreement. Next example, audit prioritization and remediation is critical to know which aspects of operations run the highest business and technical risk, so which can be articulated and addressed. An efficient audit solution allows executive to share insight into such risk by enabling them to create a single system of audit and record that gives consistent live view of the business benefits of their application , e.g. inventory numbers. Quantifying these benefits will be specific to the particular organization. For example, if one large insurance company could discover that 15% of its insurance applications could be decommissioned immediately with no impact to its insurance business, resulting in substantial savings. Then, insurance company will choose to spend 37% of its time on maintenance of insurance applications and 63% of its time on new project development, a complete reversal from how the organization divided its time three years ago. Thus, prediction what will occur to cause any business loss or cost increasing that can influence the business have more benefits to decide to spend more time to choose to do the more beneficial projects in order to reduce long term cost spending and raise long term benefits. So, behavioral rationalization can influence the business's correct time spending to which aspects of investment projects to earn more returns.

● Brand strategy

Managers need to consider the customer and other stakeholder with their branding efforts to make appropriate making decisions because brands is such at the strategic organizational assets. Management at this valuable asset needs to strategic thinking and position. The fast innovation, increased service levels and diminishing brand loyalty characterizing today's marketplaces have led to corporate branding becoming a strategic marketing tool (Xie and Boggs, 2006).

A successful brand can be defined an identifiable product, service, person or place augmented in such a way that the buyer or user perceives relevant, unique added values which match their needs most closely. What kinds of product brand can influence consumer choice? For example, product like milk, tin, iron ore and potatoes , vegetables come to mind where purchase decisions tend to be taken on the basis of price or availability and not on the expensive products brand can influence consumer choice, e.g. cars , wash machines, televisions , air conditioners etc. manufacturing products.

Conceptually, branding appears to be a necessary means of building sales by identifying products and services. Branding is the initial means to build consumer awareness by naming the offer, but also by distinguishing the offer from other similar products or services within an established category. Branding is about being different (Kay, 2006). When a company can create strong brand , it can attract customer preference and company is more protected against a company initiatives, and company can plan a growth through the penetration of new markets. So, if a business can have a strong brand, it can ensure a company's long-term success in possible. It can create goodwill value in consumption market to influence each consumer choice when who needs to buy the kind of manufacturing product. A brand combines physical and psychological element both. The physical aspect creates the linkage between differentiating them from other enterprises or products. The psychological aspect of a brand constitutes the maintenance of uniformity in terms of communications, guarantees ad behaviors as well as consistency and conformity to particular requirements (Chovancova, 2012).

Brand strategy refers to the ways that firms mix and match their brand's name on their products and a firms through its products, presents itself to the world. Corporate brand strategy must be developed to deliver the highest gains to all stakeholders and corporate public (Shahri, 2011). The brands as strategic assets and resources of competition advantages for organizations in changing and high competition world need to strategic attention and consideration from them. Strategic management organizational strengthens and weaknesses (internal factors) and environmental opportunities and threats (external factors) and environmental opportunities and threats (external factors). Also, strategic brand management can be viewed from these internal (identify) and external (image) perspective. So, establishment of balance is needed between the brand identity and image , e.g. LG brand mobile phones will be built different attractive mobile images, e.g. mobile phone products design of any model choices as well as correct identity attributes ,e.g. music sound choices attributes, internet attributes, phone call attributes by the LG brand mobile phone manufacturer. So, the suggested LG brand models can help multi-business companies operating and guideline to selection and choice of LG mobile phone branding strategy to enter the global competition mobile phone sale market, e.g. mobile phone mature market , e.g. Hong Kong, US, UK, mobile phone potential (developing market) , e.g. India, Africa.

It is evident that this LG brand different model mobile phone products can be chosen to enter to emerging or developing markets. It can be a proper guidance to individual (single) mobile phone business companies (from developed) economies entering to emerging or developing economies or companies operating in emerging markets. So, LG brand mobile phone can have the strength of relationship between influencing factors and choice of branding strategy is moderated by other situation-dependent influences if it chose to join to be another brand of mobile phone partner. Because of broader the stakeholders' interest, the LG non famous brand mobile phone firm can operate in emerging markets , e.g. US market more likely will phone corporate branding with any one famous brand mobile phone firm in US.

In emerging market, such as US mobile phone brand market, there are many different stakeholders that affect LG brand mobile phone organization enters to US mobile phone market. In this US mobile phone market , corporate image is emphasized by stakeholders more and more, therefore entrants from developed countries , such as US, is possible to choose corporate branding more likely. Developing economies experience political and legal instabilities daily, as a result, it can be suppose that corporate branding can manage these instabilities and decrease their effects. Because lack of valid and reliable information , media and other communication channels to Korea , LG brand mobile phone company, the marketing costs are very high in developing economies , such as Korea and companies prefer corporate branding strategy with US any one famous brand mobile phone company. So, such as one Korea, non famous LG brand mobile phone company which can choose to enter the developed country, such as US market to corporate with any one famous brand mobile phone company to build corporate brand strategy if which believed its LG brand mobile models have unique functions (attributes), when US any famous brand mobile phone companies' models of mobile phones have lack of these unique functions from LG brand mobile phone products.

● Human resource plans to space
exploration organization

The European space exploration decides on investment in space science. I shall indicate how it is carrying on implementing strategic human resource plan presence in space mission to achieve its space exploration aim. Application-oriented space programs, such as telecommunications, navigation and Earth observation are fully served by robotic (i.e. fully automated) satellites. Where a strategic human resource presence plan would be demanded environmental requirement of these state-of-the art instruments. Yet the exploration of the nearby solar system , for example, the Moon and Mar mission may be conducted in principle by either robotic vehicles and/or a human presence. Hence, an excellent strategic human resource plan is really needed if European space exploration expected its space exploration mission can be success. To justify future space exploration, especially in the area where robotic and human spaceflight capabilities overlap. To provide guidance, we must examine some strategy aspects of this potentially powerful robot-human partnerships long-term strategic human partnership plan.

Scientific enquiry(including life and engineering sciences), broader consideration of technology and economy as well as more philosophical and political aspects. European space exploration must need different international scientists cooperation from different scientific professionals to cooperate to research different scientific skills to achieve space exploration more easily. Because European space exploration mission is expected to earn economic and societal benefits of funding pure science and space science missions. Indeed, a strategic human resource plan for the cost share between robotic and manned missions in European space exploration, capitalizing on technological advance and international cooperation, but without negative impacting the future of pure scientific research, would be highly desirable. Hence international different scientists need to cooperate to achieve this space science exploration mission more easily. First European space exploration needs have clear strategic plan for human space flight missions. Such as: achieving scientific, political, and commercial activities dealing with the Earth, e.g. meteorology, climate , resources, communications, navigation, military and surveillance, achieving activities related to the exploration of the solar systems typically scientific , and which may be either robotic or manned. Thus, European policies and activities are needed reasonable well focused and organized of with the selections of missions in each of areas being determined by evolving scientific developments and commercial priorities, when European needs to cooperate with some space exploration countries, such as China, England, Japan, US, India etc. countries. For example, an objective and strategic consideration of some aspects of the future of solar system exploration might begin process with a significant impact on long-term European ambitions and policies.

European space exploration needs to consider how to develop a strategic view. The term space exploration represents to extension of human reach beyond the Earth's atmosphere using spacecraft to access unknown environments and to acquire knowledge about space planets, stars by human and robotic means.

From a purely scientific perspective, the exploration of the solar system mission is such as, understanding the formation of the solar system and of the Earth, and questions of plane more generally. It also addresses questions related to he beginning of life on Earth, and the search for evidence for (past) life and biological activity, elsewhere in the solar system and beyond.

From a human space flight perspective, space exploration mission represents the outward continuation of Earth based exploration, which has advanced over many centuries. These activities, ranging from the Apollo program, the current international space station activities, and future plans for manned missions to Mars have a strong impact on the public, at the same time, associated costs are very large.

From long term plan, from a economical benefit human space flight perspective, European space exploration organization objectives include: To raise students knowledge and learning to understand the solar system and of the universe as whole, to assist university to increase space science course (subjects school fee income and to encourage student numbers to choose to study this space exploration course (subjects as well as provides many different kinds of space exploration job chance for students space science employment market, for civilized and advanced society for universities education, employers capital investment and research to earn long term economic benefits to overall European economic development; space science research is as an extension of the pursuit of pure research , entirely unexpected and unpredictable economic development can eventually deliver substantial benefits to European society, and related economic dividend, more calculated approaches to exploiting potential arising from space research are being increasingly well coordinated.

Space technology transfer program (and its associated business incubations center), for example, has been set up to share the benefits of its research and development, making space sector technologies available to European industry, technology development has more immediately, space exploration provides new challenges, requiring the direct development of new technologies. These technological development can create new possibilities for innovation and economic growth , spanning business opportunities for industry as well as access to new resources. This provides the strong motivation both for politicians and tax payers to commit to their very high costs, space exploration encourages industrial development return is the strong industrial interest to develop large-scale facilities and capabilities for space exploration, space exploration has the capability of spectacularly demonstrating national and international capabilities, and has the potential of fostering international cooperation in ambitions projects of international human resource cooperation . At the same time, industrial countries and Europe as a whole, do not want to be left behind in the commercial aspects of space exploration, but rather want to be considered as viable collaborative partners by other space faring countries and organizations . For Europe, this means maintaining a level of space exploration know how such that other key players (USA, Japan, China, Russia, as well as emerging investors like India and Brazil) consider that it provides. Thus, European space exploration needs different countries scientists cooperation to achieve space business objectives, space research objectives, space education objections. It needs have human resources strategic plan to assist to any related space technological aspect research if European expected its space exploration mission can be achieves on one day. Thus, strategic human resource plan is very important to European space exploration organization.

For strategic human resource plan, I shall indicate these aspects as below:

In the area of human health, international space station (ISS) research is providing in the understanding of ageing, disease and the environment. Biological and human investigations have provided an improved understanding of basis physiological processes normally masked by gravity and the development of new medical technology driven by the need to support telemedicine, disease models, psychological stress response systems, nutrition, cell behavior and environmental health . So, human strategic plan needs this medical, biological, environmental health, psychological health, medicine, cell behavior, nutrition scientists employees in the world. In the area of micro-gravity science, the ISS has been central to the understanding of many phenomena in life sciences and technology.

In the area of human flight element of the European space program. It has become a reliable facility, with experiments that can be planned with experiments that can be planned with some confidence of execution. Fields now covered include micro-gravity research, medical and engineering sciences, chemistry, material developments, and fluid physics with the number of experiments carried out having increased substantially over recent years. The European program for life and physical sciences has produced many advanced in a variety of scientific disciplines since its inception in 2001 year, since the bulk of the substantial infrastructure costs for in the past, its use for science, which has been greatly improved in recent years, should continue to be optimized.

Thus, European space exploration human strategic plan can't only concentrate on flight (aviation) technology space professionals. It needs to seek other professionals, such as medical, psychology, science, biology, cell science, environment protection, life science , chemistry etc. professionals. Because this organization's mission is not only space science exploration, it includes other are related to space exploration research. If European space exploration only concentrate on researching space exploration, it will have risk , due to it spends existing funding be diverted from robotic missions to the intrinsically, even more expensive human space exploration program, single space exploration is much risk more than variety space exploration, e.g. space medicine, space medical, space tourism, space nature resource exploration, space cells exploration etc. different related space exploration businesses. Thus, strategic plan can't only concentrate on Moon or Mars space exploration . Because space has much potential business opportunities to let human to discover to gain any new business benefits to human.

In the future, human space exploration possible mission will include: defining the infrastructure priorities for servicing and cargo transportation whether by Ariane 5, by Soyuz launched from Centre Spatial Guyanais (CSG) , or by other commercial vehicles, strategically maintaining the options for human access to low Earth orbit more effective exploitation of the ISS for the physical , life science, engineering science and by the scientific community more generally (for example, involving announcements of opportunity for engineering sciences, articulating the role of the ISS in terms of human biology, especially in the context of future missions to the Moon or Mars, defining more what the ISS can contribute to the long term development of human space flight (such transportation systems, robot-human interfaces, and advanced life-support systems, expanding and enhancing its capabilities for education , which the astronauts on board have undertaken with great success, and further publishing its scientific work and potential. Finally, how to reduce risk cost to space exploration, as soon as human space flight is considered the currently accepted wisdom is that risk to human life (in terms of launchers, survival systems, space tool and return to Earth) must be suppressed to extremely low levels of profitability. For example, the lowing possibility of a factor from 10% to 1% might increase the cost by a factor of 10 or more, but whether the formal probability estimates, significant advances in space exploration will always carry some risk to human life quantifying these risks will always be. However, difficult but a comparison with the historical levels of risk as commercial aviation development might provide a useful guide. Thus, why not single space exploration business (related space science businesses) can reduce risk as well as European and other countries space exploration cooperation can bring human benefits more than European (single) space exploration business investment. Thus, global strategic human resource plan must be need to European space exploration business.

Why does organizational development need strategic plan? Strategic plan is similar with a pyramid planning. At the low level of strategies/ tactics operations: How will the organization accomplish its goals? At the middle level of goals/ objectives direction: what does the organization want to achieve? At the top level of principles beliefs: What does the organization mission and purpose? Why does the organization exist?

A well-developed strategic plan describes a vision for the future, strengths and weaknesses of the organization, the nature of the changes for sustainable growth and development, the sequence of these changes, those who are responsible for guiding change, the resources required, whether which currently exist within the organization or must be generated from external resources.

In a strategic plan, it consists mission , such as what we hope to accomplish , capabilities, resources, strengths and weaknesses, such as what you are capable of doing. Opportunities and threats , include needs of clients, and stakeholders, competitors and social , economic , political and technological forces. When all elements combine the strategic plan can be the fit. Long term strategic plan needs usually 5 to 10 years, focuses of future achievement, weighs a series of alternatives to make choices, resources mobilization with activities, operational plan needs short term (one year or less) , achievement to targets annual, alternatives are not considered, tend focus one unit or related such of activities, no formal action.

- The direction between business

and tactic models and tactics

Nowadays, business model has been used by strategy to refer to the logic of the firm, the way it operates and how it creates value for its stakeholders. What is the relationship between business model and strategy? Can business model reflect a clear separation between tactics and strategy. This distinction is possible because strategy and business model are different constructs.

Any strategy can help a firm to learn to analyze its competitive environments defined its position, develops competitive corporate advantages and understands threats to sustaining advantage in the face of challenging competitive threats. However, external environment changing (variable) factor can influence a firm's development. Such as globalization, deregulation to technological change. So, any firm can't neglect to change to compete differently and innovate in its business model. For examples, IBM computer firm's 2006 year and 2008 year " Global CEO study", showed that top management in a broad range of computer industries are actively seeking guidance on how to innovate to its computer business model to improve its ability to both create and capture value.

Advances in information and communication technologies have driven the recent interest on business model innovation. Many e-businesses constitute new business models. Of course, not all business model innovations are IT driven; other forces , such as globalization and deregulation, have also resulted in new business models and fed the interest on this area. In fact, socially motivated enterprises that aim to reach the bottom of the pyramid constitute an important source of business model innovations. In truth, there is not yet agreement on what are the distinctive features of super business models. We believe that the dispute has arisen, because of lack of clear distinction between the strategy and business model and tactics.

Business model refers to the logic of the firm, the way, it operates and how it creates value of its stakeholders. Strategy refers to the choice of business model through which the firm will compete in the marketplace. Tactics refers to the residual choices open to a firm by the business model that it employs. What is the difference between the concepts of strategy , business models and tactics? In the first stage, firms need to choose a login of value creation and value capture (chose their business model). In the second stage, firms make tactical choices guided by their goals (in most cares, goals expect some form of stakeholder value maximization). So, the object of strategy is the choice of business model and the business model employed determines the tactics available to the firm to compete against, or cooperate with other firms in the marketplace. However, any business needs to know how the connection between strategy and business model and tactics can be clearly separated.

How to define a good business model? Two questions need to concern to answer : who is the customer and what does the customer value? what is the economic to customers at an appropriate cost? My idea is that business model refers to the logic by which that any business model should answer, one related to related to the value provided to the customer and the other to the organization's ability to capture value in the process of serving customers. For example, e-business can be an innovative technological business model to value chain analysis, the resource-based view of the firm, dynamic capabilities, transaction cost economies and strategic network. So, why business model is the first stage to design before strategy and tactics achievement.

Business model is similar to machine logic of operation system: any machine has a particular logic of operation (the way, the different components are assembled and related to one another), it runs in a particular way and in operating, it creates value for whomever uses it. For example, every automobile has a particular logic of operation, conventional automobiles operate quite differently than hybrids, and standard transmission automobiles. Different automobile models create different value for their stakeholders, the drivers. Some drivers may prefer standard transmission. Others may prefer a small car that allows them to easily navigate the streets of a congested city, others may prefer a powerful explosion engine to enjoy the countryside to the fullest. Different operation and create different value for their drivers. Likewise, to better understand business models, one needs to look at their component parts and understand how who relate to one another: The question arises: What are business models made of? I contend that business models are composed of two different elements. The concrete choices are made by management on how the organization must operate and the consequences of the choices both.

In fact, choices may include compensation, policy, contracts decision making, outsourcing decision, location of facilities, assets employed, extent of vertical integration, or sale and marketing methods. Every choice has consequence. For example, the provision of high-powered incentives (a choice) has implications regarding the willingness to exert effort or to cooperate with workers (consequences). Likewise, pricing policies (choices) regard sale volumes, affect the economies of scale and bargaining power is enjoyed by the firm both (two consequences).

In strategic plan view point, I indicate three types of choices: polices, assets and governance structure. Policies refer action that the firm adopts for all aspects of its operation, e.g. unions complain dealing, locating plants in rural or city areas choice, encouraging employees to fly tourist class, providing fee shares, bonus monetary incentives, or flying to secondary airports as a way to cut expenses to employee welfare. Asset refers to tangible resources, such as manufacturing facilities, a satellite system for communicating between offices or the use of a particular aircraft model by an airline. Governance of assets and policies refers to the structures of contractual arrangements that confer decision rights for policies or assets. For example, a given business model may contain as a choice to the certain assets, such as a fleet of tracks. The firm can own the fleet or lease it from a third part. The transaction cost economies can reduce the firm to pay asset purchase expenditure at same time because it only pay rent to lease to the fleet of trucks per month.

So, business model is as the logic of the firm, the way , it operates and how it creates value for its stakeholders. The make operational , we argue that business models are composed of choices (policies, assets, governance) and the consequences derived from the choices. For example, Ryanair airline business model includes: flying to secondary airports as lowest ticket prices, low commissions to travel agents, standarized fleet of Boeing 737s,treating all passengers equally, high powered incentives, none meals, nothing free. Consequences of these choices are: secondary airport changes low airport fees, lowest ticket prices can sell large volume, low commissions cost charges to travel agents, standardized fleet of Bosing 737 s has bargaining power with suppliers, all passengers treated equally to achieve economic of scale, high powered incentives to attract combative team, none meals provision to cause faster turnaround, nothing free causes addition revenue, headquarter is low fixed cost, and no unions will be flexibility.

Ryanair airline business model is similar to a machine is assembled and how it works. There are many ways in which a machine to performance a given task can be designed and assembled: Different levels of specific mechanisms, quality of components. Different machine have different direct consequences to affect the overall level of efficiency of the machine (speed, input, efficiency, noise, quality of output) etc. Other airlines are assembled differently than Ryanair airline , which have a different logic , a different way to operate and to create value for their stakeholders. These different ways to put together airlines correspond to different business models. In the case of Ryanair airline, the business model will have three cycles. The first cycle is : The lowest fares causes low quality service expected, to cause none meals, to cause low variable cost and to cause the consequence of lowest fares fare. The second cycles is: The lowest fare causes large volume, to cause high aircraft utilization, to cause low fixed cost/passenger, and to cause the consequence of lowest fares again. The third cycle is: The lowest fares causes large volume, to cause bargaining power with supplier, to cause low fixed fares again.

It is important to evaluate different cycles consequences. If the consequences are valuable , cycles develop valuable resources and capabilities. For example, as Ryanair airline's volume increases because of its low fares, bargaining power with its suppliers (airport authorities, Boeing, Airbus) grows resulting in improvement in Ryanair airline's advantage.

In fact, every organization has some business models. This is because organization makes some choices and these choices have the some consequences. Of course, this does not mean that every business model is satisfactory or even viable in long run. Some authors indicated business model has four elements: a customer value proposition, a profit formula, key resources ,and key processes. So, business model can articulate the value proposition. It can identify a market segment, if can define the structure of the value chain. It can estimate the cost structure and profit potential. How business model design involves assessment with respect to determine. It includes that the identify of market segment to be targeted, the benefits to rise to the enterprise will deliver to the clients, the technologies and features that are of the product and service, how the revenue and cost structure of a business design to meet client need, the way in which technologies are to be offered to the client. So, every organization will choose to decide how to determine the logic of the firm , the way in operates and how it creates value for its shareholders.

Tactics refers to the residual choices open to a firm of the business model that it employs. For example, for newspaper publishing's choice of tactics. A newspaper publishing firm can't change price of the newspaper because its business model is ad-sponsored and the newspaper must be sold at zero price. Put differently the newspaper publishing business model precludes from using "price of the newspaper" as a variable that can be changed depending on the intensity of competition and other external factors. Thus, price of the newspaper is not part of the newspaper publishing business's set of tactics. For another example, some business school for MBA student, every student gets a personalized MBA curriculum, depending on whose background and professional goals. Some business schools used in many of the school's executive education programs with several faculty members co-teaching the core courses and with assets, such as classrooms, with set up for case discussions for large groups educational method; another some business schools are impossible to provide similar education methods which business model do not have as an element in whose tactical set the offering of a tailored MBA course.

These business schools modify whose businesses models. So that those tactical choices would become available, but with the current businesses models, which are not possible for them to match the other business schools' similar business models for education method to MBA course. We conclude that different business models give rise to different tactics available for competition and /or cooperation. However, tactical play an important role in determining how and value is created and captured by firms. For newspaper publishing industry example, advertising rates and the precise number of ads. displayed in the free newspaper and up affecting the readership and advertising revenues. So, likewise, of some free charge newspaper publishing's advertising rate increases, fewer advertisers with want to advertise in these free charge newspaper publishing's revenue, profit and value capture. Therefore, not only the business model employed by the firm determines factor, but also tactics play a central role in how much value the firm will be able to create and capture of the end of the day.

Tactical interaction refers to the way organizations affect each other by acting within the bounds set by their business models. Using this imagery of business model, representations, tactical interaction occur when one firm's business model is in contact will that of another firm. When this happens, there are consequences in both firms business models, where feedback to be determined not only by the focal firms choices, but by the choices of the other firm as well. For a discount retailer store example, it competes with another local retailer store, both engage in a tactical pricing competition to win customers. The interaction between the discounted and the non-discounted retailer stores can be captured to display both business models connected at market share. In this example of discount retailer stores and non-discount retailer stores, when both stores use prices in their tactical interaction. The discount retailer stores bring superior weapons to fight because of the business model that it employs to compete.

Specially, the range of prices, discount retailer stores can profitably set is much broader the profitability other non-discount retailer store competitors with a high cost operating model. So, the non-discount retailer stores can choose to sell the products or foods at higher or non-discounted price. When the discount retailer stores lack to sell whose same of similar products or foods. It means cooperation retail method of tactical interaction will be needed in this store retail market.

Strategy is often defined as a contingent plan of action designed to achieve a particular goal. Strategy is the creation of a unique and valuable position, involving a different set of activities. Creation implies choice of the particular way in which the firm competes. So, strategy is not the activity system itself, but the creation of the activity system itself, but the creation of the activity system. So, strategy refers in our development, for the contingent plan as to what business model to use. Strategy in a higher order choice that has profound implications on competitive outcomes. Choosing a particular business model means choosing a particular way to compete, a particular logic a particular way to compete, a particular logic of the firm, a particular way to operate and to create value for the firm's stakeholders. For example, model means choosing a particular way to compete, particular logic of the firm, a particular way to operate and to create value for the firm's stakeholders. For Ryanair airline example, it was encountering bankruptcy in the early 1990 year, its strategy was a plan of action to transform its airline business model from that of a standard full-service (through small) airline to a radically different one by adopting the Southwest's no-frills business model. In the mid 1990 year , after the transformation had taken place, Ryanair airline strategy. Ryanair 's top management considered four alternative plans of action to solve bankruptcy challenge. (1) becoming the Southwest of Europe, (2) Adding business class , (3) Becoming a feeder airline operating from Shannan 's airport, or (4) Existing the airline industry. Each of the entailed a different business model, a different logic of the airline firm, the way , it operates and how it creates value for its stakeholder. The high level election of becoming the Southwest of Europe (as opposed to adding business class or operating as a feeder airlines was strategy (a plan of action to create a unique and valuable position, involving a different set of activities).

Furthermore, the particular way in which Ryanair airline executed such plans was its realized strategy. The resulting new Ryanair airline with its new logic, new way to operate, and new way to create value for its stakeholders , was business model. What is the different between business model and strategy? A firm's business model is a reflection of its realized strategy. What do organization gain from having two separate concepts. There is the choice of business model because, there is a over time mapping from strategy onto business models. This means business model, an outside observer knows the firm's strategy. Some authors felt the substantive different between strategy and business models arises when the firm's plan of action calls for modifications to the business model (changes in policies and/ or assets and/or governance) when particular contingencies take place. However, there are many possible sources of contingencies upon which strategies may be based. One such source is the realization of an event outside the control of the firm. For example, one contingency the many firm are currently considering is the possibility of a recovery from the recession. Firms have plans as to how their business models must be kept of a strong economic recovery (changes in polities, asset, and/or governance). Such as plans are part of firms' strategies.

How will business model be changes by firm's strategy? What is a strategy in this economic recession situation? so, business model is prior to achieve any strategic plans. It is a logic organization design or mind to prepare to achieve any strategic plans as well as tactical operation plans. Has it difference between strategy and strategic management? When reviewing strategic thinking , using realize how this phenomenon differs in any organizations. In military view point, strategy can be used in a military campaigns. It means a way of prevailing over the adversary, a fool of victory i war . In organization view point, strategy can be applied to human relations, political, economics, business. The concept of strategy has evolved into a field of knowledge in management. Otherwise, strategy management, with content, concepts and practical reasoning, role in the academic and business fields.

Whether do concept of strategy and strategic management are understood by business managers? What is strategy and strategic management to future managers? Are who understood and recognized? To answer these two questions? We need to seek these specific objectives. (i) To build a model explaining the definition of strategy (ii) To identify which concept of strategic management in the literature. To understand these difference of two concepts. We need to adopt organizational phenomenon in different situations. In this case, the development of organizational strategy depends on what strategy and strategic management depend on understanding the perceptions of their managers on what strategy and strategic management actually is. It concerns how to predict consumer behaviors. In the field of strategy, managers represent an innovation, and a new alternative for research.

Strategy and strategic management concepts can be explained what differ from historical perspective. In any enterprises, creating and managing strategic enable them to meet the challenges of the market, reaching their objectives in the short, medium and long term. Strategic concerns great development within the corporate environment. Phenomena , such as corporate restructuring , joint decisions and actions impacting on organization size, financing were driven by the technological advance in means of communication and transport and an interactive dynamic global level have become predominant. Nowadays, thinking strategically has acquired the status of a factor in leading and managing organizations, whether for profit or otherwise. After all, strategy addresses the link between the inner world of business and its external environment.

Considering strategy is as a business logic rational and sequential, to the most dynamic that understand this process is as associated with cultural and learning factors, political and power relations. Strategy is not only one way of dealing in competition environment or market, as treated not only summarize the ideas, proposal, guidelines, indicative of paths and solutions. It has the concept of operational efficiency. In summary, strategy is what matters for the effectiveness of the organization, the external point of view, which stresses the research of the objectives against the environment, in term of internal stresses, the balance communication between members of the organization and a willingness contribute towards actions and the achievement of the common objectives; it is a series of actions to a particular situation, it is analyzing the present situation and changing it whenever necessary. It is the determinant of the basis long term goals of a firm and the adoption of action how to allocate resource necessary for carrying out these goals; it is a rule for making decisions determined by product/market scope, growth competitive advantage and synergy, it is addition of the decisions taken by an organization in all aspects , as much commercial as structural with the learning process to management, it is the directional action decisions to achieve firm's objectives. Hence, strategy is long term or short term plan to aim to achieve any missions or objectives for any organizations.

Otherwise, strategic management defines key attributes: directed towards the overall organization objectives, includes multiple stakeholders in decision making, requires incorporating short and long term perspectives and involves the recognition of trade offs between effectiveness and efficiency. Strategy management is as an ongoing process involving the efforts of strategic managers to adjust the organization to the environment in which it operates when developing competitive advantages. These competitive advantages enable the company to seize opportunities and minimize environmental threats. It is a broad term that includes determining the mission and objective of the organization in the external and internal environment.

● Strategic communication plan

How can organizational communication influence effectiveness and efficiency? What are the most effective pathways for delivering organizational messages to priority audiences? Is it the suitable media? Face-to-face meeting? Direct mail? The internet ? How will organization deliver message efficiently?

Without a plan to guide organizational communication activities, the organization runs the risk of focusing on the wrong audiences, of using messages that simply do not work. In other words, without a well-thought-through plan, your organization runs the risk of becoming irrelevant with key audiences, even of failing to meet organizational mission.

How to strategic communication plan? Your organization needs to proactively focus the activities of your organization, where there is the greatest potential for success; ensures your limited resources (time and financial most effectively applied) imposes discipline and clear thinking about why it is the best interest for your communication method to your organization to pursue certain communication initiatives; to integrate all of your public relations efforts; media, government, donor to corporate etc. ; to ensure that every member in your organization staff board, volunteers are on the same level fairly, to achieve results that more your members towards realizing your organization's goals and to encourage creative thinking about new ways to address old challenges.

So, communication plan is simply a written statement that outlines communication goals, provides some situational analysis and proposes approaches and activities to achieve the identified goals given the identified current situation. An effective communication plan can be set out the timeframe for carrying and these activities, details the resources and supports that will be necessary to achieve your organizational goals, and identifies how results will be measured. It can be a summary document of only a few pages or a 40 pages on more. Part of length and depth of a plan depends on whether it is a five year organizational plan or a plan designed to support a particular campaign or strategic goal. In the private and government sectors, communication plans are typically development on support of detailed organizational strategic plan. In the non-profit aim organization sector, it is most common to see strategic communication plans as a organizational and communication planning processes. An effective strategic communication plan focuses on many different ways of reaching all of the external and internal audiences, your organization will need to hear your messages.

How to create communication plan for your organization to improve: the ability to create a strong and positive reputation for your organization and public relations; building relationship and reputation with the media and with reputation with government at all levels; building relationship with employees and volunteer, e.g. internal communications; ability to attract an maintain strong donor support relations; building sponsorship and funding opportunities with business corporate relations; building organization's policies and direction board-staff relations; outreach about programs and services (constituency any client relations).

How to build morals within team by communication plan? Establishing goals to staff and volunteers, understanding every staff can meet is energized and ready to take on more ambitious goals. Communication plan aims to effective facilities meetings, a creative brainstorm and a focus group. Organizing effective communication plan has these stages: Stage one includes that defining organization goals, defining communication objectives, situation analysis to organizational background and external environment. Stage two includes that determining who your organizational audiences are and what messages are delivered before you move to messages. Stage three determining what your organization strategies , what tactics are. Stage four, evaluation of ideas for strategies and tactics, implementation budget before investing time in developing the timing and timeline sections, identifying certain strategic and tactics resources, producing multiple communication opportunities having a communication plan will make it easier to determine whose to allocate limited resources.

How to develop strategic environment plan? It will largely be determined by the level of buy-in that key staff and board have for the plan. Buy-in is easiest to achieve when staff have had a role in developing the plan and feel some level of ownership of ideas contained within it. All of the pieces of a communication plan are represented in the following pages. They have been laid and in a logical order by moving from organizational goals to situation analysis to audiences and messages.

- Reasons need strategic plan

Why organizations need strategic plan

American Management Association defines and differentiates between strategy, policy and objective. It indicates that policies get procedures into roles. Strategies get into tactics, resulting in an-end-means. For example, it supposes a company decides upon a sales growth of between 35 and 45 per cent and desires to achieves this by acquiring other companies, instead of introducing new products, instead of introducing new products. So, it seems strategic plan can help organization has ability to predict how to achieve its strategy to achieve sale growth aim.

For example, acquisition can be considered as a strategy is chosen by the company. The company will then have to decide on the size of the firm to be required. If it decides on acquiring a small company. This becomes the objectives. In general, strategy means the determination of the basic long term goals and objectives of an enterprise and the adoption of the action and the allocation of resources necessary for carrying out these goals.

In micro organization view, strategy is the pattern of objectives and plans for achieving these goals, purposes and goals and the major policies and plans for achieving these goals stated in such a way, so it is defined what business, the company is in or is to be and the kind of company, it is or is to be. Also, some authors define a strategy is a set of decision-making rules for the guidance of organizational behaviors. Because firm's internal and external environment change over time, the strategy also changes consequently, the idea that strategy is dynamic.

Otherwise, in macro organization view, strategic management is a science of choosing the alternatives from the designed and available actions. The managers have to decide on a process that will be most suitable to their conditions and what could enable them to achieve a desired position of their organization in overall. Large organizations which use detailed strategic management models whereas smaller businesses concentrate on planning steps compared to larger companies in the same industry. In short, the most highly rated benefits of strategic management are: charity of strategic vision for the organization, focus on what is strategically important to the organization, better understanding of the rapidly changing business environment.

- What is strategic management?

How can strategic management assist organizational development? Some management psychologists indicate any large organizational participant members needed to be trained a widely varying traditions, some in economic departments, some in strategic management departments, some is organizational behavior, some in marketing etc. departments. Trained strategic management organizations can be more efficiently and effectively to compare to non-trained strategic management organizations.

Exactly what is it? Strategic management owning organizations can know how to raise internal strengths and reduce internal weaknesses as well as can know how to predict or avoid external threats occur and absorb or raise opportunities more easily.

Strategic management can be assumed that scientific knowledge is socially constructed and is the fundamental medium that makes that social construction possible. What are the differences between strategic management organization and non strategic organization? We were interested in identifying the fundamental definition , not the monetary fashions or cycles of the field, such as micro-organizational behavior or human resource to explain what differences are between of them.

In an effort to distinguish strategic management organizations from other subfields of management organizations, consideration of how strategic management differs from or relates to other academic fields, such as economy, marketing or sociology. We would have liked to include strategy-oriented organizations from these other related field, but which are too rare to allow the type of analysis we conducted.

Has it relationship between strategic management and top management team, capital intensity and market structure. We need to examine these existing definitions and comparing them to conceptual categories. Some management professionals defined strategic management is as imputed from the distinction of the field: The field of strategic management deals with the major intended and emergent initiatives, involving utilization of resources, enhancing the performance to their external environments. They also indicated six elements make up the definition of the fields of strategic management. The first definitional element is the major intended and emergent initiatives, such as strategy, acquisition and diversification, which refer to relatively deliberate, planned initiatives, but it also includes such as learning, and innovation, which represent the move emergent activities that occur in a firm. The second definitional element is taken by general managers on behalf of owners to concern the key actors who are the focus of attention strategy research. Terms such CEO, directors, board represents the upper level. The third definitional element is involving utilization of resources that managers use in their strategic initiatives, e.g. capability and knowledge represent the resources that are internal to the firm, whereas, terms , such primarily as ties resources that link the firm to its environment and the performance. The fourth element is enhanced the performance, conceptualizes the key objectives or outcomes that are of interest to strategic management scholars, e.g. growth performance to achieve advantages. The fifth definition element indicates firms which reflects the focal unit of analysis of strategic management. Finally, the sixth element is in their external environments and is represented by market competitor and industry, which refer to the immediate environment of a firm as well as by uncertainty environment contingency, which indicate a potentially broader external context.

Porter Michael (1986) , long time Harvard professor and editor of the Harvard Business Review, published the first edition of the competitive strategy, who explained "strategy means the pattern of decision in a company that determines and reveals its objective purposes or goals, produces the principal policies and plans for achieving these goals, and defines the range of business the company is to pursue, the kind of economic and human organization, it is or intends to be, and the nature of the economic and non-economic contribution it intends to make to its shareholders, employees, customers, and communities".

In the military, the strategy for a battle refers to a general plan of attack or defense. In civil terms, strategy is concerned with the deployment of resources, this is amounts to the allocation of resources. Tactics, then is concerned with the employment of resources already deployed. In the civilian sector, this equates to operations in the board sense of the terms. Generally speaking, tactical re-expected to occur in the context of strategy, so as to ensure the attainment of strategic intent. However, strategy can fail end, when it does tactics dominate the action. Execution becomes strategy. Thus, it is always one part intended (the plan as conceived beforehand) and one part emergent (on adaption to the conditions encountered). As a consequence, there are always two versions of a given strategy: (1) strategy is as intended and (2) strategy (c) realized.

In fact, a strategy or general plan of action might be formulated for broad, long-term corporate goals and objectives, for more specific business goals and objectives, or for a functional unit, even one as small as a cost center. Such goals might or might not cause the nature of the organization, its culture. The kind of company its leadership wants it to be the markets, it will or won't enter. The basic on which it will compete or any other attribute quality or characteristic of the organization. Because strategies can do exist at various levels of the organization, it is conceivable and appropriate for the corporation to have a strategic plan , for a business unit to have one too, and for a functional unit to have one. Strategic plan can import to all organizational levels. So, it is intended to address matters of great importance. For those concerned with the enterprise, strategic issues, initiatives and plans are those that affect the entire enterprise is important ways. So the top, middle and low levels ought need to have short term and long term strategic plans to implement.

What is the direction and destination of the firm? Where is it headed and what is it to become? Not all strategic issues are long term, although may be. A short term crisis can be of strategic significance and should be dealt with accordingly.

Plans of action, whether for business always have two fundamental aspects: ends and means . What is to be achieved and how it is to be achieved? What are the firm's future results, e.g. goals, aims , targets or objectives consequences . Firms can choose either program or action or step or initiative to achieve enterprise level or business unit level or functional level future result. Those combination of ends and means firm can find any plans in all these levels of organizations. Strategies are too exist at all three levels. Consequently, one can and should find strategic thinking, planning and management at all three levels.

However, planning has been defined in various ways, ranging from thinking about the future to specifying in advance who is to do what and when. For firm plan, it can define the activity of preparing a plan, a set of intended outcomes (ends). Planning can be formal or informal , an involve lots of documentation or very little. The information base can be large and captured in a wide range of reports, studies, databases and analyses, or it can rest entirely on the personal knowledge of a few people or even just one. Plans and thus the planning activities that produce them, frequently with address timeframe, either generally or in the form of perhaps detailed schedules, resources too, might be addressed, whether in terms of money, space, equipment or people. There are no predetermined guideline to follow, it is a matter of doing what is appropriate for the task at hand.

In conclusion, strategic planning characteristics includes: establishing and periodically confirming the organization's mission and its corporate strategy what has been termed the contest for managing ; setting strategic or enterprise level financial and non-financial goals and objective; developing broad plans of action necessary to attain these goals and objectives; allocating resources on a basis consistent with strategic directions and goals and objectives and managing the various lines of business as an investment portfolio; deploying the mission and strategy. That is articulating and communicating it, as well as developing action plans at lower levels that are supportive of those at the enterprise level , one very specific method of policy or strategy deployment; monitoring results, measuring progress, and making such adjustments as are required to achieve the strategic intent specified in the strategic goals and objectives; reassessing mission, strategy, strategic goals and objectives and plans at all levels and if requires , revising any or all of them.

● Why needs strategic versus non-strategic cooperation

On reason why organization needs strategic plan because it can not revist to compare whether what it can improve or change to be better between the strategic cooperation stage and non-strategic cooperation stage if it choose to achieve strategic plan. What are the difference between strategic cooperation and non-strategic cooperation within any organizations? What are the benefits to strategic cooperation organizations? The strategic motivations are in play in finitely repeated in any organizations. Clearly, cooperation can drop because strategically-motivated individuals, who reciprocate others' cooperation solely when there is future interaction. However, it can also drop because non-strategically-motivated individuals, who reciprocate others' cooperation even in the absence of future interaction, believe others will stop cooperating in the last period. In other word, since both strategically - and non-strategically motivated individuals can cause the decline in cooperation , it is difficult to know what the contribution of each type of motivation is. So, it seems that if any organization can review to measure any staff individual motivated effect with team cooperation, it will improve strategic plan to be more successfully or more better to compare prior year and current year strategic plans.

Some psychologists have done this experiment, for example, one team member could take the increase in cooperation between repeated games and (repetitions of) one short game as being caused by strategically -motivated individuals who now have a reason to cooperate. However, this increase can also be driven by non-strategically-motivated individuals who cooperate more because who expect that within repeated interaction others will be more cooperative. Similarly, the observation that cooperation is more frequent when it is more profitable can be attributed to strategic behavior and the existence of additional cooperative equilibria. However, the increase in cooperation can able be , due to an increase in non-strategically-motivated cooperation that results from intrinsically-motivated individuals who now find cooperation relatively more attractive or from rational individual who make relatively more mistakes.

How to distinguish strategic from non-strategic motivations for cooperation in organizations? Psychologists conclude that strategic behavior has a more pronounced effect than learning in explaining the usually-observed decline in contributions in public good games. On the basis of experiment treatments, who observed cooperation is strategically motivated. However, the relative importance of non-strategic motivations increases with the profitability of cooperation. So, psychologists indicate different organization departments cooperation can encourage individual staff motivations after strategic cooperation. Otherwise, non-strategic cooperation different departments will be more unsuccessful. It seems that how to encourage department cooperation factor which can influence the organization can raise productivity or improve service performance more easily.

● Strategic plan tangible and intangible benefits

Why will inefficient and effective strategic plan bring disadvantages or lack benefits to any organizations? Motivating staff and volunteers, thinking about the future is a stimulating and energizing process. It can create a shared vision, with ideas about how to achieve that vision. Building a planning team with a common vision. The strategy plan that emerges from the process is generally more realistic and achievable and working or interdependent relationships within the organization are strengthened. Confronting key issues and solving problems. Strategic planning sets in motion a dynamic process that allows the organization to continually reassess, confront change, and grow within an agreed-upon framework. Defining roles and responsibilities , measurable performance objectives are set and the person(s) who is responsible for specific activities is identified. Challenging the status, the process creates an open atmosphere. How can organization do things better in a more systematic and thorough way. Allowing busy managers and policy makers to concentrate on the organization's future for a short period of time, meaning that who will be able to focus their expertise and insights on self-assessment and planning future directions. Explaining organization to others , a thoughtful and clear strategic plan is often a good marketing tool and can encourage shares issues support for the organizational mission that individual perspectives, roles and problems are subsumed by an overall plan that coordinates all staff members and volunteers , so that agreed upon goals and objectives are achieved in a timely manner.

The steps of strategic plan suggesting: First step, analyzing the shared valued and experiences of staff and board. Planning a meeting or workshop to facilitate strategic planning. Second step, review and update or prepare a mission statement for the organization. Third step, analyzing the organization's external environment, political , economic, social and technological factors and internal environment: resources or input, processes, and performance or outputs. Fourth step, conducting a SWOT analysis (assessing the organization's internal strengths and weaknesses and its external opportunities and threats). Fifth step, creating smaller groups for in-depth planning activities in key areas. Sixth step, reviewing the organization's existing strategic plan if there is one to identify aspects of the plan that are still strategic, those are as longer strategic plan, due to changing environments, and gaps or new issues that should be addressed in a revised plan. Seventh step, outlining a vision of where the organization should be outlining three to five years from today (the vision of success). Eighth step, identifying the strategic issues facing the organization. Ninth step, formulating goals and strategic objectives to address major issues facing the organization and ensuring its longer term growth and sustainability. Tenth step, developing work plans showing specific activities, persons responsibility resources needed and indicators why which performance will be measured. Eleventh step, identifying next step for resource mobilization and creating a approaches for generating sufficient revenue funding. Twelve step, preparing the written detailed 5 years strategic plan mission statements. Final step, identifying next steps for resources mobilization and creating a financial plan that cost, and outlines approaches for sufficient revenue or funding .

Reference

Chovancova, M. (2012), " Building a strong brand to support company competitiveness"., from www.sba.org.pl.content/ 50647.

Davis, Gerald, 1991, " Agents without principles: The Spread Of The Poison Pill Through The Intercorporate Network." Administrative Science Quarterly, 36: 583-613.

Obembe, D. understanding individual action: whn employees contravence management directives to faster knowledge sharing. Management research review. 2010, vol. 33, issue. 6 , pp. 656-666. ISSN 2040-8269.

Poister, Theodore H. Streib, gregory (2005), "Elements of strategic planning and management in municipal government, Status after two decades", Public Administration Review, 65(1), pp.45.

Hickson, D. J. Miller, S.C. , Wilson , D.C. Planned on prioritized, implementation of strategic decisions. J. Manage, Stud , 2003, 40, 1803-1836.

Johnston, R., Clack, G., 2001. Service operations management, Prentice-Hall, Harlow, UK.

Kay, J.M. (2006). "Strong brands and corporate brands", European Journal Of Marketing, vol. 40, no.7/8, pp. 742-760. Porter, Michael (1986). Competitive Strategies. Harvard Business School Press.

Shahri, M.H. (2011), " The effectiveness of corporate branding strategy in multi- business companies", Australia Journal of Business And Management Research, vol. 1 no 6, pp. 51-59.

Stanhope, M. & Lancaster, J. (2000). Community & Public Health, St. Louis, Mo, Mobsy.

Xie, Y.H. and Boggs, J.D. (2006), " corporate branding vs. product branding in emerging markets, a conceptual framework", Marketing intelligence & planning, vol. 24 no. 24, pp. 347-364.

XII

The relationship between human behavior and service need

Human Behavioral network job brings social economic benefits

What does human network job mean ? Why may human network job be popular? Why human network job behavior may influence economy ?

Nowadays internet is popular to use. We can apply internet to find data , search any new things, even earn money. Why does internet

may become huma network job source. For example, e-publish may be one kind of new human network job. Any authors may apply internet

channel to help them to sell electronic or paper books from e-publisher web store. They may apply facebook, you tub etc. any online

channel to promote themselves new books to let new readers to know whether when they may buy themselves favourable new topic books to read

from electronic publisher web store.

Thus, future electronic publisher industry may help any authors to build internet network platform to help them to sell and promote

ot advertise their any one new electronic or paper book topic to let global any one reader to choose to buy their any new topic books from electronic publisher web store easily and conveniently. However, it implies that electronic network platform author may be one kind of future new human network job in our societies.

How electronic network platform author job may bring economy benefit in macro economy view? A person can have few friends, contacts and still be very influential if these few

friends and contacts are themselves highly influential, e.g. one author must not need to know any one reader in global society. When they like to choose any electronic books from electronic internet network platform. They may become the author's any one topic book buyer, when they feel the author's any one topic book is fun and attract they make decision to buth the strange author whose the topic book from electronic book publisher's platform web store conventiently in short time. Although, they are strangers, they do not know themselves , but the reader can understand what it way that made Google from writing platofrm to create new creative mind and typing network job method to replace traditional hand writing book method for global authors. It will be one kind of new human network writing job.

Hence, global any one reader can apply an innovative search engine , such as google.com to find whether whom author personal new topic books are value to read from internet.

Then, the electroniuc publisher's web store may be new book store platform sale network to help the author to sell

many electronic or paper books from electronic network platform
in short time. So, internet may be future new network plaform to help global any one author to create network writing job absolutely. Furthermore, internet may be popular social media
to help any one author to build goold relationship between his/her readers. It is one kind of new network, human network job. New authors do not need to buy many paper books to prepare to put in any one book shop warehouse. Their every book can print on demand to reduce out of book stock in any one book shop. They may choose to sell either electronic books or paper books both from any one book publisher web store. So, electronic network platform may be one kind of good writing channel to help human authors to create income and it can also help authors to bring new creative mind and new topic fun content books to let readers to know and buy to read from electronic publisher network platform.

Why does human behavior may be one kind of new human network job to bring global economic advantages. ALthough, it may be free income or without inocme, but the person does the network behavior, his/her behavior may be bring advantages to influence many other people's health. For this case, when a worker in a coffee shop in an airport gets a vaccination againnst the flu, it does not only helps him or her stay healthy, but also helps the many travellers who might otherwise have been inflected if that workers caught the flu. So, the externality , the result implies the vaccination of even a part of a community conveys benefits to the whole community. For example, governments pay special attention to the vaccinations of school children, teachers, health mothers, and the elderly, categories of people particularly susceptible not only to catching, but also to transmitting a disease.

It is not accidental that governments are heavily involved with vaccination . When there are externalities, free market, fail to persuade individual incentives with society's
their the worker's decision of whether to get a vaccine ends up attracting whether other people get sick. The workers might not fully take all these other people's potential suffering into account when making her or his vaccination decision.

As Stanford University does many suggestions, understand this and tries to help them make the right decisions and so providers free flu vaccines for its staff and students.
Small pockets of unvaccinated individuals can allow a disease to gain a spread more widely well-being. For example, parent weighing the costs and benefits of a vaccine for their child is not always thinking of the consequences of that vaccination to other people. THese are markets in which subsidizing or regulating behavior can make everyone better off. Because the reason for requiring that a child be vaccinated before enrolling in school is not just to protect that child, because each child's vaccination affects others via potential contagions.
Robots take our jobs behavioral and economy influences
Robot job behavior brings economy influences

If one day robots can replace human to do simple, even complex jobs. They will bring what influences to our global societial economy.The popular economic refrain declares that the
global middle class is dying and robots will soon take our jobs, e.g. shopping center customer service jobs, library service jobs, cinema ticket sale jobs, restaurant kitchen cooker jobs,
even, bus drivers, taxi drivers etc. public transport driving jobs, accountant, doctors etc. professional jobs. Whether it is beautiful or petty matter if our future societies have many human jobs can be replaced to do from robots. Businessman must may reduce to employ employees and reduce to pay salary or wage, when robots can be replaced to do their employees tasks. But, societies must bring unemployement rate rises , due to societies will have many people loss jobs when their employers choose to buy robots to serve their clients or do any office tasks or customer service or cleaning etc. tasks.

In micro economy view, employers may save money in long term, but in macro economy view, it will cause unemployment ratio rises , even crime rate rises when there are many people lose
jobs in societies. These models of doom, though, fail to account for the hundreds of businesses riding the waves of change in their industries when robots may be invented to replace human to do many simple , even complex tasks in our future societies.

WE may image that one small factory needs to manufacture fishes canes to sell to supermarket, the small , cheaper stuff and higher margin parts of the fishes manufacture industry. Before, this factory needs to employ many human factory workers need to help every fresh customer makeing the perfect fishing gear, designed for performance, durability, and cost in order to achieve to manufacture every fish cane in whole fished processing manufacturing stages. Every worker needs to spend about 15 to twenty minutes to finish every fish cane , till to delivery to any supermarket to sell. If this fish canes manufacturing factory can apply manufacturing robots to help them to finish any one working tasks , every robot can only spend five minutes to finish whole fresh fish cane manufacturing process. Thus, every robot can

help this factory save 10 to 15 minutes time to finsh every fish cane manufacturing process. IN fact, time is money, because when every robot can help this factory to reduce 10 to 15 minutes time to compare human worker. Then, this factory can finish about 20 fish canes in one hour if it can use robot to help it to manufacture fish canes. Otherwise, if this factory still use human workers to help it to manufacture fish canes, then it can finsh about 3 to 4 fish canes in one hour. SO, the manufacturing efficiency ensures that robots must help this fish manufacturing factory to raise fish canes number more than human workers. So, in robotic behavioral economy view, manufacturing robots must help this fish canes manufacturing factory to raise fish canes manufacturing number and deliver increasing number to supermarkets to prepare to sell every day. Robots can help this fish canes manufacturing factory bring manufacturing time saving, rising manufacturing efficiency, improving performance and reducing wages expenditure long time advantages in micro economy view. However, manufacturing robots can also bring disadvanages to society, e.g. increasing unemployment ratio, increasing crime rate,

this factory workers will lose jobs and income, they need earn social welfare from government and increasing government finance pressure in short time, even long time in macro economic view.

Stanford University graduate program in economics, Scott lecturer explained that "in demand and supply economic theory for robots supply and demand case, robots supply number increasing may influence human workers demand number decrease. It sometimes calls " the efficient frontier".

No specific human beings were mentioned in any of economics classes. As robots supply and demand in market case, They (robots) may be purely theoretical " agents" who reached to the most reasonable sale prices in order to persuade any one businessman buyer to make manufacturing robot buying decision whether robots can help him / her to bring how much saving time , saving money, saving cost, improving performance, efficiency economic benefit before he/she plans to reduce workers number when he/she decides to apply robots to replace human workers in his/her factory or office or any service department, e.g. cinema ticket sale service, shopping center customer service, shopping center cleaning , supermarket customer service etc. service or sale tasks. When robots can replace human to do any one of these tasks in any organizations. So, robots may be human worker agents who reached to prices the way robots would react to a software

command. There was nothing that explained why some people thrived and others did n't or why truly brilliant, hardworking people could fail when much lazier folks succeeded." Having been admitted to the Stanford University graduate program in economics, Scott lecturer hoped to get his answers there.

How robots influence our future social changing? Using the right technology can be a boon to your business in this economy. For internet example, it is easier than ever to find well-matched customers all around the world, to stay in contact with them, and to more quickly design the products they want. If you focus solely on being cutting -edge, though you risk letting the technology

take over what should be very robust relationships with your customers , employees, and colleagues. IN nowaddays society, technoligical advances and cutomation, personal

relationships in business are more crucial than ever. I mean that robots can not replace human to serve clients to let them to feel more comfortable and passion more easily. For shoe shop case example, if the shoe shop apply one robot to serve its clients to replace human shoe salesperson to serve its shoe customers. Robots ensure that they can not persuade every shoe potential buyer to make shoe buying decision more easily when robots need to contact every shoe potential buyer. The reason is simple, because robots can not touch any one shoe buyer individual emotion very easier.

If the shoe buyer needs the robots to help him/her to choose any right shoe styles when he/she can not feel himself / herself can make the most right shoe style choice decision. The robots can not replace human shoe salesperson to make shoe style choice judgement more easily. They must need longer time to analyze whether which shoe style may be the most suitable to the shoe buyer. Otherwise, human shoe salesperson may attempt to make the most right shoe style choice decision to help any one shoe buyer to chooce the most right style shoe because he/she owns shoe style sale experience, shoe style knowledge, the most important reason is that they can feel every shoe customer individual emotion to touch whether he/she will feel comfortable or happy when they attempt to help every shoe customer to seek the most right shoe style in every shoe customer whole shoe searching processing. Othwerwise, serving robots are only one machine, they can not touch or feel every shoe customer individual emotion whether he/she feel comfortable or unhappy or happy when they need to contact them in whole shoe searching processing. Hence, I believe that some tasks robots can

not repalce human staff to do very easily. Otherwise, robots may bring disadvanatges to let any one businessman to loss his/her customers, due to robots can not touch every customer

emotion to compare human staff in service tasks more easily. Robots serving customer behaviors may cause money lose and customers number lose to the shop in micro economic view.

Intellectual human economic behaviors

What does intellectual human economic behaviors mean ? I believe that when we choose or decide to do intellectual behaviors, then our societies will be influenced to bring economic growth in consequence.I shall attempt to indicate pollution case to explain how and why eithet our intellectual or foolish behaviors may bring economic growth or recession in consequence as below:

On one hand, for air pollution social case aspect example, if we only consider to buy cars to drive for working aimr or holiday leisure aim. Then, our societies air will be polluted. Our health will be influenced to bad. Our car driving behaviors may cause global environment air pollution serously. In long tiem, global air pollution will bring our bodies health to be bad. Although, ourselves car driving behaviors may bring our driving travelling leisure enjoyment and comfortable feeling in short time, also we so not need to pay public transport fare often, but we need to compensate ourselves health economic intangible loss due to air pollution , when cars number increases, dirty air will cause ouselves health to become bad.

In the result, we will need to pay more medical expenditure when we are old age, due to ourselves bodies will become bad, due to we breathe global dirty air every day, due to ourselves cars pollute air in long time, e.g. 10 to 20 years, even 30 more without limited air pollution environment. So, driving cars behavior may be one kind of human foolish behavior and our foolish behavior may bring ourselves future long time medical expenditure absolutely.

One the other hand, water pollution social aspect, if we often keep much rubblish to pollute sea, oil exploration porcessing pollute ocean , ships gas pollute ocaen, then fishes will eat polluted food and drive dirty water, due to global ocean is polluted.

In fact, because human only to conside how to buy boats to carry on leisure enjoyment activities, or catch cruises to travel on the sea. Also, oil manufacturers only consider researching anywhere to find new oil exploration places to manufacture oil product, when their oil exploration processes pollute ocarn . Consequently, global fishes drink polluted warer or eat polluted food. They will have poison. SO, human will have high chance to eat poison polluted fishes, due to fishes are poison or are polluted.

So, human is doing foolish activities, we only hope to find oil exploration places to pollute ocean or we only spend money to buy ticket to catch ships to travel anywhere in global ocean. All of these human foolish behaviors will bring pollution to global ocean. On consequently, we will need to compensate to eat polluted or dirty or poision fishes, ourselves bodies health will be bad. In long time, we need have high chance to pay medical expenditure when we are old. So, pollution case may be one good example to explain how and why human foolish behavior may influence ourselves future need to compensate serious medical loss.

All of these human foolish behavior will bring pollution to global ocean. On consequently, we will need to compensate to eat polluted or dirty or poison fished , ourselves bodies health will be bad. In long time, we will have high chance to pay medical expenditure, when we are old. So, pollution case may be one good example to explain how and why human ourselves intellectual or foolish behaviors may influence future long time economic loss or economic growth or recession in micro and micro economic view.

On another water pollution aspect hand, if we often keep rubbish to sea, oil exploration processing pollutes ocean and ships' gas pollute ocean, then fishes will eat polluted food and drink dirty water, due to fishes will eat polluted food and drink dirty sea water because the global ocean is polluted seriously.

In fact, because human only consider how to buy boats to carry on any leisure water activities, or catches cruises to travel on the sea. Also, oil manufacturers only consider any where to find oil exploratin places to manufacture oil products from ocean, when their pol exploration processes can plooute ocean. Consequently, global fishes drink polluted water or eat direty food. They will have poison. So, human will have high chance to eat poison fishes.

Otherwise, such as pollutin case, it can infuence inflation or deflation. Consequently, the reason indicates supply and demand theory. If air pollution is serious, then we will consider health issue, global cars demand number may be influenced to reduce, when global cars number demand will reduce, global car prices and supply number will need to change to fall down in order to attract or persuade global car consumers choose to make car purchase decision.

Hence, global car manufacture number and car price will be influenced to reduce, due to global air pollution issue. Consequently, deflation will occur because when the country citizen usually does not spend much extra saving money to buy car expensive goods. Money value will be low. Otherwise, if global cair pollution is not serious, human considers to buy cars to enjoy driving leisure lives. So, global car demand is influenced to increase , also global car price will also influenced to increase.

Consequently, gobal human will choose to buy cars to drive. Due to we accept to spend extra saving to buy expensive car goods. Car sale price and supply may be influenced to rise up. Money value is influenced to reduce. Inflation may be influenced, due to global car consumers number increases, we would not have extra money to spend easily. Car expensive goods expenditure influences our spending habit to avoid to make car purchase decision more easily. So, human intellectual or foolish activities may bring inflation or deflation consequency in possible indirectly in macro economic view.

On conclusion, above pollution case explain that how and why human intellectual or foolish economic behaviors may bring inflation or deflation consequency as wll as economic growth or recession consequency as well as any goods demand and supply increasing or decreasing consequency. It implies that human behavior may have indirect relationship to influence any goods demand and supply number to either increase or decrease result as well as any goods price will be influenced to increase or decrease in micro and macro economic view.

The relationship between social change and human behavior

Why does economic changes may influence human individual behavioral change? I shall attempt to indicate shopping behavior and staying at home behavior to explain their case and effect relationsip as below:

Human behavior can be influenced by economic change or economic change can be influenced by human behavior? Why does recession may influence consumers reduce shopping desire? In social recession suitation, it is possible that many people lose jobs suddenly, due to businessmen lose many customers. They need to make decision to reduce employees number in order to continue to keep businesses. Consequently, many firms (organizations) their employees may lose jobs. When they have much time, due to lose jobs, they will feel to avoid to spend too much time and money to go to shopping often. Many losing jobs people, they will often stay at homes.

So, they will reduce time to go to shopping, then non essential products won't their preferable choice purchase products. Hence, recession will change many losing jobs people their shopping or consumption desires to avoid to buy non essential products often . Usually when economic boom, many people have jobs to do because consumers number must increase when many people have jobs to do. Then, many people can accept to spend money to buy non essential products often. Many people feel spend time to go to shopping can satisfy their purchase of any kinds of new products useful psychology or desire. So, recession is one good example to explain it can influence many people do not like often to leave homes to go to shopping easily. Many people like to stay at homes, becaue they feel worry about spending too much shopping time when they leave homes. Their staying home time is one good negative shopping behavior example. So, economic change may influence human individual behavior changes , they have direct cause and efect relationship in behavioral economic view.

May human behavior influence economic change? Is it possible that human behavior may bring the country social economic change in macro economic or micro behavioral economic view ? I shall indicate publishing industry example. Do you feel that if there are many students feel learning is very important when they read many books or many of students feel interesting to read or they have reading new books in habit, then it is possible that the country will have many students like to spend time to go to any book shops to choose the books, they feel that they can help they learn new knowledge. Then the country will increase students number, they often spend time to visit any one book shop every week. Their visiting book shops behavior which may become their habits. So, the country will increase students number, they often spend time to visit book shops. Also, it implies that visiting book shops behaviors may be their behavioral habits.

So, when the country has many students often spend time to visit book shops , their visiting book shops behaviors may help any one book shop to raise books sale chance. So, the country's student individual often visiting book shop behaviors, their habitual visiting book shops behaviors must may assist help any one book shop to increase books sale number absolutely.

Consequently, any one book shop , its books sale bumber must be influenced to increase to increase because the country will have many students like or feel need visit book shops habit in order to choose any suitable books to buy to read at home in order to raise themselves learning effort. When the country has many bok shops often have many students visit their book shops, then their books sale number may be influenced to increase. It explain why student individual visiting book shop behavior may help any one book shop sale number increases also.

How human productive behavior may influence economic development

May any country which citizen behavior assist themselves country development? It is one cause and effect economic question. I mean that if the country itself citicen can not concentrate mind or energy to choose to do one kind of industry in order to let themselves country can bring the most benefit, then whether the counry itself economy can bring the most serious economic benefit. I shall attempt to indicate these countries themselves indistry choice to explain whether these countries themselves citizen productive behavior may help themselves countries to achieve the largest economic benefits. I shall indicate as below:

New Zealand farmer individual wine productive behavior

For New Zealand country example, this country concerns itself effort is foucs on farming agricultural aspect. So, this country has many farmers concentrate on farming agricultural aspect. May New Zealanders choose to spend time to produce different kinds of wines, e.g. wine or red grape wine is for the people are eating meat, or they are eating dinner.

When these New Zealanders their behaviors choose to do farming or agriculture to grow and produce different kinds of taste of white or red grape wine drinking products job. Themselves grape agriculture behavior will influence these New Zealanders themselves, they can learn how to improve different kinds of grape wine drinking products in order to achieve every kinds of white or read grape wines taste improving aim during their white or red grape producing process.

Why can New Zealander every individual white or read grape wine producers improve their white or read grape wine taste more easily? In behavioral economic view, it can explain that why any one New Zealander white or read grape wine producer can be encouraged or excited or persuaded to concentrate nervous and energy and effort to learn how to improve their white or red grape wine products easily.

In fact, New Zealand is one agricultural food export country. It has good natural environment resource , e.g. land, seed to provide any one farmer to produce themselves any kinds of agricultrual food products, e.g. fruit, or wine food products. Because New Zealanders know themselves country has enough natural resource . So, in common, many New Zealanders choose to attempt to do farming agricultural jobs in order to export themselves any kinds of fruit or meat or wine products to overseas or sell to domestic in order to earn profit.

So, when these New Zealand farmers number has been increasing every year. This country farmers will feel themsleves competition between this New Zealand farmers themselves are serious due to they may feel New Zealanders choose to do agriculture businesses in order to export themselves different kinds of farming food to overseas or sell to local to earn profit.

Hence, when many New Zealand farmers feel that farmers number has been increasing every year. They will feel themselves competition is serious. They must need to spend much time and nervous and effort to research what method is the best how to produce the best taste of white or red grape wine products in order to let local or overseas wine buyers to choose to buy his/her producing white or read grpae products to drink.

Hence, in competition psychological view, may influence many New Zealand white or reaad wine producers had been beginning to change their learning behavior on researching what method is the best in order to produce the best quality of taste red or white wine products to sell in order to attract overseas or local white or read grape wine drinkers to choose to buy his/her wine products. Their behavior will focus on learning how to raising or improving white or read grape wine taste method more than only focus on producing a large number white or red grape wine products. They believe wine quality is more important to compare wine producing number. So, New Zealand wine producers themselves wine producers behaviors have been changing on concentrating on researching wine quality method aspect more then wine producing number aspect in behavioral economic view.

America high technological productive behavior

For America example, US is one high technological country, it owns many high technological knowledge talent inventors, e.g. computer science inventors. Hence, US must attract many diferent countries owning high technological computer inventors choose to go to US to develop their computer science profession career. Also, it seems that when many computer science inventors or professions choose to go to US to develop themselves computer science new career. In behavioral economic view, due to their leaving themselves countries choice, which may bring influence themselve country job behaviors need to be changed. They must need to adapt US new live. Because they will forgive their past computer science job. These computer science professionals need to spend time to adapt US new lives. They " past computer science job behaviors" will need to be changed to their new US any computer employer's new computer science job model.

Because their traditional computer science jobs needed to be forgot in their themselves countries. They will feel their old computer science job knowledge and behavior needed to change in order to let their US any one new of computer company employer feels satisfactory to accept their new working behavior in any one US computer organization.

So, on the other hand, many US computer company employer will feel that they must need time to accept any one new overseas computer science professions their working behaviors, their working attitude daily, because these foreign comouter science professional, their past computer working behaviors and working attitude must be different to US domestic computer science professions.

In behavioral economic view, these overseas computer science professions, their working behaviors and attitude must be needed to change in order to adapt any one US new computer company itself domestic or local computer science professional stafs themselves daily working behaviors and attitude because these overseas and local computer science professionals must need to team work together.

In behavioral economic view, it is only one way that foreign computer science professionals must need to change themselves past country traditiona daily working behaviors and attitude in order to cooperate with these US local computer science professionals in teams more easily.

Consequently, if these foreign compute science professionals can change their past working behaviors and attitude to let any one US local computer science professional feels to cooperate with them easily in short time. Then, the US computer company itself whole computer professional teams themselves efficiencies will be influenced to raised or improved by the changing past working attitude and working behaviors of these foreign computer science professionals. So, in behavioral economic view, only if US any one computer company hopes itself computer teams themselves efficiency can be raised or improved when it decides to employ foreign computer science professionals and US domestic computer science professionals. They need to work in teams together. They must need to let these foreign computer science professionals to know how to change their working behaviors and attitude to let their domestic computer science professionals feel easy to work together. Then, the US computer company itself whole team efficiency must be rasied or improved easily in short time.

● China share market investing behavior

For China share market example, economic development depends on financial market. Because if many Chinese have interest to invest to carry on shares buying and selling activities in orde to learn how to earn shares interest and share profit when the China shareholder can make decision to sell himself/herself shares in the the high price, then he/she can earn money when he/she can sell the China company's shares in the high sale share price position.

If China has many Chinese like to spend time to carry on investing shares activities. Themselves shares buying and selling behaviors will influence China has many companies can increase fund from many Chinese shareholders in order to have enough money to expand or develop themselves businesses in China in long term.

Consequently, when China can have many Chinese like to attempt to carry on buying and selling shares investing behaviors in China share market. Themselves buying and selling shares behaviors can help many Chinese companies have effort to increase enough money or capital in order to continue to do their businesses in long term absolutely. So, it explains why when many Chinese become shareholders , they can assist China will have many companies continue to develop their businesses if many Chinese like to carry on shares buying and selling investing behaviors in long time in China financial investment market nowadays in behavioral economic view.

Why has any individual country have many people invest share behavior which can influence the country's macro consumption desire?

I shall apply shares market buying and selling investment behavior to explaiin why shares investment behavior which may impact the country's overal consumption desire as below:

In behavioral economic view, I assume that when the coutry has many people have interest to attempt to carry on shares buying and selling investment behavior, then their frequent shares buying and selling behaviors which may bring negactive consumption desire or shopping desire of these shares investors their consumer behavior.

The reason is simple, when the country has many share buyers number suddenly been increasing rapidly. Consequently, these large group share investors must need to spend much time to research any kinds of company shares variations, whether when their share prices will rise up of fall down in order to achieve buying the company's shares in the lowest price and selling the company's shares in the highest price level in order to earn profit.

Basic on this reason, they must need to spend much extra time to research share prices changing behavior every day, e.g. one working person will wait to leave his/her job, after he/she can spend time to gather data to research the day's share price changing behavior after dinner. So, the working person's right time may be his/her share price market research behavior. Before he/she may spend his/her night time to go to shopping after dinner, but nowadays, he/she will fogive to do his/her shopping behavior before dinner or after dinner at hight sometime. He/she will make decision to spend much night time to turn on computer to click on share market website to research his/her share purchase choice to investigate whether his/her share price whether it rises up or falls down at the moment in order to make his/her share buying or selling decision at ever night time.

I mean the when the country has many people are share investors, their shares investment behavioral spenging time which will influence many shops lose customers at might often because the country will have many people feel need to spend night time to turn on computer or watch television to investigate share price variation. So, the country will have many people / share investors choose to stay at home in order to carry on share price variation investigation behavior, they need to listen share market update news from radios or watch the share market update news from computer or TV at home every night. Consequenly, they must reduce times to leave themselves homes at night. So, their shopping behavior also will be reduced. Because these share investors feel need to spend time to investigate share price variation news at homes which can bring economic benefits (high opportunity benefits) when they choose to forgive to leave homes to go to shopping times (opportunity cost) every night.

On conclusion, it seems that when the country has many people are share investors, then their share price investigating behavior may bring negative shopping emotion at night. Consequently, the country's any one shop may lose many customers from this share investor consumer group in behavioral economic view. Hence, when the country's share investors number had been increasing rapidly, it will influence any shops lose many customers from this share investing customer group at night frequenly in short time, even long time in behavioral economic view, because their shopping desires or shopping emotion will be brought negative feeling when they make decisions to spend much time to listen radios or watch TV or computers share price update nes at night. Hence, share market will bring negative impact to influence consumer shopping desire or negative shopping emotion in behavioral economic view.

Can technology influence human shopping behavioral change?

Nowadays, technological development has reached mature stage, whether technological mature stage may bring positive or negative shopping emotion influence to global consumers. I shall aplly internet inventin or ecommerce shopping channel tool to explain whether internet technology can bring postive or negative influence to global consumer behavior in behavioral economic view.

Internet is a good technological tool, it brings e-commerce business chance. In fact, commonly, global has have many businessmen choose to use internet channel to carry on their products transactions between global online-buyers and their electronic websites. So, global many shoppers had begun to feel online shopping is more convenient to compare visiting shops shopping. Their shopping behaviors have been changed from internet technological tool. Global has many shoppers choose to buy any products from any overseas or local businessmen their web stores. They only need to spend time to find any businessmen their webstores to choose the most suitable products to pay visa to buy from their webstores. at homes. So, in general, global had have may shoppers had changed their shopping behaviors from visiting shops to visiting webstores at homes often.

So, it seems that internet technological tool had influenced global many shops disappear, but internet webstores will be replaced their actual shops on streets. Some of businessmen either they choose webstores to replace shops or choose websotes and shops both or still keep shops only. Hence, internet tool influences global businessmen have three kinds of products sale channels to let globa local and overseas consumers to choose how to buy their products. However, in fact, many of global shoppers, youngers and olders had begun to accept to buy any products from webstores. They feel to spend time to leave homes to visit shops , their shopping behaviors will be wasted time to not essential part to their daily lives. Hence, since internet technological invention, it had changed many consumers their traditional visiting shops shopping habit to change to buying products from webstores channel.

However, on the one hand, internet creates webstores ecommerce shopping channel to let global many consumers do not need to leave homes to go to shopping. It brings negative visiting shops shopping emotion to global general consumers nowadays. But on the other hand, it also brings positive visiting internet webstores shopping emotion to global general consumer nowadays. So, it seems that global many consumers feel that they often do not need to spend much time to go out shopping. Many global consumers feel convenient and enjoy to choose any products to buy from different internet webstores, when the online buyer chooses the most suitable product, he she only needs to pay visa card to buy the product from the online seller's webstore conveniently at home.

Hence, online shopping can bring economic benefit to online buyers, e.g. avoiding walking time or spending transport fare to visit the shop to go to shopping, shortening or reducing shopping time to do another important matter.

On conclusion, global many consumers began feel online shopping can bring more economic benefits on shortening shopping time, avoiding transport fare spending aspect. So, online shopping will be popular shopping behavior for future long time. It may encourage global many shoppers can make rapid shopping decision in short time in order to carry on any products buying transaction to global any one online shopper in short time easily in behavioral economic view. So, global many businessmen had begun to build themselves one attraction webstore in order to persuade different countries consumers to choose to click themselves webstores from internet channel to buy any kinds of products in short time easily.

So, internet technology had changed consumers traditional shopping behaviors to build positive online shopping emotion as well as raise online sellers' any products sale chance easily in behavioral economic view.

Why and how human behavior may influence the country's economic growth or recession?

When one country has many people choose to do the same matter for one period, whether their behavior may influence the country's pvera; economic growth or recession . I shall attempt to indicate cases toexplain their relationship as below:

For flowing rubblish behavioral case example, do you feel that when the country has many people often flow rubblish on the streets, instead of their flowing rubblish behavior may bring streets dirty? But, their flowing rubblish behavior may explain that this country has people may have enough money to buy food to ear, or enough cloths to wear, enough bottles of water to drink, even they may have enough money to buy new television, radio, refrigeraters , washing machines, desktops or laptops electronic home products from old to new to use in order to satisfy their living needs. So, when they flow old electronic home products, their flowing old home electronic products behaviors may seem that they have enough money to buy other new home electronic products to replace old home electronic products to use at homes.

However, it seems thaat this country ought have many people have jobs to do. So, many of them, they can easy to make purchase decison to flow any old home electronic products and buy any new home electronic products to use . Because this country has many people have jobs to do. So, they can often not use old home electonic products to become rubblishs to flow on streets after they had bought any kinds of new home electronic homes.

In fact, it also implies that this country's economy grows rapidly. So, many businesses can glow up rapdly. When they expanded their businesses, they must need to increase employees number in order to let they help themselves to raise productivity or serve their clients absolutely. So, when the country has many businesses can grow up, it seems that its economy must be better or it is improved to compare past. Due to many different kinds of home electronic products had been often bought to use by this country people in this period. So, this country's any streets can be observed that expensive electronic home products were flowed on streets anywhere. then, this country will have many electronic home products sellers can sell their home electronic products very easily. When this country has many people can find any kinds of jobs to do easily. So, due to unemploymen rate had been decreasing.

In behavioral economic view, as this many electronic home products rubblish country case, we can observe this country may have many people have jobs to do. So, consumption number has been increased long time. So, cheap food, or expensive home electronic products may be rubblish on any streets. This country's people , their flowing rubblish behaviors may be explained that many of people have enough jobs to do, so they have ability to buy any good taste food to eat or buy any kinds of expensive electronic home products to use. So, this country's economy may be improved for this long period. So, in behavioral economic view, when this country can have many electronic home products rubblishs are flowed on anywherer in streets frequently. It seems that this country will have many people have jobs to do, so it causes they often change old home electronic products or replaced them easily, when they have enough income to spend to buy any kinds of new home electronic products to use at homes easily. Moreover, their flowing old electronic home products behaviors also indicate that this country has many people their salaries may be increased in possible from their emplyers. When this country can have many different kinds of home electornic products are sold. It means that this country's electronic home products needs or demand had been increasing, due to many people have jobs to do and income increases to excite their living of needs also improve. Consequently, this country may seem have better economic improvement. We can observe from this country's electronic home products rubblish increasing income in theis period.

On conclusion, this country ought experience economic growth at this period. So, " flowing expensive electronic home rubblish increasing number " may seem that this country's economic growth is rapidly in this period, due to many people have jobs to do as well as salaries increase in this period.